# CRITIQUE OF PSYCHOANALYSIS

*from*

The Collected Works of C. G. Jung

*VOLUMES 4 and 18*

BOLLINGEN SERIES XX

# CRITIQUE OF PSYCHOANALYSIS

*C. G. JUNG*

*TRANSLATED BY R. F. C. HULL*

BOLLINGEN SERIES

PRINCETON UNIVERSITY PRESS

PUBLISHED BY PRINCETON UNIVERSITY PRESS


*First Princeton/Bollingen Paperback Edition, 1975*

Extracted from *Freud and Psychoanalysis*, Vol. 4, and *The Symbolic Life*, Vol. 18, both in the *Collected Works of C. G. Jung*. All the volumes comprising the *Collected Works* constitute number XX in Bollingen Series, under the editorship of Herbert Read (d. 1968), Michael Fordham, and Gerhard Adler; executive editor, William McGuire.



LIBRARY OF CONGRESS CATALOGUE CARD NUMBER: 74-5639
ISBN 0-691-01801-4
MANUFACTURED IN THE UNITED STATES OF AMERICA
BY PRINCETON UNIVERSITY PRESS, PRINCETON, N. J.

# EDITORIAL NOTE

For about six years, from 1907 to 1912, Jung practiced and wrote and presumably thought as a psychoanalyst, in close association with Freud.[1] The work that was to be his major statement, *Wandlungen und Symbole der Libido*, proved instead to be a declaration of heresy, or at any rate of independence. When its relatively brief Part I appeared in 1911, Freud complimented it; but the very extensive Part II, published the next year, left no question of Jung's position, though he still professed himself an adherent of the psychoanalytic movement. In autumn 1912, he visited the United States to lecture in various cities. His chief appearance was at the Medical School of Fordham University, in the Bronx, New York, where he gave a series of nine lectures as an extension course to doctors—"a critical account of the development of the theory of psychoanalysis," he wrote Freud upon returning. "Naturally I also made room for those of my views which deviate in places from the hitherto existing conceptions, particularly in regard to the libido theory. I found that my version of psychoanalysis won over many people who until now had been put off by the problem of sexuality in neurosis. . . . I shall take pleasure in sending you a copy of my lectures in the hope that you will gradually come to accept certain innovations already hinted at in my libido paper. . . . I hope this letter will make it plain that I feel no need at all to break off personal relations with you."[2] The break nevertheless came, scarcely two months later. Freud's last letter was written on 27 January 1913.

The chief content of the present volume is the Fordham Lectures, entitled "The Theory of Psychoanalysis" though actually a presentation of Jung's version of psychoanalysis and

1 See *The Psychoanalytic Years* and (from an earlier phase of Jung's work) *The Psychology of Dementia Praecox*, both Princeton/Bollingen paperbacks.

2 *The Freud/Jung Letters*, ed. William McGuire (1974), 323 J of 11 Nov. 1912.

a criticism of the orthodox view. It is followed by four shorter works that carry forward Jung's critique and the evolution of his own system. In the paper "Psychoanalysis and Neurosis" (actually first read also in New York in 1912, as was recently discovered) and the other two of 1913, Jung's term is still "psychoanalysis"; by 1916, when he published his *Collected Papers*, the term "analytical psychology" had become current for the doctrines of the Zurich School, and Jung's prefaces to that collection pursue the reformulation of his theories.[3]

The volume also contains two later critical papers, of 1930 and 1931, and a statement written to the *New York Times* in 1953 rehearsing, forty years after the break, Jung's critique of psychoanalysis.[4]

W.M.

[3] For other critiques of the early period, see (1) *Psychology of the Unconscious*, tr. from *Wandlungen und Symbole der Libido* by B. M. Hinkle (1916, out of print)—in 1952, Jung brought out a thoroughgoing revision whose tr. is entitled *Symbols of Transformation* (CW 5); and (2) *Two Essays in Analytical Psychology* (CW 7), including the early versions in an appendix (Princeton/Bollingen paperback).

[4] Other critical comments on psychoanalysis occur frequently throughout Jung's later writings.

# TABLE OF CONTENTS

# THE THEORY OF PSYCHOANALYSIS

[Written originally in German under the title *Versuch einer Darstellung der psychoanalytischen Theorie* and translated (by Dr. and Mrs. M. D. Eder and Miss Mary Moltzer) for delivery as a series of lectures under the present title at the medical school of Fordham University, New York, in September 1912. The German text was published in the *Jahrbuch für psychoanalytische und psychopathologische Forschungen* (Vienna and Leipzig), V (1913; reprinted as a book the same year); the English, in five issues of the *Psychoanalytic Review* (New York): I (1913/14) : 1–4 and II (1915) : 1. The latter was then republished in the Nervous and Mental Disease Monograph Series, No. 19 (New York, 1915). The analysis of a child in the last chapter had been previously presented as "Über Psychoanalyse beim Kinde" at the First International Congress of Pedagogy, Brussels, August 1911, and printed in the proceedings of the Congress (Brussels, 1912), II, 332–43.

[A second edition of the German text, with no essential alterations, was published in 1955 (Zurich). The present translation is made from this edition in consultation with the previous English version.

[The text of the 1913 and 1955 editions in German is uninterrupted by headings, but at the author's request the original division into nine lectures (ascertained from an examination of the manuscript) has here been preserved. This arrangement differs from that of the previous English version, which is divided into ten lectures; the chapter and section headings there introduced have in general been retained, with some modifications. A number of critical passages inserted at a later stage into the original manuscript and included in the German editions were omitted from the previous English version, together with the footnotes. In the present version these passages are given in pointed brackets ⟨ ⟩. —EDITORS.]

## FOREWORD TO THE FIRST EDITION

In these lectures I have attempted to reconcile my practical experiences in psychoanalysis with the existing theory, or rather, with the approaches to such a theory. It is really an attempt to outline my attitude to the guiding principles which my honoured teacher Sigmund Freud has evolved from the experience of many decades. Since my name is associated with psychoanalysis, and for some time I too have been the victim of the wholesale condemnation of this movement, it will perhaps be asked with astonishment how it is that I am now for the first time defining my theoretical position. When, some ten years ago, it came home to me what a vast distance Freud had already travelled beyond the bounds of contemporary knowledge of psychopathological phenomena, especially the psychology of complex mental processes, I did not feel in a position to exercise any real criticism. I did not possess the courage of those pundits who, by reason of their ignorance and incompetence, consider themselves justified in making "critical" refutations. I thought one must first work modestly for years in this field before one might dare to criticize. The unfortunate results of premature and superficial criticism have certainly not been lacking. Yet the great majority of the critics missed the mark as much with their indignation as with their technical ignorance. Psychoanalysis continued to flourish undisturbed and did not trouble itself about the unscientific chatter that buzzed around it. As everyone knows, this tree has waxed mightily, and not in one hemisphere only, but alike in Europe and America. Official critics meet with no better success than the Proktophantasmist in *Faust,* who laments in the Walpurgisnacht:

> Preposterous! You still intend to stay?
> Vanish at once! You've been explained away.

The critics have omitted to take it to heart that everything that exists has sufficient right to its own existence, and that this holds for psychoanalysis as well. We will not fall into the error of our opponents, neither ignoring their existence nor denying their right to exist. But this enjoins upon us the duty of applying a just criticism ourselves, based on a proper knowledge of the facts. To me it seems that psychoanalysis stands in need of this weighing-up from inside.

It has been wrongly suggested that my attitude signifies a "split" in the psychoanalytic movement. Such schisms can only exist in matters of faith. But psychoanalysis is concerned with knowledge and its ever-changing formulations. I have taken as my guiding principle William James's pragmatic rule: "You must bring out of each word its practical cash-value, set it at work within the stream of your experience. It appears less as a solution, then, than as a program for more work, and more particularly as an indication of the ways in which existing realities may be changed. *Theories thus become instruments, not answers to enigmas, in which we can rest.* We don't lie back upon them, we move forward, and, on occasion, make nature over again by their aid." [1]

In the same way, my criticism does not proceed from academic arguments, but from experiences which have forced themselves on me during ten years of serious work in this field. I know that my own experience in no wise approaches Freud's quite extraordinary experience and insight, but nonetheless it seems to me that certain of my formulations do express the observed facts more suitably than Freud's version of them. At any rate I have found, in my teaching work, that the conceptions I have put forward in these lectures were of particular help to me in my endeavours to give my pupils an understanding of psychoanalysis. I am far indeed from regarding a modest and temperate criticism as a "falling away" or a schism; on the contrary, I hope thereby to promote the continued flowering and fructification of the psychoanalytic movement, and to open the way to the treasures of psychoanalytic knowledge for those who, lacking practical experience or handicapped by certain theoretical preconceptions, have so far been unable to master the method.

For the opportunity to deliver these lectures I have to thank my friend Dr. Smith Ely Jelliffe, of New York, who kindly in-

1 [*Pragmatism* (1907), p. 53.]

vited me to take part in the Extension Course at Fordham University, in New York. The nine lectures were given in September 1912. I must also express my best thanks to Dr. Gregory, of Bellevue Hospital, for his ready assistance at my clinical demonstrations.

Only after the preparation of these lectures, in the spring of 1912, did Alfred Adler's book *Über den nervosen Charakter* [*The Nervous Constitution*] become known to me, in the summer of that year. I recognize that he and I have have reached similar conclusions on various points, but here is not the place to discuss the matter more thoroughly. This should be done elsewhere.

C. G. J.

*Zurich, autumn 1912*

## FOREWORD TO THE SECOND EDITION

Since the appearance of the first edition in 1913 so much time has elapsed, and so many things have happened, that it is quite impossible to rework a book of this kind, coming from a long-past epoch and from one particular phase in the development of knowledge, and bring it up to date. It is a milestone on the long road of scientific endeavour, and so it shall remain. It may serve to call back to memory the constantly changing stages of the search in a newly discovered territory, whose boundaries are not marked out with any certainty even today, and thus to make its contribution to the story of an evolving science. I am therefore letting this book go to press again in its original form and with no essential alterations.

C. G. J.

*October 1954*

## 1. A REVIEW OF THE EARLY HYPOTHESES

203 It is no easy task to lecture on psychoanalysis at the present time. I am not thinking so much of the fact that this whole field of research raises—I am fully convinced—some of the most difficult problems facing present-day science. Even if we put this cardinal fact aside, there remain other serious difficulties which interfere considerably with the presentation of the material. I cannot offer you a well-established, neatly rounded doctrine elaborated from the practical and the theoretical side. Psychoanalysis has not yet reached that point of development, despite all the labour that has been expended upon it. Nor can I give you a description of its growth *ab ovo*, for you already have in your country, dedicated as always to the cause of progress, a number of excellent interpreters and teachers who have spread a more general knowledge of psychoanalysis among the scientifically-minded public. Besides this, Freud, the true discoverer and founder of the movement, has lectured in your country and given an authentic account of his views. I, too, have already had the great honour of lecturing in America, on the experimental foundation of the theory of complexes and the application of psychoanalysis to education.[1]

204 In these circumstances you will readily appreciate that I am afraid of repeating what has already been said or already been published in scientific journals. Another difficulty to be considered is the fact that quite extraordinary misconceptions prevail in many quarters concerning the nature of psychoanalysis. At times it is almost impossible to imagine what exactly these erroneous conceptions might be. But sometimes they are so preposterous that one is astonished that anyone with a scientific background could ever arrive at ideas so remote from reality. Obviously it would not be worth while to cite examples of these curiosities. It will be better to devote time and energy to discussing those problems of psychoanalysis which by their very nature give rise to misunderstandings.

1 [The Clark Lectures. See "The Association Method," Coll. Works, Vol. 2, and "Psychic Conflicts in a Child," Vol. 17.]

THE TRAUMA THEORY

205 Although it has been pointed out on any number of occasions before, many people still do not seem to know that the theory of psychoanalysis has changed considerably in the course of the years. Those, for instance, who have read only the first book, *Studies on Hysteria,*[2] by Breuer and Freud, still believe that, according to psychoanalysis, hysteria and the neuroses in general are derived from a so-called trauma in early childhood. They continue senselessly to attack this theory, not realizing that it is more than fifteen years since it was abandoned and replaced by a totally different one. This change is of such great importance for the whole development of the technique and theory of psychoanalysis that we are obliged to examine it in rather more detail. So as not to weary you with case histories that by now are well known, I shall content myself with referring to those mentioned in Breuer and Freud's book, which I may assume is known to you in its English translation. You will there have read that case of Breuer's to which Freud referred in his lectures at Clark University,[3] and will have discovered that the hysterical symptom did not derive from some unknown anatomical source, as was formerly supposed, but from certain psychic experiences of a highly emotional nature, called traumata or psychic wounds. Nowadays, I am sure, every careful and attentive observer of hysteria will be able to confirm from his own experience that these especially painful and distressing occurrences do in fact often lie at the root of the illness. This truth was already known to the older physicians.

206 So far as I know, however, it was really Charcot who, probably influenced by Page's theory of "nervous shock," [4] first made theoretical use of this observation. Charcot knew, from his experience of the new technique of hypnotism, that hysterical symptoms can be produced and also be made to disappear by

2 [First published 1895; partially trans. by A. A. Brill in *Selected Papers on Hysteria and Other Neuroses* (New York, 1909; later edns.); trans. in Standard Edn. of Freud, II (1955).—EDITORS.]

3 ["Five Lectures on Psycho-Analysis."]

4 [Probably Herbert W. Page, British psychiatrist, who published on this subject; see Bibliography.—EDITORS.]

suggestion. He believed something of the kind could be observed in those increasingly common cases of hysteria caused by accidents. The traumatic shock would be comparable, in a sense, to the moment of hypnosis, since the emotion it produced would cause, temporarily, a complete paralysis of the will during which the trauma could become fixed as an auto-suggestion.

207 This conception laid the foundations for a theory of psychogenesis. It was left for later aetiological researches to find out whether the same mechanism, or a similar one, existed in cases of hysteria which could not be called traumatic. This gap in our knowledge of the aetiology of hysteria was filled by the discoveries of Breuer and Freud. They showed that even in cases of ordinary hysteria which had not been regarded as traumatically conditioned the same traumatic element could be found, and that it seemed to have an aetiological significance. So it was very natural for Freud, himself a pupil of Charcot, to see in this discovery a confirmation of Charcot's views. Consequently, the theory elaborated out of the experience of that period, mainly by Freud, bore the imprint of a traumatic aetiology. It was therefore fittingly called the trauma theory.

208 The new thing about this theory, apart from the truly admirable thoroughness of Freud's analysis of hysterical symptoms, is the abandonment of the concept of auto-suggestion, which was the dynamic element in the original theory. It was replaced by a more detailed conception of the psychological and psychophysical effects produced by the shock. The shock or trauma causes an excitation which, under normal conditions, is got rid of by being expressed ("abreacted"). In hysteria, however, the trauma is incompletely abreacted, and this results in a "retention of the excitation," or a "blocking of affect." The energy of the excitation, always lying ready *in potentia,* is transmuted into the physical symptoms by the mechanism of conversion. According to this view, the task of therapy was to release the accumulated excitation, thereby discharging the repressed and converted affects from the symptoms. Hence it was aptly called the "cleansing" or "cathartic" method, and its aim was to "abreact" the blocked affects. That stage of the analysis was therefore bound up fairly closely with the symptoms—one analysed the symptoms, or began the work of analysis with the symptoms, very much in contrast to the psychoanalytical tech-

nique employed today. The cathartic method and the theory on which it is based have, as you know, been taken over by other professional people, so far as they are interested in psychoanalysis at all, and have also found appreciative mention in the text-books.

209 Although the discoveries of Breuer and Freud are undoubtedly correct in point of fact, as can easily be proved by any case of hysteria, several objections can nevertheless be raised against the trauma theory. The Breuer-Freud method shows with wonderful clearness the retrospective connection between the actual symptom and the traumatic experience, as well as the psychological consequences which apparently follow of necessity from the original traumatic situation. All the same, some doubt arises as to the *aetiological* significance of the trauma. For one thing, the hypothesis that a neurosis, with all its complications, can be related to events in the past—that is, to some factor in the patient's predisposition—must seem doubtful to anyone who knows hysteria. It is the fashion nowadays to regard all mental abnormalities not of exogenous origin as consequences of hereditary degeneration, and not as essentially conditioned by the psychology of the patient and his environment. But this is an extreme view which fails to do justice to the facts. We know very well how to find the middle course in dealing with the aetiology of tuberculosis. There are undoubtedly cases of tuberculosis where the germ of the disease proliferates from early childhood in soil predisposed by heredity, so that even under the most favourable conditions the patient cannot escape his fate. But there are also cases where there is no hereditary taint and no predisposition, and yet a fatal infection occurs. This is equally true of the neuroses, where things will not be radically different from what they are in general pathology. An extreme theory about predisposition will be just as wrong as an extreme theory about environment.

## THE CONCEPT OF REPRESSION

210 Although the trauma theory gave distinct prominence to the predisposition, even insisting that some past trauma is the *conditio sine qua non* of neurosis, Freud with his brilliant em-

piricism had already discovered, and described in the Breuer-Freud *Studies,* certain elements which bear more resemblance to an "environment theory" than to a "predisposition theory," though their theoretical importance was not sufficiently appreciated at the time. Freud had synthesized these observations in a concept that was to lead far beyond the limits of the trauma theory. This concept he called "repression." As you know, by "repression" we mean the mechanism by which a conscious content is displaced into a sphere outside consciousness. We call this sphere the unconscious, and we define it as the psychic element of which we are not conscious. The concept of repression is based on the repeated observation that neurotics seem to have the capacity for forgetting significant experiences or thoughts so thoroughly that one might easily believe they had never existed. Such observations are very common and are well known to anyone who enters at all deeply into the psychology of his patients.

211 As a result of the Breuer-Freud *Studies,* it was found that special procedures were needed to call back into consciousness traumatic experiences that had long been forgotten. This fact, I would mention in passing, is astonishing in itself, inasmuch as we are disinclined from the start to suppose that things of such importance could ever be forgotten. For this reason it has often been objected that the reminiscences brought back by hypnotic procedures are merely "suggested" and bear no relation to reality. Even if this doubt were justified, there would certainly be no justification for denying repression in principle on that account, for there are plenty of cases where the actual existence of repressed memories has been verified objectively. Quite apart from numerous proofs of this kind, it is possible to demonstrate this phenomenon experimentally, by the association test. Here we discover the remarkable fact that associations relating to feeling-toned complexes are much less easily remembered and are very frequently forgotten. As my experiments were never checked, this finding was rejected along with the rest. It was only recently that Wilhelm Peters, of the Kraepelin school, was able to confirm my earlier observations, proving that "painful experiences are very rarely reproduced correctly." [5]

5 ("Gefühl und Erinnerung," in Kraepelin, *Psychologische Arbeiten,* VI, pt. 2, p. 237.)

212 As you see, then, the concept of repression rests on a firm empirical basis. But there is another side of the question that needs discussing. We might ask if the repression is due to a conscious decision of the individual, or whether the reminiscences disappear passively, without his conscious knowledge? In Freud's writings you will find excellent proofs of the existence of a conscious tendency to repress anything painful. Every psychoanalyst knows dozens of cases showing clearly that at some particular moment in the past the patient definitely did not want to think any longer of the content to be repressed. One patient told me, very significantly: "Je l'ai mis de côté." On the other hand, we must not forget that there are any number of cases where it is impossible to show, even with the most careful examination, the slightest trace of "putting aside" or of conscious repression, and where it seems as if the process of repression were more in the nature of a passive disappearance, or even as if the impressions were dragged beneath the surface by some force operating from below. Patients of the first type give us the impression of being mentally well-developed individuals who seem to suffer only from a peculiar cowardice in regard to their own feelings. But among the second you may find cases showing a more serious retardation of development, since here the process of repression could be compared rather to an automatic mechanism. This difference may be connected with the question discussed above, concerning the relative importance of predisposition and environment. Many factors in cases of the first type appear to depend on the influence of environment and education, whereas in the latter type the factor of predisposition seems to predominate. It is pretty clear where the treatment will be more effective.

213 As I have indicated, the concept of repression contains an element which is in intrinsic contradiction with the trauma theory. We saw, for instance, in the case of Miss Lucy R., analysed by Freud,[6] that the aetiologically significant factor was not to be found in the traumatic scenes but in the insufficient readiness of the patient to accept the insights that forced themselves upon her. And when we think of the later formulation in the

6 [*Studies on Hysteria*, pp. 106ff.]

*Schriften zur Neurosenlehre*,[7] where Freud's experience obliged him to recognize certain traumatic events in early childhood as the source of the neurosis, we get a forcible impression of the incongruity between the concept of repression and that of the trauma. The concept of repression contains the elements of an aetiological theory of environment, while the trauma concept is a theory of predisposition.

214 At first the theory of neurosis developed entirely along the lines of the trauma concept. In his later investigations Freud came to the conclusion that no positive validity could be attributed to the traumatic experiences of later life, as their effects were conceivable only on the basis of a specific predisposition. It was evidently there that the riddle had to be solved. In pursuing the roots of hysterical symptoms, Freud found that the analytical work led back into childhood; the links reached backwards from the present into the distant past. The end of the chain threatened to get lost in the mists of earliest infancy. But it was just at that point that reminiscences appeared of certain sexual scenes—active or passive—which were unmistakably connected with the subsequent events leading to the neurosis. For the nature of these scenes you must consult the works of Freud and the numerous analyses that have already been published.

## THE THEORY OF SEXUAL TRAUMA IN CHILDHOOD

215 Hence arose the theory of sexual trauma in childhood, which provoked bitter opposition not because of theoretical objections against the trauma theory in general, but against the element of sexuality in particular. In the first place, the very idea that children might be sexual, and that sexual thoughts might play any part in their lives, aroused great indignation. In the second place, the possibility that hysteria had a sexual basis was most unwelcome, for the sterile position that hysteria either was a uterine reflex-neurosis or arose from lack of sexual satisfaction

[7] [By 1912, two volumes of Freud's *Sammlungen kleiner Schriften zur Neurosenlehre* had appeared, in 1906 and 1909 (another in 1913). The various contents of these volumes were trans., regrouped, in the *Collected Papers* (1924 ff.), and, further rearranged, in the Standard Edn. The precise reference here is unavailable.—EDITORS.]

had just been given up. Naturally, therefore, the validity of Freud's observations was contested. Had the critics confined themselves to that question, and not embellished their opposition with moral indignation, a calm discussion might have been possible. In Germany, for example, this method of attack made it impossible to gain any credit at all for Freud's theory. As soon as the question of sexuality was touched, it aroused universal resistance and the most arrogant contempt. But in reality there was only one question at issue: were Freud's observations true or not? That alone could be of importance to a truly scientific mind. I daresay his observations may seem improbable at first sight, but it is impossible to condemn them *a priori* as false. Wherever a really honest and thorough check has been carried out, the existence of the psychological connections established by Freud has been absolutely confirmed, but not the original hypothesis that it is always a question of real traumatic scenes.

216 Freud himself had to abandon that first formulation of his sexual theory of neurosis as a result of increasing experience. He could no longer retain his original view as to the absolute reality of the sexual trauma. Those scenes of a decidedly sexual character, the sexual abuse of children, and premature sexual activity in childhood were later on found to be to a large extent unreal. You may perhaps be inclined to share the suspicion of the critics that the results of Freud's analytical researches were therefore based on suggestion. There might be some justification for such an assumption if these assertions had been publicized by some charlatan or other unqualified person. But anyone who has read Freud's works of that period with attention, and has tried to penetrate into the psychology of his patients as Freud has done, will know how unjust it would be to attribute to an intellect like Freud's the crude mistakes of a beginner. Such insinuations only redound to the discredit of those who make them. Ever since then patients have been examined under conditions in which every possible precaution was taken to exclude suggestion, and still the psychological connections described by Freud have been proved true in principle. We are thus obliged to assume that many traumata in early infancy are of a purely fantastic nature, mere fantasies in fact, while others do have objective reality.

217 With this discovery, somewhat bewildering at first sight, the

aetiological significance of the sexual trauma in childhood falls to the ground, as it now appears totally irrelevant whether the trauma really occurred or not. Experience shows us that fantasies can be just as traumatic in their effects as real traumata. As against this, every doctor who treats hysteria will be able to recall cases where violent traumatic impressions have in fact precipitated a neurosis. This observation is only in apparent contradiction with the unreality, already discussed, of the infantile trauma. We know very well that there are a great many more people who experience traumata in childhood or adult life without getting a neurosis. Therefore the trauma, other things being equal, has no absolute aetiological significance and will pass off without having any lasting effect. From this simple reflection it is perfectly clear that the individual must meet the trauma with a quite definite inner predisposition in order to make it really effective. This inner predisposition is not to be understood as that obscure, hereditary disposition of which we know so little, but as a psychological development which reaches its climax, and becomes manifest, at the traumatic moment.

### THE PREDISPOSITION FOR THE TRAUMA

218 I will now show you, by means of a concrete example, the nature of the trauma and its psychological preparation. It concerns the case of a young woman who suffered from acute hysteria following a sudden fright.[8] She had been to an evening party and was on her way home about midnight in the company of several acquaintances, when a cab came up behind them at full trot. The others got out of the way, but she, as though spellbound with terror, kept to the middle of the road and ran along in front of the horses. The cabman cracked his whip and swore; it was no good, she ran down the whole length of the road, which led across a bridge. There her strength deserted her, and to avoid being trampled on by the horses she would, in her desperation, have leapt into the river had not the passers-by restrained her. Now, this same lady had happened to be in St. Petersburg on the bloody 22nd of January [1905], in the very street which

[8] [This case is fully reported in *Two Essays on Analytical Psychology*, pars. 8ff., 417ff.—EDITORS.]

was being cleared by the volleys of the soldiers. All round her people were falling to the ground dead or wounded; she, however, quite calm and clear-headed, espied a gate leading into a yard, through which she made her escape into another street. These dreadful moments caused her no further agitation. She felt perfectly well afterwards—indeed, rather better than usual.

219 This failure to react to an apparent shock is often observed. Hence it necessarily follows that the intensity of a trauma has very little pathogenic significance in itself; everything depends on the particular circumstances. Here we have a key to the "predisposition." We have therefore to ask ourselves: what are the particular circumstances of the scene with the cab? The patient's fear began with the sound of the trotting horses; for an instant it seemed to her that this portended some terrible doom —her death, or something as dreadful; the next moment she lost all sense of what she was doing.

220 The real shock evidently came from the horses. The patient's predisposition to react in so unaccountable a way to this unremarkable incident might therefore be due to the fact that horses have some special significance for her. We might conjecture, for instance, that she once had a dangerous accident with horses. This was actually found to be the case. As a child of about seven she was out for a drive with the coachman, when suddenly the horses took fright and at a wild gallop made for the precipitous bank of a deep river-gorge. The coachman jumped off and shouted to her to do likewise, but she was in such deadly fear that she could hardly make up her mind. Nevertheless she managed to jump in the nick of time, while the horses crashed with the carriage into the depths below. That such an event would leave a very deep impression hardly needs proof. Yet it does not explain why at a later date such an insensate reaction should follow a perfectly harmless stimulus. So far we know only that the later symptom had a prelude in childhood. The pathological aspect of it still remains in the dark.

221 This anamnesis, whose continuation we shall find out later,[9] shows very clearly the discrepancy between the so-called trauma and the part played by fantasy. In this case fantasy must predominate to a quite extraordinary degree in order to produce

9 [See infra, pars. 297ff. and 355ff.—EDITORS.]

such a great effect from so insignificant a stimulus. At first one is inclined to adduce that early childhood trauma as an explanation—not very successfully, it seems to me, because we still do not understand why the effects of that trauma remained latent so long, and why they manifested themselves precisely on this occasion and on no other. The patient must surely have had opportunities enough during her lifetime of getting out of the way of a carriage going at full speed. The moment of deadly peril she experienced earlier in St. Petersburg did not leave behind the slightest trace of neurosis, despite her being predisposed by the impressive event in her childhood. Everything about this traumatic scene has still to be explained, for, from the standpoint of the trauma theory, we are left completely in the dark.

222 You must forgive me if I return so persistently to this question of the trauma theory. I do not think it superfluous to do so, because nowadays so many people, even those closely connected with psychoanalysis, still cling to the old standpoint, and this gives our opponents, who mostly never read our writings or do so only very superficially, the impression that psychoanalysis still revolves round the trauma theory.

223 The question now arises: what are we to understand by this "predisposition," through which an impression, insignificant in itself, can produce such a pathological effect? This is a question of fundamental importance, and, as we shall see later, it plays a very important role in the whole theory of neurosis. We have to understand why apparently irrelevant events of the past still have so much significance that they can interfere in a daemonic and capricious way with our reactions in actual life.

### THE SEXUAL ELEMENT IN THE TRAUMA

224 The early school of psychoanalysis, and its later disciples, did all they could to find in the special quality of those original traumatic experiences the reason for their later effectiveness. Freud went deepest: he was the first and only one to see that some kind of sexual element was mingled with the traumatic event, and that this admixture, of which the patient was generally unconscious, was chiefly responsible for the effect of the

trauma. The unconsciousness of sexuality in childhood seemed to throw a significant light on the problem of the long-lasting constellation caused by the original traumatic experience. The real emotional significance of that experience remains hidden all along from the patient, so that, not reaching consciousness, the emotion never wears itself out, it is never used up. We might explain the long-lasting constellative effect of the experience as a kind of *suggestion à échéance,* for this, too, is unconscious and develops its effect only at the appointed time.

225 It is hardly necessary to give detailed examples showing that the real character of sexual activities in infancy is not recognized. Doctors are aware, for instance, that open masturbation right up to adult life is not understood as such, especially by women. From this it is easy to deduce that a child would be even less conscious of the character of certain actions; hence the real meaning of these experiences remains hidden from consciousness even in adult life. In some cases the experiences themselves are completely forgotten, either because their sexual significance is quite unknown to the patient, or because their sexual character, being too painful, is not admitted, in other words, is repressed.

226 As already mentioned, Freud's observation that the admixture of a sexual element in the trauma is a characteristic concomitant having a pathological effect led to the theory of the infantile sexual trauma. This hypothesis means that the pathogenic experience is a sexual one.

## INFANTILE SEXUAL FANTASY

227 At first this hypothesis was countered by the widespread opinion that children have no sexuality at all in early life, thus making such an aetiology unthinkable. The modification of the trauma theory already discussed, that the trauma is generally not real at all but essentially just fantasy, does not make things any better. On the contrary, it obliges us to see in the pathogenic experience a positive sexual manifestation of infantile fantasy. It is no longer some brutal accidental impression coming from outside, but a sexual manifestation of unmistakable clearness actually created by the child. Even real traumatic

experiences of a definitely sexual character do not happen to the child entirely without his co-operation; it was found that very often he himself prepares the way for them and brings them to pass. Abraham has furnished valuable proofs of great interest in support of this, which in conjunction with many other experiences of the same kind make it seem very probable that even real traumata are frequently aided and abetted by the psychological attitude of the child. Medical jurisprudence, quite independently of psychoanalysis, can offer striking parallels in support of this psychoanalytic assertion.

228 The precocious manifestations of sexual fantasy, and their traumatic effect, now seemed to be the source of the neurosis. One was therefore obliged to attribute to children a much more developed sexuality than was admitted before. Cases of precocious sexuality had long been recorded in the literature, for instance of a two-year-old girl who was menstruating regularly, or of boys between three and five years old having erections and therefore being capable of cohabitation. But these cases were curiosities. Great was the astonishment, therefore, when Freud began to credit children not only with ordinary sexuality but even with a so-called "polymorphous-perverse" sexuality, and moreover on the basis of the most exhaustive investigations. People were far too ready with the facile assumption that all this had merely been suggested to the patients and was accordingly a highly debatable artificial product.

229 In these circumstances, Freud's *Three Essays on the Theory of Sexuality*[10] provoked not only opposition but violent indignation. I need hardly point out that the progress of science is not furthered by indignation and that arguments based on the sense of moral outrage may suit the moralist—for that is his business—but not the scientist, who must be guided by truth and not by moral sentiments. If matters really are as Freud describes them, all indignation is absurd; if they are not, indignation will avail nothing. The decision as to what is the truth must be left solely to observation and research. In consequence of this misplaced indignation the opponents of psychoanalysis, with a few honourable exceptions, present a slightly comic picture of pitiful backwardness. Although the psychoanalytic school

10 [First published in 1905.]

was unfortunately unable to learn anything from its critics, as the critics did not trouble to examine our actual conclusions, and although it could not get any useful hints, because the psychoanalytic method of investigation was and still is unknown to them, it nevertheless remains the duty of our school to discuss very thoroughly the discrepancies between the existing views. It is not our endeavour to put forward a paradoxical theory contradicting all previous theories, but rather to introduce a certain category of new observations into science. We therefore consider it our duty to do whatever we can from our side to promote agreement. True, we must give up trying to reach an understanding with all those who blindly oppose us, which would be a waste of effort, but we do hope to make our peace with men of science. This will now be my endeavour in attempting to sketch the further conceptual development of psychoanalysis, up to the point where it reached the *sexual theory of neurosis*.[11]

[11] [See pp. 47ff.]

## 2. THE THEORY OF INFANTILE SEXUALITY

230 As you have heard in the last lecture, the discovery of precocious sexual fantasies, which seemed to be the source of the neurosis, forced Freud to assume the existence of a richly developed infantile sexuality. As you know, the validity of this observation has been roundly contested by many, who argue that crude error and bigoted delusion have misled Freud and his whole school, alike in Europe and in America, into seeing things that never existed. We are therefore regarded as people in the grip of an intellectual epidemic. I must confess that I have no way of defending myself against this sort of "criticism." For the rest, I must remark that science has no right to start off with the idea that certain facts do not exist. The most one can say is that they appear to be very improbable, and that more confirmation and more exact study are needed. This is also our reply to the objection that nothing reliable can be learnt from the psychoanalytic method, as the method itself is absurd. No one believed in Galileo's telescope, and Columbus discovered America on a false hypothesis. The method may for all I know be full of errors, but that should not prevent its use. Chronological and geographical observations were made in the past with quite inadequate instruments. The objections to the method must be regarded as so many subterfuges until our opponents come to grips with the facts. It is there that the issue should be decided —not by a war of words.

231 Even our opponents call hysteria a psychogenic illness. We believe we have discovered its psychological determinants and we present, undaunted, the results of our researches for public criticism. Anyone who does not agree with our conclusions is at liberty to publish his own analyses of cases. So far as I know, this has never yet been done, at least in the European literature. Under these circumstances, critics have no right to deny our discoveries *a priori*. Our opponents have cases of hysteria just as we have, and these are just as psychogenic as ours, so there is nothing to prevent them from finding the psychological deter-

minants. It does not depend on the method. Our opponents content themselves with attacking and vilifying our researches, but they do not know how to find a better way.

232 Many of our critics are more careful and more just, and admit that we have made many valuable observations and that the psychic connections revealed by the psychoanalytic method very probably hold good, but they maintain that our conception of them is all wrong. The alleged sexual fantasies of children, with which we are here chiefly concerned, must not be taken, they say, as real sexual functions, being obviously something quite different, since the specific character of sexuality is acquired only at the onset of puberty.

233 This objection, whose calm and reasonable tone makes a trustworthy impression, deserves to be taken seriously. It is an objection that has given every thoughtful analyst plenty of cause for reflection.

## THE CONCEPT OF SEXUALITY

234 The first thing to be said about this problem is that the main difficulty resides in the concept of sexuality. If we understand sexuality as a fully developed function, then we must restrict this phenomenon to the period of maturity and are not justified in speaking of infantile sexuality. But if we limit our conception in this way, we are faced with a new and much greater difficulty. What name are we then to give to all those biological phenomena correlated with the sexual function in the strict sense, such as pregnancy, birth, natural selection, protection of offspring, and so on? It seems to me that all this belongs to the concept of sexuality, although a distinguished colleague did once say that childbirth is not a sexual act. But if these things do pertain to the concept of sexuality, then countless psychological phenomena must come into it too, for we know that an incredible number of purely psychological functions are connected with this sphere. I need only mention the extraordinary importance of fantasy in preparing and perfecting the sexual function. Thus we arrive at a highly biological conception of sexuality, which includes within it a series of psychological functions as well as a series of physiological phenomena. Availing

ourselves of an old but practical classification, we might identify sexuality with the instinct for the preservation of the species, which in a certain sense may be contrasted with the instinct of self-preservation.

235 Looking at sexuality from this point of view, we shall no longer find it so astonishing that the roots of the preservation of the species, on which nature sets such store, go much deeper than the limited conception of sexuality would ever allow. Only the more or less grown-up cat catches mice, but even the very young kitten at least plays at catching them. The puppy's playful attempts at copulation begin long before sexual maturity. We have a right to suppose that man is no exception to this rule. Even though we do not find such things on the surface in our well-brought-up children, observation of children of primitive peoples proves that they are no exceptions to the biological norm. It is really far more probable that the vital instinct for preservation of the species begins to unfold in early infancy than that it should descend at one fell swoop from heaven, fully-fledged, at puberty. Also, the organs of reproduction develop long before the slightest sign of their future function can be discerned.

236 So when the psychoanalytic school speaks of "sexuality," this wider concept of the preservation of the species should be associated with it, and it should not be thought that we mean merely the physical sensations and functions which are ordinarily connoted by that word. It might be said that in order to avoid misunderstandings one should not call the preliminary phenomena of early infancy "sexual." But this demand is surely not justified, since anatomical nomenclature is taken from the fully-developed system and it is not usual to give special names to the more or less rudimentary stages.

## IMPORTANCE OF THE NUTRITIVE FUNCTION

237 Now although no fault can be found with Freud's sexual terminology as such, since he logically gives all the stages of sexual development the general name of sexuality, it has nevertheless led to certain conclusions which in my view are untenable. For if we ask ourselves how far the first traces of sexuality

go back into childhood, we have to admit that though sexuality exists implicity *ab ovo* it only manifests itself after a long period of extra-uterine life. Freud is inclined to see even in the infant's sucking at its mother's breast a kind of sexual act. He was bitterly attacked for this view, yet we must admit that it is sensible enough if we assume with Freud that the instinct for the preservation of the species, i.e., sexuality, exists as it were separately from the instinct of self-preservation, i.e., the nutritive function, and accordingly undergoes a special development *ab ovo*. But this way of thinking seems to me inadmissible biologically. It is not possible to separate the two modes of manifestation or functioning of the hypothetical life-instinct and assign each of them a special path of development. If we judge by what we see, we must take into consideration the fact that in the whole realm of organic nature the life-process consists for a long time only in the functions of nutrition and growth. We can observe this very clearly indeed in many organisms, for instance in butterflies, which as caterpillars first pass through an asexual stage of nutrition and growth only. The intra-uterine period of human beings, as well as the extra-uterine period of infancy, belong to this stage of the life process.

238 *This period is characterized by the absence of any sexual function,* so that to speak of manifest sexuality in infancy would be a contradiction in terms. The most we can ask is whether, among the vital functions of the infantile period, there are some that do not have the character of nutrition and growth and hence could be termed sexual. Freud points to the unmistakable excitement and satisfaction of the infant while sucking, and he compares these emotional mechanisms with those of the sexual act. This comparison leads him to assume that the act of sucking has a sexual quality. Such an assumption would be justifiable only if it were proved that the tension of a physical need, and its release by gratification, is a sexual process. But the fact that sucking has this emotional mechanism proves just the contrary. Consequently we can only say that this emotional mechanism is found both in the nutritive function and in the sexual function. If Freud derives the sexual quality of the act of sucking from the analogy of the emotional mechanism, biological experience would also justify a terminology qualifying the sexual act as a function of nutrition. This is exceeding the bounds in both

directions. What is quite evident is that the act of sucking cannot be qualified as sexual.

239 We know, however, of other functions at the infantile stage which apparently have nothing to do with the function of nutrition, such as sucking the finger and its numerous variants. Here is rather the place to ask whether such things belong to the sexual sphere. They do not serve nutrition, but produce pleasure. Of that there can be no doubt, but it nevertheless remains disputable whether the pleasure obtained by sucking should be called by analogy a sexüal pleasure. It could equally well be called a nutritive pleasure. This latter qualification is the more apt in that the form of pleasure and the place where it is obtained belong entirely to the sphere of nutrition. The hand which is used for sucking is being prepared in this way for the independent act of feeding in the future. That being so, surely no one will beg the question by asserting that the first expressions of human life are sexual.

240 Yet the formula we hit on just now, that pleasure is sought in sucking the finger without serving any nutritive purpose, leaves us feeling doubtful whether it does belong entirely to the sphere of nutrition. We notice that the so-called bad habits of a child as it grows up are closely connected with early infantile sucking, like putting the finger in the mouth, biting the nails, picking the nose, ears, etc. We see, too, how easily these habits pass over into masturbation later on. The conclusion that these infantile habits are the first stages of masturbation or of similar activities, and therefore have a distinctly sexual character, cannot be denied: it is perfectly legitimate. I have seen many cases in which an indubitable correlation existed between these childish habits and masturbation, and if masturbation occurs in late childhood, before puberty, it is nothing but a continuation of the infantile bad habits. The inference from masturbation that other infantile habits have a sexual character appears natural and understandable from this point of view, in so far as they are acts for obtaining pleasure from one's own body.

241 From here it is but a short step to qualifying the infant's sucking as sexual. Freud, as you know, took that step and you have just heard me reject it. For here we come upon a contradiction which is very hard to resolve. It would be fairly easy if we could assume two separate instincts existing side by side.

Then the act of sucking the breast would be a nutritive act and at the same time a sexual act, a sort of combination of the two instincts. This seems to be Freud's conception. The obvious co-existence of the two instincts, or rather their manifestation in the form of hunger and the sexual drive, is found in the life of adults. But at the infantile stage we find *only* the function of nutrition, which sets a premium on pleasure and satisfaction. Its sexual character can be argued only by a *petitio principii*, for the facts show that the act of sucking is the first to give pleasure, not the sexual function. *Obtaining pleasure is by no means identical with sexuality.* We deceive ourselves if we think that the two instincts exist side by side in the infant, for then we project into the psyche of the child an observation taken over from the psychology of adults. The co-existence or separate manifestation of the two instincts is *not* found in the infant, for one of the instinctual systems is not developed at all, or is quite rudimentary. If we take the attitude that the striving for pleasure is something sexual, we might just as well say, paradoxically, that hunger is a sexual striving, since it seeks pleasure by satisfaction. But if we juggle with concepts like that, we should have to allow our opponents to apply the terminology of hunger to sexuality. This kind of one-sidedness appears over and over again in the history of science. I am not saying this as a reproach: on the contrary, we must be glad that there are people who are courageous enough to be immoderate and one-sided. It is to them that we owe our discoveries. What is regrettable is that each should defend his one-sidedness so passionately. Scientific theories are merely suggestions as to how things might be observed.

242 The co-existence of two instinctual systems is an hypothesis that would certainly facilitate matters, but unfortunately it is impossible because it contradicts the observed facts and, if pursued, leads to untenable conclusions.

## THE POLYMORPHOUS-PERVERSE SEXUALITY OF INFANCY

243 Before I try to resolve this contradiction, I must say something more about Freud's sexual theory and the changes it has undergone. As I explained earlier, the discovery of a sexual

fantasy-activity in childhood, which apparently had the effect of a trauma, led to the assumption that the child must have, in contradiction to all previous views, an almost fully developed sexuality, and even a polymorphous-perverse sexuality. Its sexuality does not seem to be centred on the genital function and on the other sex, but is occupied with the child's own body, whence it is said to be autoerotic. If its sexual interest is directed outwards to another person, it makes but little difference to the child what that person's sex is. Hence the child may very easily be "homosexual." Instead of the non-existent, localized sexual function there are a number of so-called bad habits, which from this point of view appear as perverse actions since they have close analogies with subsequent perversions.

244 As a result of this conception sexuality, ordinarily thought of as a unity, was decomposed into a plurality of separate drives; and since it was tacitly assumed that sexuality originates in the genitals, Freud arrived at the conception of "erogenous zones," by which he meant the mouth, skin, anus, etc.

245 The term "erogenous zone" reminds us of "spasmogenic zone." At all events the underlying idea is the same: just as the spasmogenic zone is the place where a spasm originates, the erogenous zone is the place from which comes an afflux of sexuality. On the underlying model of the genitals as the anatomical source of sexuality, the erogenous zones would have to be conceived as so many genital organs out of which sexuality flows. This state is the polymorphous-perverse sexuality of children. The term "perverse" appeared justified by the close analogy with later perversions which are, so to speak, simply a new edition of certain "perverse" interests in early infancy. They are frequently connected with one or other of the erogenous zones and cause those sexual anomalies which are so characteristic of children.

## SEXUAL COMPONENTS AS ENERGIC MANIFESTATIONS

246 From this point of view the later, normal, "monomorphic" sexuality is made up of several components. First it falls into a homo- and a heterosexual component, then comes the autoerotic component, and then the various erogenous zones. This concep-

tion can be compared with the position of physics before Robert Mayer, when only separate fields of phenomena existed, each credited with elementary qualities whose correlation was not properly understood. The law of the conservation of energy brought order into the relationship of forces to one another, at the same time abolishing the conception of those forces as having an absolute, elementary character and making them manifestations of the same energy. The same thing will have to happen with this splitting of sexuality into the polymorphous-perverse sexuality of childhood.

247 Experience compels us to postulate a constant interchange of individual components. It was recognized more and more that perversions, for instance, exist at the expense of normal sexuality, and that increased application of one form of sexuality follows a decrease in the application of another form. To make the matter clearer I will give an example. A young man had a homosexual phase lasting for some years, during which time he had no interest in girls. This abnormal condition gradually changed towards his twentieth year, and his erotic interests became more and more normal. He began to take an interest in girls, and soon he had overcome the last traces of homosexuality. This lasted for several years, and he had a number of successful love-affairs. Then he wanted to marry. But here he suffered a severe disappointment, as the girl he adored threw him over. During the ensuing phase he gave up all idea of marriage. After that he experienced a dislike of all women, and one day he discovered that he had become homosexual again, for young men once more had a peculiarly irritating effect upon him.

248 If we regard sexuality as consisting of a fixed heterosexual and a fixed homosexual component we shall never explain this case, since the assumption of fixed components precludes any kind of transformation. In order to do justice to it, we must assume a great mobility of the sexual components, which even goes so far that one component disappears almost completely while the other occupies the foreground. If nothing but a change of position took place, so that the homosexual component lapsed in full force into the unconscious, leaving the field of consciousness to the heterosexual component, modern scientific knowledge would lead us to infer that equivalent effects would then arise from the unconscious sphere. These effects would have to

be regarded as resistances to the activity of the heterosexual component, that is, as resistances against women. But in our case there is no evidence of this. Though faint traces of such influences existed, they were of such slight intensity that they could not be compared with the previous intensity of the homosexual component.

249 On the existing theory, it remains incomprehensible how the homosexual component, regarded as so firmly fixed, could disappear without leaving any active traces behind it. ⟨Further, it would be very difficult to conceive how these transformations come about. One could, at a pinch, understand the development passing through a homosexual stage in the pubertal period in order to lay the foundation for normal heterosexuality later, in a fixed, definite form. But how are we then to explain that the product of a gradual development, to all appearances bound up very closely with organic processes of maturation, is suddenly abolished under the impact of an impression, so as to make room for an earlier stage? Or, if two active components are postulated as existing simultaneously side by side, why is only one of them active and not the other as well? One might object that the homosexual component in men does in fact show itself most readily in a peculiar irritability, a special sensitiveness in regard to other men. According to my experience the apparent reason for this characteristic behaviour, of which we find so many examples in society today, is an invariable disturbance in the relationship with women, a special form of dependence on them. This would constitute the "plus" that is counterbalanced by the "minus" in the homosexual relationship. (Naturally this is not the real reason. The real reason is the infantile state of the man's character.)⟩

250 It was, therefore, urgently necessary to give an adequate explanation of such a change of scene. For this we need a dynamic hypothesis, since these permutations of sex can only be thought of as dynamic or energic processes. Without an alteration in the dynamic relationships, I cannot conceive how a mode of functioning can disappear like this. Freud's theory took account of this necessity. His conception of components, of separate modes of functioning, began to be weakened, at first more in practice than in theory, and was eventually replaced by a conception of energy. The term chosen for this was *libido*.

## 3. THE CONCEPT OF LIBIDO

251 Freud had already introduced the concept of libido in his *Three Essays on the Theory of Sexuality,* where he says:

> The fact of the existence of sexual needs in human beings and animals is expressed in biology by the assumption of a "sexual instinct," on the analogy of the instinct of nutrition, that is of hunger. Everyday language possesses no counterpart to the word "hunger," but science makes use of the word "libido" for that purpose.[1]

252 In Freud's definition the term *libido* connotes an exclusively sexual need, hence everything that Freud means by libido must be understood as sexual need or sexual desire. In medicine the term *libido* is certainly used for sexual desire, and specifically for sexual lust. But the classical use of the word as found in Cicero, Sallust, and others was not so exclusive; there it is used in the more general sense of passionate desire.[2] I mention this fact now, because further on it will play an important part in our argument, and because it is important to know that the term *libido* really has a much wider range of meaning than it has in medicine.

253 The concept of libido—whose sexual meaning in the Freudian sense we shall try to retain as long as possible—represents that dynamic factor which we were seeking in order to explain the shifting of the psychological scenery. This concept makes it much easier to formulate the phenomena in question. Instead of the incomprehensible exchanging of the homosexual component for the heterosexual component, we can now say that the libido was gradually withdrawn from its homosexual application and that it passed over in the same measure to a heterosexual application. In the process the homosexual component disappeared almost completely. It remained only an empty possibility, signifying nothing in itself. Its very existence is quite

1 [Standard Edn., VII, p. 135.]

2 [Cf. the definition of libido in *Symbols of Transformation*, pars. 185f.]

rightly denied by the layman, just as he would deny the possibility that he is a murderer. The libido concept also helps to explain the reciprocal relationships between the various modes of sexual functioning. At the same time, it does away with the original idea of a plurality of sexual components, which savoured too much of the old philosophical notion of psychic faculties. Their place is taken by libido, which is capable of the most varied applications. The earlier "components" represent only possible modes of action. The libido concept puts in the place of a divided sexuality split into many roots a dynamic unity, lacking which these once-significant components remain nothing but potential activities. This conceptual development is of the greatest importance; it accomplishes for psychology the same advance that the concept of energy introduced into physics. Just as the theory of the conservation of energy deprived the various forces of their elementary character and made them manifestations of a single energy, so the theory of libido deprives the sexual components of their elementary significance as psychic "faculties" and gives them a merely phenomenological value.

### THE ENERGIC THEORY OF LIBIDO

254 This view is a far better reflection of reality than the theory of components. With the libido theory we can easily explain the case of the young man cited earlier. The disappointment he met with at the moment he wanted to marry drove his libido away from its heterosexual mode of application, with the result that it assumed a homosexual form again and thus reinduced the earlier homosexuality. Here I cannot refrain from remarking that the analogy with the law of the conservation of energy is very close. In both cases one has to ask, when one sees that a quantum of energy has disappeared, where this energy has re-emerged in the meantime? If we apply this point of view as an explanatory principle to the psychology of human conduct, we shall make the most surprising discoveries. We can then see that the most heterogeneous phases in an individual's psychological development are connected with one another in an energic relationship. Every time we come across a person who has a "bee in his bonnet," or a morbid conviction, or some extreme

attitude, we know that there is too much libido, and that the excess must have been taken from somewhere else where, consequently, there is too little. From this point of view psychoanalysis is a method which helps us to discover those places or functions where there is too little libido, and to restore the balance. Thus the symptoms of a neurosis must be regarded as exaggerated functions over-invested with libido.[3] The energy used for this purpose has been taken from somewhere else, and it is the task of the psychoanalyst to discover the place it was taken from or where it was never applied.

255 The question has to be reversed in the case of those syndromes characterized mainly by lack of libido, for instance apathetic states. Here we have to ask, where did the libido go? The patient gives us the impression of having no libido, and there are many doctors who take him at his face value. Such doctors have a primitive way of thinking, like a savage who, seeing an eclipse of the sun, believes that the sun has been swallowed and killed. But the sun is only hidden, and so it is with these patients. The libido is there, but it is not visible and is inaccessible to the patient himself. Superficially, we have here a lack of libido. It is the task of psychoanalysis to search out that hidden place where the libido dwells and where the patient himself cannot get at it. The hidden place is the "non-conscious," which we may also call the "unconscious" without attributing to it any mystical significance.

### *UNCONSCIOUS FANTASY SYSTEMS*

256 Psychoanalysis has taught us that there are non-conscious psychological systems which, by analogy with conscious fantasies, can be described as unconscious fantasy systems. In states of neurotic apathy these unconscious fantasy systems are the objects of libido. We are fully aware that when we speak of unconscious fantasy-systems we are speaking only figuratively. By this we mean no more than that we accept as a necessary postulate the conception of psychic entities outside consciousness. Experience teaches us, we might say daily, that there are non-conscious

3 We meet with a similar view in Janet.

psychic processes which perceptibly influence the libido economy. Those cases known to every psychiatrist, in which a complicated system of delusions breaks out with comparative suddenness, prove that there must be unconscious psychic developments that have prepared the ground, for we can hardly suppose that such things come into being just as suddenly as they enter consciousness.

257 I have allowed myself to make this digression concerning the unconscious in order to point out that, with regard to the changing localization of libidinal investments, we have to reckon not merely with the conscious but with another factor, the unconscious, into which the libido sometimes disappears. We can now resume our discussion of the further consequences resulting from the adoption of the libido theory.

### THE CONSERVATION OF LIBIDO

258 Freud has taught us, and we see it in the everyday practice of psychoanalysis, that there exist in early childhood, instead of the later normal sexuality, the beginnings of many tendencies which in later life are called "perversions." We have had to admit Freud's right to apply a sexual terminology to these tendencies. Through the introduction of the libido concept, we see that in adults those elementary components which seemed to be the origin and source of normal sexuality lose their importance and are reduced to mere potentialities. Their operative principle, their vital force, so to speak, is the libido. Without libido these components mean practically nothing. Freud, as we saw, gives the libido an unquestionably sexual connotation, something like "sexual need." It is generally assumed that libido in this sense comes into existence only at puberty. How, then, are we to explain the fact that children have a polymorphous-perverse sexuality, and that the libido activates not merely one perversion but several? If the libido, in Freud's sense, comes into existence only at puberty, it cannot be held accountable for earlier infantile perversions—unless we regard them as "psychic faculties," in accordance with the theory of components. Quite apart from the hopeless theoretical confusion this would lead to, we would be sinning against the methodological axiom

that "explanatory principles are not to be multiplied beyond the necessary."

259 There is no alternative but to assume that before and after puberty it is the same libido. Hence the infantile perversions arise in exactly the same way as in adults. Common sense will object to this, as obviously the sexual needs of children cannot possibly be the same as those of sexually mature persons. We might, however, compromise on this point and say with Freud that though the libido before and after puberty is the same it is different in its intensity. Instead of the intense sexual need after puberty there would be only a slight sexual need in childhood, gradually diminishing in intensity until, at about the first year, it is nothing but a trace. We could declare ourselves in agreement with this from the biological point of view. But we should also have to assume that everything that comes within the realm of the wider concept of sexuality discussed in the previous lecture is already present in miniature, including all those emotional manifestations of psychosexuality, such as need for affection, jealousy, and many other affective phenomena, and by no means least the neuroses of childhood. It must be admitted, however, that these affective phenomena in children do not at all give the impression of being "in miniature"; on the contrary, they can rival in intensity those of an adult. Nor should we forget that, as experience has shown, the perverse manifestations of sexuality in childhood are often more glaring, and even seem to be more richly developed, than in adults. In an adult showing a similar state of richly developed perversion we could rightly expect a total extinction of normal sexuality and of many other important forms of biological adaptation, as is normally the case with children. An adult is rightly called perverse when his libido is not used for normal functions, and the same can reasonably be said of a child: he is polymorphous-perverse because he does not yet know the normal sexual function.

260 These considerations suggest that perhaps the amount of libido is always the same and that no enormous increase occurs at sexual maturity. This somewhat audacious hypothesis leans heavily, it is clear, on the law of the conservation of energy, according to which the amount of energy remains constant. It is conceivable that the peak of maturity is reached only when the infantile, subsidiary applications of libido gradually discharge

themselves into one definite channel of sexuality and are extinguished in it. For the moment we must content ourselves with these suggestions, for we must next pay attention to one point of criticism concerning the nature of the infantile libido.

261 Many of our critics do not concede that the infantile libido is simply less intense but of essentially the same nature as the libido of adults. The libidinal impulses of adults are correlated with the genital function, those of children are not, or only in exceptional cases, and this gives rise to a distinction whose importance must not be underestimated. It seems to me that this objection is justified. There is indeed a considerable difference between immature and fully developed functions, just as there is between play and seriousness, between shooting with blank and with loaded cartridges. This would give the infantile libido that undeniably harmless character which is demanded by common sense. But neither can one deny that blank-shooting is shooting. We must get accustomed to the idea that sexuality really exists, even before puberty, right back into early childhood, and we have no grounds for not calling the manifestations of this immature sexuality sexual.

262 This naturally does not invalidate the objection which, while admitting the existence of infantile sexuality in the form we have described, nevertheless contests Freud's right to designate as "sexual" early infantile phenomena such as sucking. We have already discussed the reasons which may have induced Freud to stretch his sexual terminology so far. We mentioned, too, how this very act of sucking could be conceived just as well from the standpoint of the nutritive function and that, on biological grounds, there was actually more justification for this derivation than for Freud's view. It might be objected that these and similar activities of the oral zone reappear in later life in an undoubtedly sexual guise. This only means that these activities can be used later for sexual purposes, but proves nothing about their originally sexual character. I must, therefore, admit that I can find no ground for regarding the pleasure-producing activities of the infantile period from the standpoint of sexuality, but rather grounds to the contrary. It seems to me, so far as I am capable of judging these difficult problems correctly, that from the standpoint of sexuality it is necessary to divide human life into three phases.

### THE THREE PHASES OF LIFE

263 The first phase embraces the first years of life; I call this period the *presexual stage.*[4] It corresponds to the caterpillar stage of butterflies, and is characterized almost exclusively by the functions of nutrition and growth.

264 The second phase embraces the later years of childhood up to puberty, and might be called the *prepubertal stage.* Germination of sexuality takes place at this period.

265 The third phase is the adult period from puberty on, and may be called the period of *maturity.*

266 It will not have escaped you that the greatest difficulty lies in assigning limits to the presexual stage. I am ready to confess my great uncertainty in regard to this problem. When I look back on my own psychoanalytic experiences with children—insufficiently numerous as yet, unfortunately—at the same time bearing in mind the observations made by Freud, it seems to me that the limits of this phase lie between the third and fifth year, subject, of course, to individual variation. This age is an important one in many respects. The child has already outgrown the helplessness of a baby, and a number of important psychological functions have acquired a reliable hold. From this period on, the profound darkness of the early infantile amnesia, or discontinuity of consciousness, begins to be illuminated by the sporadic continuity of memory. It seems as if, at this stage, an essential step forward is taken in the emancipation and centring of the new personality. So far as we know, the first signs of interests and activities which may fairly be called sexual also fall into this period, even though these indications still have the infantile characteristics of harmlessness and naïveté.

### THE SEXUAL TERMINOLOGY

267 I think I have sufficiently explained why a sexual terminology cannot be applied to the presexual stage, so we may now consider the other problems from the standpoint we have just

[4] [Cf. *Symbols of Transformation,* par. 206.]

reached. You will remember that we dropped the problem of decreased libido in childhood because it was impossible in that way to reach any clear conclusion. We now take up this question once again, if only to see whether the energic conception fits in with our present formulations.

268 We saw that the difference between infantile and mature sexuality can be explained, according to Freud, by the diminishing intensity of sexuality in childhood. But we have just advanced reasons why it seems doubtful that the life-processes of a child, with the exception of sexuality, are any less intense than those of adults. We could say that, sexuality excepted, the affective phenomena, and the nervous symptoms if there are any, are quite as intense as in adults. Yet, on the energic view, they are all manifestations of libido. It is therefore difficult to believe that the intensity of libido can make the difference between mature and immature sexuality. Rather the difference seems to be conditioned by a change in the localization of libido (if such an expression be permitted). In contradistinction to its medical definition, the libido of a child is occupied far more with subsidiary functions of a mental and physical nature than with local sexual functions. This being so, one is tempted to withdraw the predicate "sexualis" from the term "libido" and to strike out the sexual definition of libido given in Freud's *Three Essays on the Theory of Sexuality*. The necessity for this becomes really urgent when we ask ourselves whether the intense joys and sorrows of a child in the first years of his life, that is, *at the presexual stage,* are conditioned solely by his sexual libido.

269 Freud has pronounced himself in favour of this supposition. There is no need for me to repeat here the reasons which compelled me to postulate a presexual stage. The caterpillar stage possesses an alimentary libido but no sexual libido; we have to put it like that if we want to retain the energic view which the libido theory offers us. I think there is nothing for it but to abandon the sexual definition of libido, or we shall lose what is valuable in the libido theory, namely the energic point of view. For a long time now the need to give the concept of libido breathing-space and to remove it from the narrow confines of the sexual definition has forced itself on the psychoanalytical school. One never wearied of insisting that sexuality was not to

be taken too literally but in a wider sense; yet exactly *how* remained obscure and so could not satisfy the serious critics.

270 I do not think I am going astray if I see the real value of the concept of libido not in its sexual definition but in its energic view, thanks to which we are in possession of an extremely valuable heuristic principle. We are also indebted to the energic view for dynamic images and correlations which are of inestimable value to us in the chaos of the psychic world. Freudians would be wrong not to listen to those critics who accuse our libido theory of mysticism and unintelligibility. We were deceiving ourselves when we believed that we could make the *libido sexualis* the vehicle of an energic conception of psychic life, and if many of Freud's school still believe that they are in possession of a well-defined and, so to speak, concrete conception of libido, they are not aware that this concept has been put to uses which far exceed the bounds of any sexual definition. Consequently the critics are right when they object that the libido theory purports to explain things which do not properly belong to its sphere. This really does evoke the impression that we are operating with a mystical entity.

## THE PROBLEM OF LIBIDO IN DEMENTIA PRAECOX

271 In my book *Wandlungen und Symbole der Libido* I tried to furnish proof of these transgressions and at the same time to show the need for a new conception of libido which took account only of the energic view. Freud himself was forced to admit that his original conception of libido might possibly be too narrow when he tried to apply the energic view consistently to a famous case of dementia praecox—the so-called Schreber case.[5] This case is concerned among other things with that well-known problem in the psychology of dementia praecox, the loss of adaptation to reality, a peculiar phenomenon consisting in the special tendency of these patients to construct an inner fantasy world of their own, surrendering for this purpose their adaptation to reality.

272 One aspect of this phenomenon, the absence of emotional

5 ["Psycho-Analytic Notes on an Autobiographical Account of a Case of Paranoia (Dementia Paranoides)."]

rapport, will be well known to you, as this is a striking disturbance of the reality function. By dint of much psychoanalytic work with these patients we established that this lack of adaptation to reality is compensated by a progressive increase in the creation of fantasies, which goes so far that the dream world becomes more real for the patient than external reality. Schreber found an excellent figurative description for this phenomenon in his delusion about the "end of the world." He thus depicts the loss of reality in a very concrete way. The dynamic explanation is simple: we say that libido has withdrawn more and more from the external world into the inner world of fantasy, and there had to create, as a substitute for the lost world, a so-called reality equivalent. This substitute is built up piece by piece, so to speak, and it is most interesting to see out of what psychological material this inner world is constructed.

273 This way of looking at the displacement of libido is based on the everyday use of the term, its original, purely sexual connotation being very rarely remembered. In actual practice we speak simply of *libido,* and this is understood in so innocuous a sense that Claparède once remarked to me that one could just as well use the word "interest." The customary use of the term has developed, quite naturally and spontaneously, into a usage which makes it possible to explain Schreber's end of the world simply as a withdrawal of libido. On this occasion Freud remembered his original sexual definition of libido and tried to come to terms with the change of meaning that had quietly taken place in the meantime. In his paper on Schreber he asks himself whether *what the psychoanalytic school calls libido and conceives as "interest from erotic sources" coincides with interest in general.* You see that, putting the problem in this way, Freud asks himself the question which Claparède had already answered in practice.

274 Freud thus broaches the question of whether the loss of reality in schizophrenia, to which I drew attention in my "Psychology of Dementia Praecox," [6] is due entirely to the withdrawal of erotic interest, or whether this coincides with objective interest in general. We can hardly suppose that the normal "fonction du réel" (Janet) is maintained solely by erotic interest. The fact

6 [The first paper in *The Psychogenesis of Mental Disease,* Collected Works, Vol. 3.]

is that in very many cases reality disappears altogether, so that not a trace of psychological adaptation can be found in these patients. (In these states reality is replaced by complex contents.) We are therefore compelled to admit that not only the erotic interest, but all interest whatsoever, has got lost, and with it the whole adaptation to reality.

275 Earlier, in my "Psychology of Dementia Praecox," I tried to get round this difficulty by using the expression "psychic energy," because I could not base the theory of dementia praecox on the theory of displacements of libido sexually defined. My experience—at that time chiefly psychiatric—did not permit me to understand this latter theory: only later did I come to realize its partial correctness as regards the neuroses, thanks to increased experiences in the field of hysteria and obsessional neurosis. Abnormal displacements of libido, quite definitely sexual, do in fact play a great role in these illnesses. But although very characteristic repressions of sexual libido do take place in the neuroses, the loss of reality so typical of dementia praecox never occurs. In dementia praecox the loss of the reality function is so extreme that it must involve the loss of other instinctual forces whose sexual character must be denied absolutely, for no one is likely to maintain that reality is a function of sex, Moreover, if it were, the withdrawal of erotic interest in the neuroses would necessarily entail a loss of reality comparable to that which occurs in dementia praecox. But, as I said before, this is not the case.

276 ⟨Another thing to be considered—as Freud also pointed out in his work on the Schreber case—is that the introversion of sexual libido leads to an investment of the ego which might conceivably produce that effect of loss of reality. It is indeed tempting to explain the psychology of the loss in this way. But when we examine more closely the various things that can arise from the withdrawal and introversion of sexual libido, we come to see that though it can produce the psychology of an ascetic anchorite, it cannot produce dementia praecox. The anchorite's whole endeavour is to exterminate every trace of sexual interest, and this is something that cannot be asserted of dementia praecox.[7]⟩

7 ⟨It might be objected that dementia praecox is characterized not only by the introversion of sexual libido but also by a regression to the infantile level, and

277 These facts have made it impossible for me to apply Freud's libido theory to dementia praecox. I am also of the opinion that Abraham's essay on this subject [8] is theoretically untenable from the standpoint of Freud's conception of libido. Abraham's belief that the paranoid system, or the schizophrenic symptomatology, is produced by the withdrawal of sexual libido from the outside world cannot be justified in terms of our present knowledge. For, as Freud has clearly shown, a mere introversion or regression of libido invariably leads to a neurosis and not to dementia praecox. It seems to me impossible simply to transfer the libido theory to dementia praecox, because this disease shows a loss of reality which cannot be explained solely by the loss of erotic interest.

### THE GENETIC CONCEPTION OF LIBIDO

278 The attitude of reserve which I adopted towards the ubiquity of sexuality in my foreword to "The Psychology of Dementia Praecox," despite the fact that I recognized the psychological mechanisms pointed out by Freud, was dictated by the position of the libido theory at that time. Its sexual definition did not permit me to explain functional disturbances which affect the indefinite sphere of the hunger drive just as much as that of sex solely in the light of a sexual libido theory. Freud's libido theory had long seemed to me inapplicable to dementia praecox. In my analytical work I noticed that, with growing experience, a slow change in my conception of libido had taken place. Instead of the descriptive definition set forth in Freud's *Three Essays*, there gradually took shape a genetic definition of libido, which enabled me to replace the expression "psychic energy" by "libido." I had to tell myself: if the reality function consists nowadays to only a very small extent of sexual libido

---

that this constitutes the difference between the anchorite and the schizophrenic. This is certainly correct, but it would still have to be proved that in dementia praecox it is regularly and exclusively the erotic interest which goes into a regression. It seems to me rather difficult to prove this, because erotic interest would then have to be understood as the "Eros" of the old philosophers. But that can hardly be meant. I know cases of dementia praecox where all regard for self-preservation disappears, but not the very lively erotic interests.)

8 ["The Psycho-Sexual Differences between Hysteria and Dementia Praecox."]

and to a far greater extent of other instinctual forces, then it is very important to consider whether, phylogenetically speaking, the reality function is not, at least very largely, of sexual origin. It is impossible to answer this question directly, but we can seek to approach it by a circuitous route.

279 A cursory glance at the history of evolution suffices to show that numerous complicated functions, which today must be denied all trace of sexuality, were originally nothing but offshoots of the reproductive instinct. As we know, an important change occurred in the principles of reproduction during the ascent through the animal kingdom: the vast numbers of gametes which chance fertilization made necessary were progressively reduced in favour of assured fertilization and effective protection of the young. The decreased production of ova and spermatozoa set free considerable quantities of energy for conversion into the mechanisms of attraction and protection of offspring, etc. Thus we find the first stirrings of the artistic impulse in animals, but subservient to the reproductive instinct and limited to the breeding season. The original sexual character of these biological phenomena gradually disappears as they become organically fixed and achieve functional independence. Although there can be no doubt that music originally belonged to the reproductive sphere, it would be an unjustified and fantastic generalization to put music in the same category as sex. Such a terminology would be tantamount to treating of Cologne cathedral in a text-book of mineralogy, on the ground that it consisted very largely of stones.

280 Up to now we have spoken of libido as the instinct for propagation or for the preservation of the species, and have kept within the confines of a view which contrasts libido with hunger in the same way as the instinct for the preservation of the species is contrasted with the instinct for self-preservation. In nature, of course, this artificial distinction does not exist. There we see only a continuous life-urge, a will to live, which seeks to ensure the continuance of the whole species through the preservation of the individual. Thus far our conception of libido coincides with Schopenhauer's Will, inasmuch as a movement perceived from the outside can only be grasped as the manifestation of an inner will or desire. Once we have arrived at the bold conjecture that the libido which was originally employed in the

production of ova and spermatozoa is now firmly organized in the function of nest-building, for instance, and can no longer be employed otherwise, we are compelled to include every striving and every desire, as well as hunger, in this conception. There is no longer any justification for differentiating in principle between the desire to build nests and the desire to eat.[9]

281 I think you will already see where our argument is leading us. We are in the process of carrying through the energic point of view consistently, putting the energic mode of action in the place of the purely formal functioning. Just as the older sciences were always talking of reciprocal actions in nature, and this old-fashioned point of view was replaced by the law of the conservation of energy, so here too, in the realm of psychology, we are seeking to replace the reciprocal action of co-ordinated psychic faculties by an energy conceived to be homogeneous. We thus take cognizance of the justified criticism that the psychoanalytic school is operating with a mystical conception of libido.

282 For this reason I must dispel the illusion that the whole psychoanalytic school has a clearly understood and concrete conception of libido. I maintain that the libido with which we operate is not only not concrete or known, but is a complete X, a pure hypothesis, a model or counter, and is no more concretely conceivable than the energy known to the world of physics. Only in this way can we escape those violent transgressions of the proper boundaries, which happen time and again when we try to reduce co-ordinated forces to one another. ⟨We shall never be able to explain the mechanics of solid bodies or of electromagnetic phenomena in terms of a theory of light, for mechanics and electromagnetism are not light. Moreover, strictly speaking, it is not physical forces that change into one another, but the energy that changes its outward form. Forces are phenomenal manifestations; what underlies their relations with one another is the hypothetical idea of energy, which is, of course, entirely psychological and has nothing to do with so-called objective reality.⟩ This same conceptual achievement that has taken place in physics we seek to accomplish for the libido theory. We want to give the concept of libido the position that really belongs to it, which is a purely energic one, so that we can conceive the

9 [Pars. 278–80 and 274–75 reappear with certain modifications and additions in *Symbols of Transformation*, pars. 192ff.—EDITORS.]

life-process in terms of energy and replace the old idea of reciprocal action by relations of absolute equivalence. We shall not be disturbed if we are met with the cry of vitalism. We are as far removed from any belief in a specific life-force as from any other metaphysical assertion. Libido is intended simply as a name for the energy which manifests itself in the life-process and is perceived subjectively as conation and desire. It is hardly necessary to defend this view. It brings us into line with a powerful current of ideas that seeks to comprehend the world of appearances energically. Suffice it to say that everything we perceive can only be understood as an effect of force.

283 In the diversity of natural phenomena we see desire—libido—taking the most variegated forms. In early childhood it appears at first wholly in the form of the nutritive instinct which builds up the body. As the body develops, new spheres of activity are opened up successively for the libido. A definitive and extremely important sphere of activity is sexuality, which to begin with appears closely bound up with the function of nutrition (one has only to think of the influence of nutritional factors on propagation in the lower animals and plants). In the sphere of sexuality the libido acquires a form whose tremendous importance gives us the justification for using the ambiguous term "libido" at all. Here it appears at first in the form of an undifferentiated, primary libido, as the energy of growth that causes cell-division, budding, etc. in individuals.

284 Out of this primary, sexual libido, which produces from one small organism millions of ova and spermatozoa, there developed, by a tremendous restriction of fertility, offshoots whose function is maintained by a specifically differentiated libido. This differentiated libido is now "desexualized" by being divested of its original function of producing eggs and sperm, nor is there any possibility of restoring it to its original function. Thus the whole process of development consists in a progressive absorption of the primary libido, which produced nothing but gametes, into the secondary functions of attraction and protection of offspring. This development presupposes a quite different and much more complicated relation to reality, a genuine reality function which is inseparably connected with the needs of reproduction. In other words, the altered mode of reproduction brings with it, as a correlate, a correspondingly enhanced

adaptation to reality. This, of course, does not imply that the reality function owes its existence exclusively to the differentiation in reproduction. I am fully aware of the indefinitely large role played by the nutritive function.

285 In this way we gain some insight into the factors originally conditioning the reality function. It would be a fundamental error to say that its driving force is a sexual one. It *was* in large measure a sexual one originally, but even then not exclusively so.

286 The process of absorption of primary libido into secondary functions probably always occurred in the form of "libidinal affluxes," that is to say sexuality was diverted from its original destination and part of it used for the mechanisms of attraction and protection of the young—functions which gradually increase the higher you go in the phylogenetic scale. This transfer of sexual libido from the sexual sphere to subsidiary functions is still taking place. (Malthusianism, for instance, is an artificial continuation of the natural tendency.) Wherever this operation occurs without detriment to the adaptation of the individual we call it "sublimation," and "repression" when the attempt fails.

287 The descriptive standpoint of psychoanalysis views the multiplicity of instincts, among them the sexual instinct, as partial phenomena, and, in addition, recognizes certain affluxes of libido to nonsexual instincts.

288 The genetic standpoint is different. It regards the multiplicity of instincts as issuing from a relative unity, the libido; it sees how portions of libido continually split off from the reproductive function, add themselves as libidinal affluxes to the newly formed functions, and finally merge into them.

289 From this point of view we can rightly say that the schizophrenic withdraws his libido from the outside world and in consequence suffers a loss of reality compensated by an increase in fantasy activity.

## INFANTILE PERVERSIONS

290 We shall now try to fit this new conception of libido into the theory of infantile sexuality, which is so very important for the

theory of neurosis. In infants we find that libido as energy, as a vital activity, first manifests itself in the nutritional zone, where, in the act of sucking, food is taken in with a rhythmic movement and with every sign of satisfaction. With the growth of the individual and development of his organs the libido creates for itself new avenues of activity. The primary model of rhythmic movement, producing pleasure and satisfaction, is now transferred to the zone of the other functions, with sexuality as its ultimate goal. A considerable portion of the "alimentary libido" has to convert itself into "sexual libido." This transition does not take place quite suddenly at puberty, but only very gradually during the course of childhood. The libido can free itself only with difficulty and quite slowly from the modality of the nutritive function in order to pass over into the sexual function.

291 In this transitional stage there are, so far as I am able to judge, two distinct phases: the phase of sucking, and the phase of displaced rhythmic activity. Sucking belongs by its very nature to the sphere of the nutritive function, but outgrows it by ceasing to be a function of nutrition and becoming a rhythmic activity aiming at pleasure and satisfaction without intake of nourishment. At this point the hand comes in as an auxiliary organ. It appears even more clearly as an auxiliary organ in the phase of displaced rhythmic activity for pleasure, which then leaves the oral zone and turns to other regions. As a rule, it is the other body-openings that become the first objects of libidinal interest; then the skin, or special parts of it. The activities carried out in these places, taking the form of rubbing, boring, picking, pulling, and so forth, follow a certain rhythm and serve to produce pleasure. After lingering for a while at these stations, the libido continues its wanderings until it reaches the sexual zone, where it may provide occasion for the first attempts at masturbation. In the course of its migrations the libido carries traces of the nutritional phase into its new field of operations, which readily accounts for the many intimate connections between the nutritive and the sexual function.[10] This migration of libido takes place during the presexual stage, whose special distinguishing-mark is that the libido gradually sloughs off the

10 [Pars. 290–91 likewise recur with small changes in *Symbols of Transformation*, par. 206.—EDITORS.]

character of the nutritive instinct and assumes that of the sexual instinct.[11] At the stage of nutrition, therefore, we cannot yet speak of a true sexual libido.

292 In consequence, we are obliged to qualify the so-called polymorphous-perverse sexuality of early infancy. The polymorphism of libidinal strivings at this period can be explained as the gradual migration of libido, stage by stage, away from the sphere of the nutritive function into that of the sexual function. Thus the term "perverse," so bitterly attacked by our critics, can be dropped, since it creates a false impression.

293 When a chemical substance breaks up into its elements, these elements are, under those conditions, products of disintegration. But it is not permissible to describe all elements whatsoever as products of disintegration. Perversions are disturbed products of a developed sexuality. They are never the initial stages of sexuality, although there is an undoubted similarity between the initial stage and the product of disintegration. As sexuality develops, its infantile stages, which should no longer be regarded as "perverse" but as rudimentary and provisional, resolve themselves into normal sexuality. The more smoothly the libido withdraws from its provisional positions, the more quickly and completely does the formation of normal sexuality take place. It is of the essence of normal sexuality that all those early infantile tendencies which are not yet sexual should be sloughed off as much as possible. The less this is so, the more perverse will sexuality become. Here the expression "perverse" is altogether appropriate. The basic conditioning factor in perversion, therefore, is an infantile, insufficiently developed state of sexuality. The expression "polymorphous-perverse" has been borrowed from the psychology of neurosis and projected backwards into the psychology of the child, where of course it is quite out of place.

11 ⟨I must ask the reader not to misunderstand my figurative way of speaking. It is, of course, not libido as energy that gradually frees itself from the function of nutrition, but libido as a function, which is bound up with the slow changes of organic growth.⟩

## 4. NEUROSIS AND AETIOLOGICAL FACTORS IN CHILDHOOD

294 Now that we have ascertained what is to be understood by infantile sexuality, we can follow up the discussion of the theory of neurosis, which we began in the first lecture and then dropped. We followed the theory of neurosis up to the point where we ran up against Freud's statement that the predisposition which makes traumatic experiences pathogenically effective is a sexual one. Helped by our reflections since then, we can now understand how that sexual predisposition is to be conceived: it is a retardation, a check in the process of freeing the libido from the activities of the presexual stage. The disturbance must be regarded in the first place as a temporary fixation: the libido lingers too long at certain stations in the course of its migration from the nutritive function to the sexual function. This produces a state of disharmony because provisional and, as it were, outworn activities still persist at a period when they should have been given up. This formula can be applied to all those infantile features which are so prevalent in neurotics that no attentive observer can have failed to notice them. In dementia praecox the infantilism is so striking that it has even given a telltale name to one particular syndrome—*hebephrenia* (literally, 'adolescent mind').

295 The matter is not ended, however, by saying that the libido lingers too long in the preliminary stages. For while the libido is lingering, time does not stand still, and the development of the individual is proceeding apace. Physical maturation heightens the discrepancy between the perseverating infantile activity and the demands of later years with their changed conditions of life. In this way the foundation is laid for a dissociation of the personality, and hence for a conflict, which is the real basis of a neurosis. The more the libido is engaged in retarded activities, the more intense will the conflict be. The particular experience

best suited to make this conflict manifest is a traumatic or pathogenic one.

296 As Freud has shown in his early writings, one can easily imagine a neurosis arising in this way. It was a conception that fitted in quite well with the views of Janet, who attributed a neurosis to some kind of defect. From this standpoint one could regard neurosis as a product of retarded affective development, and I can easily imagine that this conception must seem self-evident to anyone who is inclined to derive the neuroses more or less directly from a hereditary taint or congenital degeneracy. Unfortunately the real state of affairs is much more complicated. In order to give you some idea of these complications, I shall cite a very ordinary example of hysteria, which I hope will show you how characteristic and how extremely important they are theoretically.

297 You will probably remember the case of the young hysteric I mentioned earlier, who, surprisingly enough, did not react to a situation which might have been expected to make a profound impression on her, and yet displayed an unexpected and pathologically violent reaction to a quite ordinary occurrence. We took this occasion to express our doubt as to the aetiological significance of the trauma, and to investigate more closely the so-called predisposition which rendered the trauma effective. The result of that investigation led to the conclusion just mentioned, that it is by no means improbable that the origin of a neurosis is due to a retardation of affective development.

298 You will now ask in what way the patient's affective development was retarded. The answer is that she lived in a world of fantasy which can only be described as infantile. It is unnecessary for me to give you a description of these fantasies, for, as neurologists or psychiatrists, you undoubtedly have a daily opportunity to listen to the childish prejudices, illusions, and emotional demands of neurotics. The disinclination to face stern reality is the distinguishing feature of these fantasies; there is a lack of seriousness, a playfulness in them, which sometimes frivolously disguises real difficulties, at other times makes mountains out of molehills, always thinking up fantastic ways of evading the demands of real life. We immediately recognize in them the intemperate psychic attitude of the child to reality, his precarious judgment, his lack of orientation, his dislike of un-

pleasant duties. With such an infantile mentality all manner of wishful fantasies and illusions can grow luxuriantly, and this is where the danger comes in. By means of these fantasies people can easily slip into an unreal and completely unadapted attitude to the world, which sooner or later must lead to catastrophe.

### THE TRAUMA THEORY CRITICIZED

299 If we follow the patient's infantile fantasy-life back into earliest childhood, we find, it is true, many obviously outstanding scenes which might well serve to provide fresh food for this or that fantastic variation, but it would be vain to search for the so-called traumatic elements from which something pathological, for instance her abnormal fantasy activity, might have originated. There were plenty of "traumatic" scenes, but they did not lie in early childhood; and the few scenes of early childhood which were remembered did not appear to be traumatic, being more like accidental experiences which passed by without having any effect worth mentioning on her fantasies. The earliest fantasies consisted of all sorts of vague and half-understood impressions she had received of her parents. All sorts of special feelings clustered round the father, fluctuating between fear, horror, aversion, disgust, love, and ecstasy. The case was like so many other cases of hysteria for which no traumatic aetiology can be found; they are rooted instead in a peculiar, premature fantasy activity which permanently retains its infantile character.

300 You will object that it is just that scene with the bolting horses that represents the trauma, and that this was obviously the model for that nocturnal scene eighteen years later, when the patient could not get out of the way of the horses trotting along behind her and wanted to throw herself into the river, following the model of the horses and carriage plunging down the ravine. From this moment on she also suffered from hysterical twilight states. But, as I tried to show you in my earlier lecture, we find no trace of any such aetiological connection in the development of her fantasy system. It is as though the danger of losing her life, that first time with the bolting horses, passed by without noticeable effect. In all the years following

that experience there was no discernible trace of that fright. It was as though it had never happened. In parenthesis let me add that perhaps it never happened at all. There is nothing to prevent it from being sheer fantasy, for here I have only the statements of the patient to rely on.[1]

301 Suddenly, after eighteen years, this experience becomes significant, is reproduced and acted out in all its details. The old theory says: the previously blocked affect has suddenly forced its way to the surface. This assumption is extremely unlikely and becomes still more inconceivable when we consider that the story of the bolting horses may not even be true. Be that as it may, it is almost inconceivable that an affect should remain buried for years and then suddenly explode at an unsuitable opportunity.

302 It is very suspicious, too, that patients often have a pronounced tendency to account for their ailments by some long-past experience, ingeniously drawing the analyst's attention away from the present to some false track in the past. This false track was the one pursued by the first psychoanalytical theory. But to this false hypothesis we owe an insight into the determination of neurotic symptoms which we should never have reached if the investigators had not trodden this path, guided into it, really, by the tendency of the patient to mislead. I think that only those who regard the happenings in this world as a concatenation of errors and accidents, and who therefore believe that the pedagogic hand of the rationalist is constantly needed to guide us, can ever imagine that this path was an aberration from which we should have been warned off with a signboard. Besides the deeper insight into psychological determination, we owe to this "error" a method of inquiry of incalculable importance. It is for us to rejoice and be thankful that Freud had the courage to let himself be guided along this path. Not thus is the progress of science hindered, but rather by blind adherence to insights once gained, by the typical conservatism of authority, by the childish vanity of the savant and his fear of making mistakes. This lack of courage is considerably more injurious to the name of science than an honest error. When

1 ⟨It may not be superfluous to remark that there are still people who believe that psychologists swallow the lies of their patients. That is quite impossible. Lies are fantasies, and we deal in fantasies.⟩

will there be an end to the incessant squabbling about who is right? One has only to look at the history of science: how many have *been* right, and how few have *remained* right!

### THE PARENTAL COMPLEX

303 But to return to our case. The question that now arises is this: if the old trauma is not of aetiological significance, then the cause of the manifest neurosis is obviously to be sought in the retardation of affective development. We must therefore regard the patient's statement that her hysterical twilight states were caused by the fright she got with the horses as null and void, although that fright was the starting-point for her manifest illness. This experience merely *seems* to be important without being so in reality, a formulation which is true of most other traumata. They merely *seem* to be important because they provide occasion for the manifestation of a condition that has long been abnormal. The abnormal condition, as we have already explained, consists in the anachronistic persistence of an infantile stage of libido development. The patients continue to hang on to forms of libido activity which they should have abandoned long ago. It is almost impossible to catalogue these forms, so extraordinarily varied are they. The commonest, which is scarcely ever absent, is an excessive fantasy activity characterized by a thoughtless overvaluation of subjective wishes. Excessive fantasy activity is always a sign of faulty application of libido to reality. Instead of being used for the best possible adaptation to the actual circumstances, it gets stuck in fantastic applications. We call this state one of partial introversion when libido is used for the maintenance of fantasies and illusions instead of being adapted to the actual conditions of life.

304 A regular concomitant of this retardation of affective development is the *parental complex*. When the libido is not used for purposes of real adaptation it is always more or less introverted.[2] The material content of the psychic world consists of

2 ⟨Introversion does not mean that libido simply accumulates inactively. But it is used for the creation of fantasies and illusions when the introversion results in regression to an infantile mode of adaptation. Introversion can also lead to action on a rational plane.⟩

memories, that is, of material from the individual's past (aside from actual perceptions). If the libido is partially or totally introverted, it invests to a greater or lesser degree large areas of memory, with the result that these reminiscences acquire a vitality that no longer properly belongs to them. The patients then live more or less entirely in the world of the past. They battle with difficulties which once played a role in their lives but which ought to have faded out long ago. They still worry, or rather are forced to worry, about things which should long since have ceased to be important. They amuse or torment themselves with fancies which, in the normal course of events, were once significant but no longer have any significance for adults.

305 Among the things that were of the utmost significance at the infantile period the most influential are the personalities of the parents. Even when the parents have long been dead and have lost, or should have lost, all significance, the situation of the patient having perhaps completely changed since then, they are still somehow present and as important as if they were still alive. The patient's love, admiration, resistance, hatred, and rebelliousness still cling to their effigies, transfigured by affection or distorted by envy, and often bearing little resemblance to the erstwhile reality. It was this fact that compelled me to speak no longer of "father" and "mother" but to employ instead the term "imago," because these fantasies are not concerned any more with the real father and mother but with subjective and often very much distorted images of them which lead a shadowy but nonetheless potent existence in the mind of the patient.

306 The complex of the parental imagos, that is, the whole tissue of ideas relating to the parents, provides an important field of activity for the introverted libido. I should mention in passing that the complex in itself leads but a shadowy existence if it is not invested with libido. In accordance with the earlier usage worked out in my *Studies in Word Association,* the word "complex" denoted a system of ideas already invested with libido and activated by it. But this system also exists *in potentia,* ready for possible action, even when not temporarily or permanently invested with libido.

## PARENTAL INFLUENCES ON CHILDREN

307 At the time when psychoanalytic theory was still dominated by the trauma concept and, in conformity with that view, was inclined to look for the *causa efficiens* of the neurosis in the past, it seemed to us that the parental complex was, as Freud called it, the "nuclear complex" of neurosis. The role of the parents seemed to be so powerful a factor that we were apt to blame them for all the subsequent complications in the life of the patient. Some years ago I discussed this in my paper, "The Significance of the Father in the Destiny of the Individual." [3] Once again we had allowed ourselves to be guided by the tendency of the patient to revert to the past, following the direction of his introverted libido. This time, certainly, it was no longer an external, accidental experience or event which seemed to produce the pathogenic effect; it was rather a psychological effect apparently arising out of the individual's difficulties in adapting to the conditions of the family milieu. The disharmony between the parents on the one hand and between the parents and the child on the other seemed especially liable to produce psychic currents in the child which were incompatible with his individual way of life.

308 In the paper just alluded to I cited a number of instances, taken from a wealth of material on this subject, which show these effects particularly clearly. The effects apparently emanating from the parents are not limited to the endless recriminations of their neurotic offspring, who constantly lay the blame for their illness on their family circumstances or bad upbringing, but extend even to actual events in the life of the patients, where no such determining influence could have been expected. The lively imitativeness which we find in primitives as well as in children can give rise, in particularly sensitive children, to a peculiar inner identification with the parents, to a mental attitude so similar to theirs that effects in real life are sometimes produced which, even in detail, resemble the personal experiences of the parents.[4]

3 [See *Freud and Psychoanalysis*, pars. 693ff., and *The Psychoanalytic Years*.]

4 ⟨I am discounting the inherited organic similarity which is naturally responsible for many things but by no means all.⟩

309 For the empirical material on this subject, I must refer you to the literature, but should just like to remind you that one of my pupils, Dr. Emma Fürst, has adduced valuable experimental proofs in regard to this problem. I have already referred to her researches in my lectures at Clark University.[5] By applying the association test to whole families, Dr. Fürst established the great conformity of reaction type among all members of one family. These experiments show that very often there exists an unconscious concordance of association between parents and children, which can only be explained as an intensive imitation or identification. The results of these researches indicate a far-reaching parallelism of biological tendencies that readily explains the sometimes astonishing similarity in the destinies of parents and children. Our destinies are as a rule the outcome of our psychological tendencies.

310 These facts enable us to understand why not only the patients themselves, but the theories that have been built on these researches, tend to assume that neurosis is the result of the characterological influence of the parents on the children. This assumption is, moreover, supported by the experience which lies at the base of all education, namely, the plasticity of the child's mind, which is commonly compared with soft wax, taking up and preserving all impressions. We know that the first impressions of childhood accompany us inalienably throughout life, and that, just as indestructibly, certain educational influences can keep people all their lives within those limits. In these circumstances it is not surprising that conflicts break out between the personality moulded by educational and other influences of the infantile milieu and one's own individual style of life. It is a conflict which all those must face who are called upon to live a life that is independent and creative.

311 Owing to the enormous influence which childhood has on the later development of character, you will readily understand why one would like to attribute the cause of a neurosis directly to the influences of the infantile environment. I must confess

5 [Fürst, "Statistical Investigations on Word-Associations and on Familial Agreement in Reaction Type among Uneducated Persons" (orig. 1905). Jung's discussion of her work occurred in the second of the Clark Lectures under the title "Familial Constellations"; see *Experimental Researches*, Coll. Works, Vol. 2.—EDITORS.]

that I have known cases in which any other explanation seemed to me less plausible. There are indeed parents whose own contradictory nature causes them to treat their children in so unreasonable a fashion that the children's illness would appear to be unavoidable. Hence it is almost a rule among nerve specialists to remove neurotic children, whenever possible, from the dangerous family atmosphere and place them among more healthy influences, where, even without any medical treatment, they thrive much better than at home. There are many neurotic patients who were clearly neurotic as children and so have never been free from illness since childhood. In such cases the view outlined above seems generally valid.

## THE INFANTILE MENTALITY

312 This knowledge, which for the time being seemed to us definitive, was considerably deepened by the researches of Freud and the psychoanalytic school. The parent-child relationship was studied in all its details, since it was just this relationship which was considered aetiologically important. It was soon noticed that these patients really did live partly or entirely in their childhood world, although themselves quite unconscious of this fact. On the contrary, it was the arduous task of psychoanalysis to investigate the psychological mode of adaptation so thoroughly that one could put one's finger on the infantile misunderstandings. As you know, a striking number of neurotics were spoiled as children. Such cases offer the best and clearest examples of the infantilism of their psychological mode of adaptation. They start out in life expecting the same friendly reception, tenderness, and easy success to which they were accustomed by their parents in their youth. Even very intelligent patients are incapable of seeing that from the very beginning they owe the complications of their lives as well as their neurosis to dragging their infantile emotional attitude along with them. The small world of the child, the family milieu, is the model for the big world. The more intensely the family sets its stamp on the child, the more he will be emotionally inclined, as an adult, to see in the great world his former small world. Of course this must not be taken as a conscious intellectual process. On the contrary,

the patient feels and sees the difference between now and then, and tries as well as he can to adapt himself. Perhaps he will even believe himself perfectly adapted, since he may be able to grasp the situation intellectually, but that does not prevent his emotions from lagging far behind his intellectual insight.

313 It is scarcely necessary to give you examples of this phenomenon, for it is an everyday experience that our emotions never come up to the level of our insight. It is exactly the same with the neurotic, but greatly intensified. He may perhaps believe that, except for his neurosis, he is a normal person, fully adapted to the conditions of life. It never crosses his mind that he has still not given up certain infantile demands, that he still carries with him, in the background, expectations and illusions of which he has never made himself conscious. He indulges in all sorts of pet fantasies, of which he is seldom, if ever, so conscious that he knows that he has them. Very often they exist only as emotional expectations, hopes, prejudices, and so forth. In this case we call them unconscious fantasies. Sometimes they appear on the fringe of consciousness as fleeting thoughts, only to vanish again the next moment, so that the patient is unable to say whether he had such fantasies or not. It is only during psychoanalytic treatment that most patients learn to retain and observe these fugitive thoughts. Although most fantasies were once conscious, for a moment, as fleeting thoughts, it would not do to call them *conscious,* because most of the time they are practically *unconscious.* It is therefore right to call them unconscious fantasies. Of course there are also infantile fantasies which are perfectly conscious and can be reproduced at any time.

## 5. THE FANTASIES OF THE UNCONSCIOUS

314 The realm of unconscious infantile fantasies has become the real object of psychoanalytic research, for it seems to offer the key to the aetiology of neurosis. Here, quite otherwise than with the trauma theory, we are forced by all the reasons we have mentioned to assume that the roots of the psychological present are to be found in the family history of the patient.

315 The fantasy systems which patients present on being questioned are mostly of a composite nature and are elaborated like a novel or a drama. But, despite their elaboration, they are of relatively little value in investigating the unconscious. Just because they are conscious, they defer too much to the demands of etiquette and social morality. They have been purged of all painful personal details, and also of everything ugly, thereby becoming socially presentable and revealing very little. The more valuable and evidently more influential fantasies are not conscious, in the sense previously defined, and so have to be dug out by the psychoanalytic technique.

316 Without wishing to enter fully into the question of technique, I must here meet an objection that is constantly heard. It is that the so-called unconscious fantasies are merely suggested to the patient and exist only in the mind of the analyst. This objection is on the same vulgar level as those which impute to us the crude mistakes of beginners. Only people with no psychological experience and no knowledge of the history of psychology are capable of making such accusations. No one with the faintest glimmering of mythology could possibly fail to see the startling parallels between the unconscious fantasies brought to light by the psychoanalytic school and mythological ideas. The objection that our knowledge of mythology has been suggested to the patient is without foundation, because the psychoanalytic school discovered the fantasies first and only then became acquainted with their mythology. Mythology, as we know, is something quite outside the ken of the medical man.

317 As these fantasies are unconscious, the patient is naturally unaware of their existence, and to question him about them directly would be quite pointless. Nevertheless it is said over and over again, not only by patients but by so-called normal persons: "But if I had such fantasies, surely I would know it!" But what is unconscious is in truth something that we do *not* know. Our opponents, too, are firmly convinced that such things do not exist. This *a priori* judgment is pure scholasticism and has no grounds to support it. We cannot possibly rest on the dogma that consciousness alone is the psyche, for we have daily proof that our consciousness is only a part of the psychic function. When the contents of our consciousness appear they are already in a highly complex state; the constellation of our thoughts from the material contained in our memory is a predominantly unconscious process. We are therefore obliged to assume, whether we like it or not, the existence of a non-conscious psychic sphere, even if only as a "negative borderline concept," like Kant's *Ding an sich.* Since we perceive effects whose origin cannot be found in consciousness, we are compelled to allow hypothetical contents to the sphere of the non-conscious, which means presupposing that the origin of those effects lies in the unconscious precisely because it is not conscious. This conception of the unconscious can hardly be accused of "mysticism." We do not pretend to know or to assert anything positive about the state of psychic elements in the unconscious. Instead, we have formulated symbolical concepts in a manner analogous to our formulation of conscious concepts, and this terminology has proved its value in practice.

## THE CONCEPT OF THE UNCONSCIOUS

318 This way of thinking is the only possible one if we accept the axiom that "principles are not to be multiplied beyond the necessary." We therefore speak about the effects of the unconscious just as we do about the phenomena of consciousness. Great objection was taken to Freud's statement: "The unconscious can only wish." This was regarded as an unheard-of metaphysical assertion, something like a tenet from von Hartmann's *Philosophy of the Unconscious.* The indignation was

due simply to the fact that these critics, unknown to themselves, evidently started from a metaphysical conception of the unconscious as an *ens per se,* and naïvely projected their epistemologically unclarified ideas on to us. For us the unconscious is not an entity in this sense but a mere term, about whose metaphysical essence we do not permit ourselves to form any idea. In this we are unlike those arm-chair psychologists who are not only perfectly informed about the localization of the psyche in the brain and the physiological correlates of mental processes, but can assert positively that beyond consciousness there are nothing but "physiological processes in the cortex."

319 Such naïvetés should not be imputed to us. When Freud says that the unconscious can only wish, he is describing in symbolical terms effects whose source is not conscious, but which from the standpoint of conscious thinking can only be regarded as analogous to wishes. The psychoanalytic school is, moreover, aware that the discussion as to whether "wishing" is a suitable analogy or not can be reopened at any time. Anybody who knows a better one will be welcome. Instead of which, our opponents content themselves with denying the existence of these phenomena or else, if certain phenomena have to be admitted, they abstain from all theoretical formulations. This last point is understandable enough, since it is not everyone's business to think theoretically.

320 Once one has succeeded in freeing oneself from the dogma of the psyche's identity with consciousness, thus admitting the possible existence of extra-conscious psychic processes, one cannot, *a priori,* either assert or deny anything about the potentialities of the unconscious. The psychoanalytic school has been accused of making assertions without sufficient grounds. It seems to us that the abundant, perhaps too abundant case-material contained in the literature offers enough and more than enough grounds, yet it does not seem sufficient for our opponents. There must be a good deal of difference as to the meaning of the word "sufficient" in regard to the validity of these grounds. So we must ask: Why does the psychoanalytic school apparently demand far less exacting proofs of its formulations than its opponents?

321 The reason is simple. An engineer who has built a bridge and calculated its load needs no further proof of its holding

capacity. But a sceptical layman, who has no notion how a bridge is built, or what is the strength of the material used, will demand quite different proofs of its holding capacity, since he can have no confidence in it. It is chiefly the profound ignorance of our opponents about what we are doing that screws their demands up to such a pitch. In the second place, there are the countless theoretical misunderstandings: it is impossible for us to know them all and to clear them up. Just as we find in our patients new and ever more astounding misconceptions about the ways and aims of psychoanalysis, so our critics display an inexhaustible ingenuity in misunderstanding. You can see from our discussion of the concept of the unconscious just what kind of false philosophical assumptions can vitiate understanding of our terminology. Obviously a person who thinks of the unconscious as an absolute entity is bound to require proofs of a totally different kind, utterly beyond our power to give, as our opponents in fact do. Had we to offer proof of immortality, mountains of proofs of the weightiest nature would have to be furnished, very different from what would be required to demonstrate the existence of plasmodia in a malaria patient. Metaphysical expectations still bedevil scientific thinking far too much for the problems of psychoanalysis to be seen in their own frame of reference.

322 But, in fairness to our critics, I must admit that the psychoanalytic school has itself given rise to plenty of misunderstandings, even though in all innocence. One of the principal sources is the confusion that reigns in the theoretical sphere. Regrettable though it is, we have no presentable theory. You would understand this if you could see in concrete instances the enormous difficulties we have to wrestle with. Contrary to the opinion of nearly all the critics, Freud is anything rather than a theorist. He is an empiricist, as anyone must admit who is willing to go at all deeply into Freud's writings and to try to see his cases as he sees them. Unfortunately, our critics are not willing. As we have repeatedly been told, it is "repulsive and disgusting" to see them as Freud does. But how can anyone learn the nature of Freud's method if he allows himself to be put off by disgust? Just because people make no effort to accommodate themselves to Freud's point of view, adopted perhaps as a necessary working hypothesis, they come to the absurd conclusion

that he is a theorist. They readily assume that *Three Essays on the Theory of Sexuality* is simply a theory, invented by a speculative brain, and that everything is put into the patient's head by suggestion. But that is turning things upside down. This makes it easy for the critics, which is just what they want. They pay no attention at all to the "couple of case-histories" with which the psychoanalyst conscientiously documents his theoretical statements, but only to the theory and the formulation of technique. The weak spots of psychoanalysis are not to be found here—for psychoanalysis is essentially empirical—though here, undoubtedly, is a large and insufficiently cultivated field where the critics can romp to their heart's content. In the field of theory there are many uncertainties and not a few contradictions. We were conscious of this long before our learned critics began to honour us with their attentions.

### THE DREAM

323 After this digression we will return to the question of unconscious fantasies which occupied us before. Nobody, as we have seen, has the right to assert their existence or define their qualities unless effects of unconscious origin are observed which can be expressed in terms of conscious symbolism. The only question is whether effects can in fact be found that comply with this expectation. The psychoanalytic school believes it has discovered such effects. I will mention the principal phenomenon at once: the dream.

324 Of this it may be said that it enters consciousness as a complex structure compounded of elements whose connection with each other is not conscious. Only afterwards, by adding a series of associations to the individual images in the dream, can we show that these images had their origin in certain memories of the recent past. We ask ourselves: Where have I seen or heard that? And then, by the ordinary process of association, comes the memory that certain parts of the dream have been consciously experienced, some the day before, some earlier. So far there will be general agreement, for these things have been known for a long time. To that extent the dream presents itself to us as a more or less unintelligible jumble of elements not at

first conscious and only recognized afterwards through their associations.[1] It should be added that not all parts of the dream have a recognizable quality from which their conscious character can be deduced; they are often, and indeed mostly, unrecognizable at first. Only afterwards does it occur to us that we have consciously experienced this or that part of the dream. From this standpoint alone we may regard the dream as a product of unconscious origin.

325 The technique for exploring the unconscious origin is the one I have just mentioned, used as a matter of course long before Freud by every dream-investigator. We simply try to remember where the parts of the dream came from. The psychoanalytic technique of dream elucidation is based on this very simple principle. It is a fact that certain parts of the dream are derived from our waking life, from events which, on account of their obvious unimportance, would have fallen into oblivion and were already on the way to becoming definitely unconscious. It is just these parts that are the effects of "unconscious ideas." Exception has been taken to this expression too. Naturally we do not take things nearly so concretely, not to say ponderously, as our critics. Certainly this expression is nothing more than conscious symbolism—we were never in any doubt on that point. But it is perfectly clear and serves very well as a sign for an unknown psychic fact. As I have said before, we have no alternative but to conceive the unconscious by analogy with the conscious. We do not pretend that we understand a thing merely because we have invented a sonorous and all-but-incomprehensible name for it.

## THE METHOD OF DREAM-ANALYSIS

326 The principle of psychoanalytic elucidation is, therefore, extraordinarily simple and has actually been known for a long time. The subsequent procedure follows logically along the

1 (This might be disputed on the ground that it is an *a priori* assertion. I must remark, however, that this view conforms to the one generally accepted working hypothesis concerning the origin of dreams: that they are derived from the experiences and thoughts of the recent past. We are, therefore, moving on known ground.)

same lines. If we get really absorbed in a dream—which naturally never happens outside analysis—we shall succeed in discovering still more reminiscences about the individual dream-parts. But we are not always successful in finding reminiscences about some of them. These must be put aside for the time being. (When I say "reminiscences" I do not mean only memories of actual experiences; I also mean the reproduction of meaningful associations and connections.) The reminiscences so gathered are called the "dream-material." We treat this material in accordance with a generally accepted scientific principle. If you have any experimental material to work up, you compare its individual parts and classify them according to their similarities. You proceed in exactly the same way with dream-material; you look for the *common features, whether of form or content.*

327 In doing this one has to get rid, so far as possible, of certain prejudices. I have observed that the beginner is always looking for some special feature and then tries to force his material to conform to his expectations. I have noticed this particularly with colleagues who, because of the well-known prejudices and misunderstandings, were once passionate opponents of psychoanalysis. If it was my fate to analyse them, and they at last obtained real insight into the method, the first mistake they generally made in their psychoanalytic work was to do violence to the material by their own preconceived opinions. That is, they now vented their previous attitude to psychoanalysis on their material, which they could not assess objectively but only in terms of their subjective fantasies.

328 Once embarked on the task of examining the dream-material, you must not shrink from any comparison. The material usually consists of very disparate images, from which it is sometimes very difficult to extract the *tertium comparationis.* I must refrain from giving detailed examples, as it is quite impossible to discuss such voluminous material in a lecture. I would, however, like to call your attention to a paper by Rank on "a dream which interprets itself."[2] There you will see how extensive is the material that must be taken into account for purposes of comparison.

329 Hence, in exploring the unconscious, we proceed in the

2 "Ein Traum, der sich selbst deutet" (1910).

usual way when conclusions are to be drawn by the comparative method. It has often been objected: Why should a dream have any unconscious content at all? This objection is in my view about as unscientific as it could possibly be. Every psychological element has its special history. Every sentence I utter has, besides the meaning consciously intended by me, its historical meaning, which may turn out to be quite different from its conscious meaning. I am expressing myself somewhat paradoxically on purpose: I do not mean that I could explain the historical meaning of every individual sentence. That is easier in the case of larger and more complex structures. Thus, it will be clear to everyone that, apart from the manifest content of a poem, the poem itself is especially characteristic of the poet in regard to its form, content, and manner of origin. While the poet merely gave expression in his poem to the mood of the moment, the literary historian will see things in it and behind it which the poet would never have suspected. The analysis which the literary historian makes of the poet's material is exactly comparable with the method of psychoanalysis, not excluding the mistakes that may creep in.

330 The psychoanalytic method can be compared with historical analysis and synthesis in general. Suppose, for instance, we did not understand the meaning of the baptismal rite practised in our churches today. The priest tells us: baptism means the admission of the child into the Christian community. But this does not satisfy us. Why is the child sprinkled with water? In order to understand this ceremony, we must gather together from the whole history of ritual, that is, from mankind's memories of the relevant traditions, a body of comparative material culled from the most varied sources:

1. Baptism is clearly a rite of initiation, a consecration. Therefore we have to collect all memories in which any initiation rites are preserved.

2. The act of baptism is performed with water. For this special form another series of memories must be collected, namely, of rites in which water is used.

3. The person to be baptized is sprinkled with water. Here we have to collect all those rites in which the neophyte is sprinkled, immersed, etc.

4. All reminiscences from mythology, folklore, as well as

superstitious practices, etc., have to be recalled, in so far as they run in any way parallel to the symbolism of the baptismal act.

331 In this way we build up a comparative study of the act of baptism. We discover the elements out of which the baptismal act is formed; we ascertain, further, its original meaning, and at the same time become acquainted with the rich world of myths that have laid the foundation of religions and help us to understand the manifold and profound meanings of baptism. The analyst proceeds in the same way with a dream. He collects the historical parallels to every part of the dream, even the remotest, and tries to reconstruct the psychological history of the dream and its underlying meanings. Through this monographic elaboration we obtain, just as in the analysis of baptism, a profound insight into the marvellously delicate and meaningful network of unconscious determination—an insight that may legitimately be compared with the historical understanding of an act which we had hitherto regarded in a very superficial and one-sided way.

332 This excursus seemed to me unavoidable. In view of the numerous misunderstandings of all those who constantly seek to discredit the psychoanalytic method, I felt obliged to give you a very general account of the method and its position within the methodology of science. I do not doubt that there are superficial and improper applications of this method. But an intelligent critic should not allow this to detract from the method itself, any more than a bad surgeon should be used to discredit the value of surgery in general. I do not doubt, either, that not all the expositions of dream-psychology by psychoanalysts are entirely free from misunderstandings and distortions. But much of this is due to the fact that, precisely because of his training in the natural sciences, it is difficult for the medical man to get an intellectual grasp of a very subtle psychological method, even though he instinctively handles it correctly.

333 The method I have described is the one I adopt and the one to which I hold myself scientifically responsible. To give advice about dreams and to make direct attempts at interpretation is, in my opinion, absolutely wrong and scientifically inadmissible. It is not a methodological but a quite arbitrary proceeding which defeats itself by the sterility of its results, like every false method.

334 If I have made the attempt to illustrate the principles of the psychoanalytic method by means of dream-analysis it is because the dream is one of the clearest examples of psychic contents whose composition eludes direct understanding. When someone knocks in a nail with a hammer in order to hang something up, we can understand every detail of the action; it is immediately evident. It is otherwise with the act of baptism, where every phase is problematic. We call these actions, whose meaning and purpose are not immediately evident, symbolic actions, or symbols. On the basis of this reasoning we call a dream symbolic, because it is a psychological product whose origin, meaning, and purpose are obscure, and is therefore one of the purest products of unconscious constellation. As Freud aptly says, the dream is the *via regia* to the unconscious.

## THE ASSOCIATION EXPERIMENT

335 There are many products of unconscious constellation besides dreams. In the association experiment we have a means of determining exactly the influence of the unconscious. We see these effects in the disturbances which I have called "complex indicators." The task which the association test sets the subject of the experiment is so extraordinarily simple that even children can accomplish it without difficulty. It is all the more surprising that, despite this, so many disturbances of the intended action should be registered. The only things that can regularly be shown to be causes of these disturbances are the partly conscious, partly unconscious constellations caused by complexes. In the majority of cases the connection of these disturbances with feeling-toned complexes can be demonstrated without difficulty. But very often we must have recourse to the psychoanalytic method in order to explain the connection; that is, we must ask the patient what associations he can give to the disturbed reactions.

336 In this way we obtain the historical material on which to base our judgment. It has been objected that the patient could then say whatever he liked—in other words, any old nonsense. This objection is made, I believe, on the unconscious assumption that the historian who gathers material for his monograph

is an imbecile, incapable of distinguishing real parallels from apparent ones and authentic reports from crude falsifications. The professional has means at his disposal for avoiding clumsy mistakes with certainty and more subtle ones with some probability. For anyone who understands psychoanalytic work it is a well-known fact that it is not so very difficult to see where there is coherence and where there is none. In addition, fraudulent statements are in the first place very significant of the person who makes them, and secondly they are easily recognized as fraudulent.

337 ⟨There is, however, another objection to be considered, which is more worth mentioning. One can ask oneself whether the reminiscences subsequently produced were really the basis of a dream. If, in the evening, I read an interesting account of a battle, and at night dream of the Balkan War, and then during analysis remember by association certain details in the account of the battle, even the most rigorous critic will fairly assume that my retrospective association is right and true. As I mentioned earlier, this is one of the most firmly entrenched hypotheses regarding the origin of dreams. All we have done is to apply this working hypothesis consistently to all the remaining associations relating to all other parts of the dream. Ultimately, we are saying no more than that this dream-element is linked with this association, that it therefore has something to do with it, that there is a connection between the two things. When a distinguished critic once remarked that, by means of psychoanalytic interpretations, one could even connect a cucumber with an elephant, this worthy showed us, by the very fact of associating "cucumber" with "elephant," that these two things somehow have an associative connection in his mind. One must have a lot of nerve and a magisterial judgment to declare that the human mind produces entirely meaningless associations. In this instance, only a little reflection is needed to understand the meaning of the association.⟩

338 In the association experiment we can ascertain the extraordinarily intense effects emanating from the unconscious precisely through the interference of complexes. The slips and faults in the experiment are nothing but prototypes of the mistakes we make in everyday life, the majority of which must be regarded as due to the interference of complexes. Freud has gathered

this material together in his book *The Psychopathology of Everyday Life.* It includes the so-called symptomatic actions—which from another point of view might equally well be called "symbolic actions"—and real slips like lapses of memory, slips of the tongue, and so on. All these phenomena are effects of unconscious constellations and are therefore so many gateways to the realm of the unconscious. When they are cumulative, we have to call them a neurosis, which from this point of view looks like a dysfunction and must be understood as the effect of an unconscious constellation.

339 Thus the association experiment is, not infrequently, a means of unlocking the unconscious directly, although mostly it is simply a technique for obtaining a wide selection of faulty reactions which can then be used for exploring the unconscious by psychoanalysis. At least, this is its most reliable form of application at present. However, it is possible that it will furnish other, especially valuable facts which would give us direct glimpses of the unconscious, but I do not consider this question sufficiently ripe to speak about yet.

## 6. THE OEDIPUS COMPLEX

340 After what I have told you about our method you may have gained rather more confidence in its scientific character, and will be inclined to agree that the fantasies which have been brought to light by psychoanalytic research are not just the arbitrary suppositions and illusions of psychoanalysts. Perhaps you will even be willing to listen patiently to what these products of unconscious fantasy can tell us.

341 The fantasies of adults are, in so far as they are conscious, immensely varied and take the most strongly individual forms. It is therefore impossible to give a general description of them. But it is very different when we enter by means of analysis into the world of unconscious fantasies. The diversity of the fantasy-material is indeed very great, but we do not find nearly so many individual peculiarities as in the conscious realm. We meet here with more typical material which is not infrequently repeated in similar form in different individuals. Constantly recurring in these fantasies are ideas which are variations of those found in religion and mythology. This fact is so striking that we may say we have discovered in these fantasies the forerunners of religious and mythological ideas.

342 I should have to enter into very much more detail to give you any adequate examples. For these problems I must refer you to my book *Symbols of Transformation*. Here I will only mention that the central symbol of Christianity—sacrifice—plays an important part in the fantasies of the unconscious. The Viennese school knows this phenomenon under the ambiguous name of "castration complex." This paradoxical use of the term follows from the special attitude of the Viennese school towards the question of sexuality, which I discussed earlier. I have devoted special attention to the problem of sacrifice in the above-mentioned book. I must content myself with this passing reference and will now proceed to say something about the origin of unconscious fantasies.

343 In a child's unconscious the fantasies are very much simpler, as if scaled to the childish milieu. Thanks to the concerted efforts of the psychoanalytic school, we have discovered that the most frequent fantasy of childhood is the so-called Oedipus complex. This term, too, seems the most unsuitable one possible. We all know that the tragic fate of Oedipus consisted in his marrying his mother and slaying his father. This tragic conflict of adult life appears far removed from the psyche of a child, and to the layman it seems quite inconceivable that a child should suffer from this conflict. But, with a little reflection, it will become clear that the *tertium comparationis* lies precisely in the *narrow restriction of the fate of Oedipus to his two parents.* This restriction is characteristic of the child, for the fate of the adult is not limited to the parents. To that extent Oedipus is the exponent of an infantile conflict magnified to adult proportions. The term "Oedipus complex" naturally does not mean conceiving this conflict in its adult form, but rather on a reduced scale suitable to childhood. All it means, in effect, is that the childish demands for love are directed to mother and father, and to the extent that these demands have already attained a certain degree of intensity, so that the chosen object is jealously defended, we can speak of an "Oedipus complex."

344 This weakening and reduction in scale of the Oedipus complex should not be understood as a diminution of the total sum of affect, but as indicating the smaller share of sexual affect characteristic of a child. To make up for this, childish affects have that peculiar intensity which is characteristic of the sexual affect in adults. The little son would like to have his mother all to himself and to be rid of his father. As you know, small children can sometimes force themselves between the parents in the most jealous way. In the unconscious these wishes and intentions assume a more concrete and more drastic form. Children are small primitive creatures and are therefore quickly ready to kill—a thought which is all the easier in the unconscious, because the unconscious is wont to express itself very dramatically. But as a child is, in general, harmless, this seemingly dangerous wish is as a rule harmless too. I say "as a rule," for we know that children can occasionally give way to their murderous impulses, not only indirectly, but in quite direct fashion. But just as the child is incapable of making systematic plans, so his intention to murder

is not all that dangerous. The same is true of his Oedipal intention towards the mother. The faint hints of this fantasy in the child's consciousness can easily be overlooked; all parents are therefore convinced that their children have no Oedipus complex. Parents, like lovers, are mostly blind. If I now say that the Oedipus complex is in the first place only a formula for childish desires in regard to the parents and for the conflict which these desires evoke—as every selfish desire must—the matter may seem more acceptable.

345 The history of the Oedipus fantasy is of special interest because it teaches us a great deal about the development of unconscious fantasies in general. People naturally think that the Oedipus problem is the problem of the son. But this, remarkably enough, is an illusion. Under certain conditions, the sexual libido reaches its final differentiation, corresponding to the sex of the individual, only relatively late in puberty. Before this time it has a sexually undifferentiated character, which could also be termed bisexual. It is therefore not surprising if little girls have an Oedipus complex too. So far as we know, the first love of a child, regardless of sex, belongs to the mother. If the love for the mother is intense at this stage, the father is jealously kept away as a rival. Of course, for the child itself, the mother at this early stage of childhood has no sexual significance worth mentioning, and to that extent the term "Oedipus complex" is not really suitable. At this period the mother still has the significance of a protecting, enfolding, nourishing being, who for this reason is a source of pleasure.

346 ⟨It is characteristic, too, that the babyish word for mother, "mamma," is the name for the maternal breast. As Dr. Beatrice Hinkle has informed me, interrogation of small children elicited the fact that they defined "mother" as the person who gives food, chocolate, etc. One could hardly assert that for children of this age food is only a symbol for sex, though this is sometimes true of adults. A superficial glance at the history of civilization will show just how enormous the nutritive source of pleasure is. The colossal feasts of Rome in its decadence were an expression of anything you like, only not of repressed sexuality, for that is the last thing one could accuse the Romans of in those days. There is no doubt that these excesses were some kind of substitute, but not for sexuality; they were far more a

substitute for neglected moral functions, which we are too prone to regard as laws forced on man from outside. Men have the laws which they make for themselves.⟩

347 As I explained earlier, I do not identify the feeling of pleasure *eo ipso* with sexuality. Sexuality has an increasingly small share in pleasure-sensations the further back we go in childhood. Nevertheless, jealousy can play a large role, for it too is something that does not belong entirely to the sexual sphere, since the desire for food has itself much to do with the first stirrings of jealousy—one has only to think of animals! Certainly it is reinforced by a budding eroticism relatively early. This element gains in strength as the years go on, so that the Oedipus complex soon assumes its classical form. The conflict takes on a more masculine and therefore more typical form in a son, whereas a daughter develops a specific liking for the father, with a correspondingly jealous attitude towards the mother. We could call this the Electra complex. As everyone knows, Electra took vengeance on her mother Clytemnestra for murdering her husband Agamemnon and thus robbing her—Electra—of her beloved father.

348 Both these fantasy complexes become more pronounced with increasing maturity, and reach a new stage only in the post-pubertal period, when the problem arises of detachment from the parents. This stage is characterized by the symbol we have already mentioned: the symbol of sacrifice. The more sexuality develops, the more it drives the individual away from his family and forces him to achieve independence. But the child has become closely attached to the family by his whole previous history, and especially to the parents, so that it is often only with the greatest difficulty that the growing individual can free himself inwardly from his infantile milieu. If he does not succeed in this, the Oedipus (or Electra) complex will precipitate a conflict, and then there is the possibility of neurotic disturbances. The libido, already sexually developed, pours into the Oedipal "mould" and gives rise to feelings and fantasies which prove beyond doubt the effectiveness of the complex, which till then had been unconscious and more or less inoperative.

349 The first consequence is the formation of intense resistances against the "immoral" impulses stemming from the now active complex. This affects the conscious behaviour in two ways.

Either the consequences are direct, in which case the son displays violent resistances against his father and a particularly affectionate and dependent attitude towards his mother; or they are indirect, that is to say compensated: instead of resistance to the father there is marked submissiveness coupled with an irritated, antagonistic attitude towards the mother. Direct and compensated consequences can sometimes alternate. All this is true also of the Electra complex. If the sexual libido were to get stuck in this form, the Oedipus and Electra conflict would lead to murder and incest. This naturally does not happen with normal people, nor in so-called "amoral" primitive communities, otherwise the human race would have perished long ago. On the contrary, it is in the natural order of things that familiar objects lose their compelling charm and force the libido to seek new objects; and this acts as an important regulative factor which prevents parricide and incest. The continuous development of libido towards objects outside the family is perfectly normal and natural, and it is an abnormal and pathological phenomenon if the libido remains, as it were, glued to the family. Nevertheless, it is a phenomenon that can sometimes be observed in normal people.

## THE PROBLEM OF INCEST

350 ⟨The unconscious fantasy of sacrifice, occurring some time after puberty, is a direct outcome of the infantile complexes. Of this I have given a circumstantial example in my book *Symbols of Transformation.* The fantasy of sacrifice means the giving up of infantile wishes. I have shown this in my book and at the same time have pointed out the parallels in the history of religion. It is not surprising that this problem plays an important role in religion, for religion is one of the greatest helps in the psychological process of adaptation. The chief obstacle to new modes of psychological adaptation is conservative adherence to the earlier attitude. But man cannot leave his previous personality and his previous objects of interest simply as they are, otherwise his libido would stagnate in the past, and this would be an impoverishment for him. Here religion is a great help because, by the bridge of the symbol, it leads his

libido away from the infantile objects (parents) towards the symbolic representatives of the past, i.e., the gods, thus facilitating the transition from the infantile world to the adult world. In this way the libido is set free for social purposes.⟩

351 Freud has a special conception of the incest complex which has given rise to heated controversy. He starts from the fact that the Oedipus complex is usually unconscious, and he conceives this to be the consequence of a moral repression. It is possible that I am not expressing myself quite correctly if I give you Freud's view in these words. At any rate, according to him the Oedipus complex seems to be repressed, that is, displaced into the unconscious through the reactive effect of conscious tendencies. It almost looks as if the Oedipus complex would rise to consciousness if the child's development were uninhibited and were not affected by cultural influences.[1]

352 Freud calls the barrier that prevents this acting out of the Oedipus complex the "incest barrier." He seems to believe, so far as one can gather from his writings, that the incest barrier is formed by the backwash of experience, that it is a correction by reality, since the unconscious strives for boundless and immediate satisfaction without regard for others. In this he agrees with Schopenhauer, who says of the egoism of the blind World-Will that it is so strong that a man could slay his brother merely to grease his boots with his brother's fat. Freud considers that the psychological incest barrier can be compared with the incest prohibitions found even among primitives. He further considers that these prohibitions are a proof that men really do desire incest, for which reason laws were framed against it even on the primitive level. He therefore takes the tendency towards incest to be an absolutely concrete sexual wish, for he calls this complex the root-complex, or nucleus, of the neuroses and is inclined, viewing this as the original one, to reduce practically the whole psychology of the neuroses, as well as many other phenomena in the realm of the mind, to this one complex.

[1] A view expressed most strongly by Stekel.

## 7. THE AETIOLOGY OF NEUROSIS

353 With this new conception of Freud's we come back to the question of the aetiology of neurosis. We have seen that psychoanalytic theory started from a traumatic experience in childhood, which later on was found to be partly or wholly unreal. In consequence, the theory made a change of front and sought the aetiologically significant factor in the development of abnormal fantasies. The investigation of the unconscious, continued over a period of ten years with the help of an increasing number of workers, gradually brought to light a mass of empirical material which showed that the incest complex was a highly important and never-failing element in pathological fantasy. But it was found that the incest complex was not a special complex of neurotic people; it proved to be a component of the normal infantile psyche. We cannot tell from its mere existence whether this complex will give rise to a neurosis or not. To become pathogenic, it must precipitate a conflict; the complex, which in itself is inactive, must be activated and intensified to the point where a conflict breaks out.

354 This brings us to a new and important question. If the infantile "nuclear complex" is only a general form, not in itself pathogenic but requiring special activation, then the whole aetiological problem is altered. In that case we would dig in vain among the reminiscences of earliest childhood, since they give us only the general forms of later conflicts but not the actual conflict. ⟨It makes no difference that there were already conflicts in childhood, for the conflicts of childhood are different from the conflicts of adults. Those who have suffered ever since childhood from a chronic neurosis do not suffer now from the same conflict they suffered from then. Maybe the neurosis broke out when they first had to go to school as children. Then it was the conflict between indulgence and duty, between love for their parents and the necessity of going to school. But now it is the conflict between, say, the joys of a

comfortable bourgeois existence and the strenuous demands of professional life. It only seems to be the same conflict. It is just as if the "Teutschen" of the Napoleonic wars were to compare themselves with the old Germans who rebelled against the Roman yoke.⟩

## UNCONSCIOUS DETERMINATION

355 I think I can best make my meaning clear if I describe the subsequent development of the theory by using the example of the young lady whose story you have heard in the earlier lectures. As you will probably remember, we found in the anamnesis that the fright with the horses led to the reminiscence of a similar scene in childhood, in which connection we discussed the trauma theory. We found that we had to look for the real pathological element in her exaggerated fantasies, which arose from her retarded psychosexual development. We now have to apply the theoretical insight we have thus gained to the genesis of this particular illness if we want to understand how, just at that moment, that childhood experience was constellated so effectively.

356 The simplest way to find an explanation for that nocturnal occurrence would be to make an exact inquiry into the circumstances of the moment. The first thing I did, therefore, was to question the patient about the company she had been keeping at the time. From this I learnt that she knew a young man to whom she thought of getting engaged; she loved him and hoped to be happy with him. At first nothing more could be discovered. But it would never do to be deterred from investigation by the negative results of the preliminary questioning. There are indirect ways of reaching the goal when the direct way fails. We therefore return to that singular moment when the lady ran headlong in front of the horses. We inquire about her companions and the sort of festive occasion she had just taken part in. It had been a farewell party for her best friend, who was going abroad to a health-resort on account of her nerves. This friend was married and, we are told, happily; she was also the mother of a child. We may take leave to doubt the statement that she was happy; for, were she really so, she would

presumably have no reason to be "nervous" and in need of a cure.

357 Shifting my angle of approach, I learnt that after her friends had caught up with her they took the patient back to the house of her host, as this was the nearest shelter. There she was hospitably received in her exhausted state. At this point the patient broke off her narrative, became embarrassed, fidgeted, and tried to change the subject. Evidently some disagreeable recollection had suddenly bobbed up. After the most obstinate resistance had been overcome, it appeared that yet another very remarkable incident had occurred that night: the amiable host had made her a fiery declaration of love, thus precipitating a situation which, in the absence of the lady of the house, might well be considered both difficult and distressing. Ostensibly this declaration of love came to her like a bolt from the blue. A modicum of criticism teaches us, however, that these things never drop from the skies but always have their history. It was now the task of the next few weeks to dig out bit by bit a long love-story, until at last a complete picture emerged which I attempt to outline as follows:

358 As a child the patient had been a regular tomboy, caring only for wild boys' games, scorning her own sex and avoiding all feminine ways and occupations. After puberty, when the erotic problem might have come too close, she began to shun all society, hated and despised everything that even remotely reminded her of the biological destiny of woman, and lived in a world of fantasy which had nothing in common with rude reality. Thus, until about her twenty-fourth year, she evaded all those little adventures, hopes, and expectations which ordinarily move a girl's heart at this age. Then she got to know two men who were destined to break through the thorny hedge that had grown up around her. Mr. A was her best friend's husband, and Mr. B was his bachelor friend. She liked them both. Nevertheless it soon began to look as though she liked Mr. B a vast deal better. An intimacy quickly sprang up between them and before long there was talk of a possible engagement. Through her relations with Mr. B and through her friend she often came into contact with Mr. A, whose presence sometimes disturbed her in the most unaccountable way and made her nervous.

359 About this time the patient went to a large party. Her friends were also there. She became lost in thought and was dreamily playing with her ring when it suddenly slipped off her finger and rolled under the table. Both gentlemen looked for it and Mr. B succeeded in finding it. He placed the ring on her finger with an arch smile and said, "You know what that means!" Overcome by a strange and irresistible feeling, she tore the ring from her finger and flung it through the open window. A painful moment ensued, as may be imagined, and soon she left the party in deep dejection.

360 Not long after this, so-called chance brought it about that she should spend her summer holidays at a health resort where Mr. and Mrs. A were also staying. Mrs. A then began to grow visibly nervous, and frequently stayed indoors because she felt out of sorts. The patient was thus in a position to go out for walks alone with Mr. A. On one occasion they went boating. So boisterous was she in her merriment that she suddenly fell overboard. She could not swim, and it was only with great difficulty that Mr. A pulled her half-unconscious into the boat. And then it was that he kissed her. With this romantic episode the bonds were tied fast. To excuse herself in her own eyes she tried all the more energetically to get herself engaged to Mr. B, telling herself every day that it was Mr. B whom she really loved. Naturally this curious little game had not escaped the keen glances of wifely jealousy. Mrs. A, her friend, had guessed the secret and fretted accordingly, so that her nerves only got worse. Hence it became necessary for Mrs. A to go abroad for a cure.[1]

361 The farewell party presented a dangerous opportunity. The patient knew that her friend and rival was going off the same evening, and that Mr. A would be alone in the house. Of course she did not think this out logically and clearly, for some women have a remarkable capacity for thinking purely with their feelings, and not with their intellects, so that it seems to them as if they had never thought certain things at all. At any rate she had a very queer feeling all the evening. She felt extraordinarily nervous, and when Mrs. A had been accompanied to the station and had gone, the hysterical twilight state came over her on the

[1] [Cf. *Two Essays*, pars. 11f. and 420. For the first two instalments of the story see supra, pars. 218ff. and 297ff.—EDITORS.]

way back. I asked her what she had been thinking or feeling at the actual moment when she heard the horses coming along behind her. Her answer was that she had only a feeling of panic, the feeling that something dreadful was approaching which she could no longer escape. The consequence was, as you know, that she was brought back exhausted to the house of her host, Mr. A.

362 To the simple mind this dénouement seems perfectly obvious. Every layman will say, "Well, that is clear enough, she only intended to return by one way or another to Mr. A's house." But the psychologist would reproach the layman for his incorrect way of expressing himself, and would tell him that the patient was not conscious of the motives of her behaviour, and that we cannot therefore speak of her *intention* to return to Mr. A's house. There are, of course, learned psychologists who could find any number of theoretical reasons for disputing the purposiveness of her action—reasons based on the dogma of the identity of consciousness and psyche. But the psychology inaugurated by Freud recognized long ago that the purposive significance of psychological acts cannot be judged by conscious motives but only by the objective criterion of their psychological result. Today it can no longer be contested that there are unconscious tendencies which have a great influence on a person's reactions and on the effect he has on others.

363 What happened at Mr. A's house bears out this observation. Our patient made a sentimental scene, and Mr. A felt obliged to react to it with a declaration of love. Looked at in the light of these concluding events, the whole previous history seems to be very ingeniously directed towards precisely this end, though consciously the patient was struggling against it all the time.

364 The theoretical gain from this story is the clear recognition that an unconscious "intention" or tendency stage-managed the fright with the horses, very probably using for this purpose the infantile reminiscence of the horses galloping irresistibly towards disaster. Seen in the light of the whole material, the nocturnal scene with the horses—the starting point of the illness—seems to be only the keystone of a planned edifice. The fright and the apparently traumatic effect of the childhood experience are merely staged, but staged in the peculiar way characteristic of hysteria, so that the *mise en scène* appears almost exactly

like a reality. We know from hundreds of experiences that hysterical pains are staged in order to reap certain advantages from the environment. Nevertheless these pains are entirely real. The patients do not merely think they have pains; from the psychological point of view the pains are just as real as those due to organic causes, and yet they are stage-managed.

## THE REGRESSION OF LIBIDO

365 This utilization of reminiscences for staging an illness or an ostensible aetiology is called a *regression of libido*. The libido goes back to these reminiscences and activates them, with the result that an apparent aetiology is simulated. In this instance, according to the old theory, it might seem as if the fright with the horses were due to the old trauma. The resemblance between the two scenes is unmistakable, and in both cases the patient's fright was very real. At all events, we have no reason to doubt her assertions in this respect, as they fully accord with our experiences of other patients. The nervous asthma, the hysterical anxiety-attacks, the psychogenic depressions and exaltations, the pains, the cramps, etc. are all quite real, and any doctor who has himself suffered from a psychogenic symptom will know how absolutely real it feels. Regressively reactivated reminiscences, however fantastic they may be, are as real as recollections of events which have actually happened.

366 As the term "regression of libido" indicates, we understand by this retrograde mode of application a reversion to earlier stages. From our example we can see very clearly how the process of regression takes place. At that farewell party, which presented a good opportunity for her to be alone with her host, the patient shrank from the idea of turning this opportunity to her advantage, but let herself be overpowered by desires which hitherto she had never admitted. The libido was not used consciously for that purpose, nor was this purpose ever acknowledged. In consequence, the libido had to carry it out by means of the unconscious, under the cover of panic in face of overwhelming danger. Her feelings at the moment when the horses approached illustrate our formulation very clearly: she felt as if something inescapable now had to happen.

367 The process of regression is beautifully illustrated in an image used by Freud. The libido can be compared with a river which, when it meets with an obstruction, gets dammed up and causes an inundation. If this river has previously, in its upper reaches, dug out other channels, these channels will be filled up again by reason of the damming below. They appear to be real river-beds, filled with water as before, but at the same time they have only a provisional existence. The river has not permanently flowed back into the old channels, but only for as long as the obstruction lasts in the main stream. The subsidiary streams carry the water not because they were independent streams from the beginning, but because they were once stages or stations in the development of the main river-bed, passing possibilities, traces of which still exist and can therefore be used again in times of flood.

368 This image can be applied directly to the development of the uses of libido. The final direction, the main river-bed, has not yet been found at the time of the infantile development of sexuality. Instead, the libido branches out into all sorts of subsidiary streams, and only gradually does the final form appear. But when the river has dug out its main bed, all the subsidiary streams dry up and lose their importance, leaving only traces of their former activity. Similarly, the importance of the child's preliminary exercises at sexuality disappears almost completely as a rule, except for a few traces. If later an obstruction occurs, so that the damming up of libido reactivates the old channels, this state is properly speaking a new and at the same time an abnormal one. The earlier, infantile state represents a normal application of libido, whereas the reversion of libido to infantile ways is something abnormal. I am therefore of the opinion that Freud is not justified in calling the infantile sexual manifestations "perverse," since a normal manifestation should not be designated by a pathological term. This incorrect usage has had pernicious consequences in confusing the scientific public. Such a terminology is a misapplication to normal people of insights gained from neurotic psychology, on the assumption that the abnormal by-path taken by the libido in neurotics is still the same phenomenon as in children.

369 The so-called "amnesia of childhood," which I would like to mention in passing, is a similar illegitimate "retrograde" appli-

cation of terms from pathology. Amnesia is a pathological condition, consisting in the repression of certain conscious contents, and this cannot possibly be the same as the anterograde amnesia of children, which consists in an incapacity for intentional memory-reproduction, such as is also found among primitives. This incapacity for memory-reproduction dates from birth and can be understood on quite obvious biological grounds. It would be a remarkable hypothesis if we were to assume that this totally different quality of infantile consciousness could be reduced to sexual repressions on the analogy of a neurosis. A neurotic amnesia is punched out, as it were, from the continuity of memory, whereas memory in early childhood consists of single islands in the continuum of non-memory. This condition is in every sense the opposite of the condition found in neurosis, so that the expression "amnesia" is absolutely incorrect. The "amnesia of childhood" is an inference from the psychology of neurosis, just as is the "polymorphous-perverse" disposition of the child.

### THE PERIOD OF SEXUAL LATENCY

370 This error in theoretical formulation comes to light in the peculiar doctrine of the so-called "period of sexual latency" in childhood. Freud observed that the early infantile sexual manifestations, which I call phenomena of the presexual stage, disappear after a time and reappear only much later. What Freud calls "infantile masturbation"—that is, all those quasi-sexual activities which we spoke about before—is said to return later as real masturbation. Such a process of development would be biologically unique. In conformity with this theory we would have to assume, for instance, that when a plant forms a bud from which a blossom begins to unfold, the blossom is taken back again before it is fully developed, and is again hidden within the bud, to reappear later on in a similar form. This impossible supposition is a consequence of the assertion that the early infantile activities of the presexual stage are sexual phenomena, and that the quasi-masturbational acts of that period are genuine acts of masturbation. Here the incorrect terminology and the boundless extension of the concept of sexuality take their

revenge. Thus it was that Freud was compelled to assume that there is a disappearance of sexuality, in other words, a period of sexual latency. What he calls a disappearance is nothing other than the *real beginning of sexuality,* everything preceding it being but a preliminary stage to which no real sexual character can be attributed. The impossible phenomenon of sexual latency is thus explained in a very simple way.

371 The theory of the latency period is an excellent example of the incorrectness of the conception of infantile sexuality. But there has been no error of observation. On the contrary, the hypothesis of the latency period proves how exactly Freud observed the apparent recommencement of sexuality. The error lies in the conception. As we have already seen, the prime error consists in a somewhat old-fashioned conception of a plurality of instincts. As soon as we accept the idea of two or more instincts existing side by side, we must necessarily conclude that, if one instinct is not yet manifest, it is still present *in nuce,* in accordance with the old theory of encasement.[2] Or, in physics, we should have to say that when a piece of iron passes from the condition of heat to the condition of light, the light was already present *in nuce* (latently) in the heat. Such assumptions are arbitrary projections of human ideas into transcendental regions, contravening the requirements of the theory of cognition. We have therefore no right to speak of a sexual instinct existing *in nuce,* as we would then be giving an arbitrary interpretation of phenomena which can be explained otherwise, in a much more suitable manner. We can only speak of the manifestation of the nutritive function, of the sexual function, and so on, and then only when that function has come to the surface with unmistakable clarity. We speak of light only when the iron is visibly glowing, but not when the iron is merely hot.

372 Freud as an observer sees quite clearly that the sexuality of neurotics cannot really be compared with infantile sexuality, just as there is a great difference, for instance, between the uncleanliness of a two-year-old child and the uncleanliness of a forty-year-old catatonic. The one is normal, the other exceedingly

2 [*Einschachtelung:* "An old theory of reproduction which assumed that when the first animal of each species was created, the germs of all other individuals of the same species which were to come from it were encased in its ova."—*Century Dictionary* (1890).—TRANS.]

pathological. Freud inserted a short passage in his *Three Essays,*[3] stating that the infantile form of neurotic sexuality is either wholly, or at any rate partly, due to regression. That is, even in those cases where we can say that it is still the same old infantile by-path, the function of this by-path is intensified by the regression. Freud thus admits that the infantile sexuality of neurotics is for the greater part a regressive phenomenon. That this must be so is evidenced by the researches of recent years, showing that the observations concerning the childhood psychology of neurotics hold equally true of normal people. At any rate we can say that the historical development of infantile sexuality in a neurotic is distinguished from that of normal people only by minimal differences which completely elude scientific evaluation. Striking differences are exceptional.

## THE AETIOLOGICAL SIGNIFICANCE OF THE ACTUAL PRESENT

373 The more deeply we penetrate into the heart of the infantile development, the more we get the impression that as little of aetiological significance can be found there as in the infantile trauma. Even with the acutest ferreting into their respective histories we shall never discover why people living on German soil had just such a fate, and why the Gauls another. The further we get away, in analytical investigations, from the epoch of the manifest neurosis, the less can we expect to find the real *causa efficiens,* since the dynamics of the maladjustment grow fainter and fainter the further we go back into the past. In constructing a theory which derives the neurosis from causes in the distant past, we are first and foremost following the tendency of our patients to lure us as far away as possible from the critical present. *For the cause of the pathogenic conflict lies mainly in the present moment.* It is just as if a nation were to blame its miserable political conditions on the past; as if the Germany of the nineteenth century had attributed her political dismemberment and incapacity to her oppression by the Romans, instead of seeking the causes of her difficulties in the actual present. It is mainly in the present that the effective causes lie, and here alone are the possibilities of removing them.

[3] Standard Edn., p. 232.

374 The greater part of the psychoanalytic school is still under the spell of the conception that infantile sexuality is the *sine qua non* of neurosis. It is not only the theorist, delving into childhood simply from scientific interest, but the practising analyst also, who believes that he has to turn the history of infancy inside out in order to find the fantasies conditioning the neurosis. A fruitless enterprise! In the meantime the most important factor escapes him, namely, the conflict and its demands in the present. In the case we have been describing, we should not understand any of the motives which produced the hysterical attacks if we looked for them in earliest childhood. Those reminiscences determine only the form, but the dynamic element springs from the present, and insight into the significance of the actual moment alone gives real understanding.

375 It may not be out of place to remark here that it would never occur to me to blame Freud personally for the innumerable misunderstandings. I know very well that Freud, being an empiricist, always publishes only provisional formulations to which he certainly does not attribute any eternal value. But it is equally certain that the scientific public is inclined to make a creed out of them, a system which is asserted as blindly on the one hand as it is attacked on the other. I can only say that from the sum total of Freud's writings certain average conceptions have crystallized out, which both sides treat far too dogmatically. These views have led to a number of undoubtedly incorrect technical axioms the existence of which cannot be postulated with any certainty in Freud's own work. We know that in the mind of a creator of new ideas things are much more fluid and flexible than they are in the minds of his followers. They do not possess his vital creativity, and they make up for this deficiency by a dogmatic allegiance, in exactly the same way as their opponents, who, like them, cling to the dead letter because they cannot grasp its living content. My words are thus addressed less to Freud, who I know recognizes to some extent the final orientation of the neuroses, than to his public, who continue to argue about his views.

376 From what has been said it should be clear that we gain insight into the history of a neurosis only when we understand that each separate element in it serves a purpose. We can now understand why that particular element in the previous history

of our case was pathogenic, and we also understand why it was chosen as a symbol. Through the concept of regression, the theory is freed from the narrow formula of the importance of childhood experiences, and the actual conflict acquires the significance which, on the empirical evidence, implicitly belongs to it. Freud himself introduced the concept of regression, as I have said, in his *Three Essays,* rightly acknowledging that experience does not permit us to seek the cause of a neurosis exclusively in the past. If it is true, then, that reminiscences become effective again chiefly because of regressive activation, we have to consider whether the apparently determining effects of the reminiscences can be traced back solely to the regression of libido.

377 As you have heard already, Freud himself in the *Three Essays* gives us to understand that the infantilism of neurotic sexuality is for the most part due to regression. This statement deserves considerably more emphasis than it received there. (Actually Freud did give it due emphasis in his later works.) The point is that the *regression of libido abolishes to a very large extent the aetiological significance of childhood experiences.* It had seemed to us very peculiar anyway that the Oedipus or Electra complex should have a determining influence in the formation of a neurosis, since these complexes are actually present in everyone, even in people who have never known their father and mother and were brought up by foster-parents. I have analysed cases of this kind, and found that the incest complex was as well developed in them as in other patients. This seems to me a good proof that the incest complex is much less a reality than a purely regressive fantasy formation, and that the conflicts resulting from it must be reduced rather to an anachronistic clinging to the infantile attitude than to real incestuous wishes, which are merely a cover for regressive fantasies. Looked at from this point of view, childhood experiences have a significance for neurosis only when they are made significant by a regression of libido. That this must be so to a very large extent is shown by the fact that neither the infantile sexual trauma nor the incest complex present in everyone causes hysteria. Neurosis occurs only when the incest complex is activated by regression.

FAILURE OF ADAPTATION

378 This brings us to the question: why does the libido become regressive? In order to answer this, we must examine more closely the conditions under which a regression arises. In discussing this problem with my patients I generally give the following example: A mountain-climber, attempting the ascent of a certain peak, happens to meet with an insurmountable obstacle, for instance a precipitous rock-face whose ascent is a sheer impossibility. After vainly seeking another route, he will turn back and regretfully abandon the idea of climbing that peak. He will say to himself: "It is not in my power to get over this difficulty, so I will climb an easier mountain."

379 Here we see a normal utilization of libido: the man turns back when he meets an insurmountable difficulty, and uses his libido, which could not attain its original goal, for the ascent of another mountain.

380 Now let us imagine that the rock-face was not really unclimbable so far as the man's physical abilities were concerned, but that he shrank back from this difficult undertaking from sheer funk. In this case two possibilities are open:

1. The man will be annoyed by his own cowardice and will set out to prove himself less timid on another occasion, or perhaps he will admit that with his timidity he ought never to undertake such daring ascents. At any rate, he will acknowledge that his moral capacity is not sufficient to overcome the difficulties. He therefore uses the libido which did not attain its original aim for the useful purpose of self-criticism, and for evolving a plan by which he may yet be able, with due regard to his moral capacity, to realize his wish to climb a mountain.

2. The second possibility is that the man does not admit his cowardice, and flatly asserts that the rock face is physically unclimbable, although he can very well see that, with sufficient courage, the obstacle could be overcome. But he prefers to deceive himself. This creates the psychological situation which is of significance for our problem.

381 At bottom the man knows perfectly well that it would be physically possible to overcome the difficulty, and that he is simply morally incapable of doing so. But he pushes this thought

aside because of its disagreeable character. He is so conceited that he cannot admit his cowardice. He brags about his courage and prefers to declare that things are impossible rather than that his own courage is inadequate. In this way he falls into contradiction with himself: on the one hand he has a correct appreciation of the situation, on the other he hides this knowledge from himself, behind the illusion of his bravery. He represses his correct insight and tries to force his subjective illusions on reality. The result of this contradiction is that his libido is split and the two halves fight one another. He pits his wish to climb the mountain against the opinion, invented by himself and supported by artificial arguments, that the mountain is unclimbable. He draws back not because of any real impossibility but because of an artificial barrier invented by himself. He has fallen into disunion with himself. From this moment on he suffers from an internal conflict. Now the realization of his cowardice gains the upper hand, now defiance and pride. In either case his libido is engaged in a useless civil war, and the man becomes incapable of any new enterprise. He will never realize his wish to climb a mountain, because he has gone thoroughly astray in the estimation of his moral qualities. His efficiency is reduced, he is not fully adapted, he has become—in a word—neurotic. The libido that retreated in face of the difficulty has led neither to honest self-criticism nor to a desperate struggle to overcome the difficulty at any price; it has been used merely to maintain the cheap pretence that the ascent was absolutely impossible and that even heroic courage would have availed nothing.

### REVERSION TO THE INFANTILE LEVEL

382 This kind of reaction is called *infantile.* It is characteristic of children, and of naïve minds generally, not to find the mistake in themselves but in things outside them, and forcibly to impose on things their own subjective judgment.

383 This man, therefore, solves the problem in an infantile way; he substitutes for the adapted attitude of the first climber a mode of adaptation characteristic of the child's mind. That is what we mean by regression. His libido retreats before the ob-

stacle it cannot surmount and substitutes a childish illusion for real action.

384 Such cases are a daily occurrence in the treatment of neurosis. I would only remind you of all those young girls who suddenly become hysterically ill the moment they have to decide whether to get engaged or not. As an example, I will present the case of two sisters. The two girls were separated by only a year in age. In talents and also in character they were very much alike. They had the same education and grew up in the same surroundings under the same parental influences. Both were ostensibly healthy, neither showed any noticeable nervous symptoms. An attentive observer might have discovered that the elder daughter was rather more the darling of her parents than the younger. Her parents' esteem was due to the special kind of sensitiveness which this daughter displayed. She demanded more affection than the younger one, was somewhat more precocious and forthcoming than she. Besides, she showed some delightfully childish traits—just those things which, because of their contradictory and slightly unbalanced character, make a person specially charming. No wonder father and mother had great joy in their elder daughter.

385 When the two sisters became of marriageable age, they both made the acquaintance of two young men, and the possibility of their marriages soon drew near. As is generally the case, there were certain difficulties in the way. Both girls were quite young and had very little experience of the world. The men were fairly young too, and in positions which might have been better; they were only at the beginning of their careers, nevertheless both were capable young men. The two girls lived in social surroundings which gave them the right to certain expectations. It was a situation in which doubts as to the suitability of either marriage were permissible. Moreover, both girls were insufficiently acquainted with their prospective husbands, and were not quite sure of their love. Hence there were many hesitations and doubts. It was noticed that the elder sister always showed greater waverings in all her decisions. On account of these hesitations there were some painful moments with the two young men, who naturally pressed for a definite answer. At such moments the elder sister showed herself much more agitated than the younger one. Several times she went weeping to her mother, bemoaning

her own uncertainty. The younger one was more decided, and put an end to the unsettled situation by accepting her suitor. She thus got over her difficulty and thereafter events ran smoothly.

386 As soon as the admirer of the elder sister heard that the younger one had given her word, he rushed to his lady and begged passionately for her final acceptance. His tempestuous behaviour irritated and rather frightened her, although she was really inclined to follow her sister's example. She answered in a haughty and rather offhand way. He replied with sharp reproaches, causing her to answer still more tartly. At the end there was a tearful scene, and he went away in a huff. At home, he told the story to his mother, who expressed the opinion that the girl was obviously not the right one for him and that he had better choose someone else. The quarrel had made the girl profoundly doubtful whether she really loved him. It suddenly seemed to her impossible to leave her beloved parents and follow this man to an unknown destiny. Matters finally went so far that the relationship was broken off altogether. From then on the girl became moody; she showed unmistakable signs of the greatest jealousy towards her sister, but would neither see nor admit that she was jealous. The former happy relationship with her parents went to pieces too. Instead of her earlier child-like affection she put on a sulky manner, which sometimes amounted to violent irritability; weeks of depression followed. While the younger sister was celebrating her wedding, the elder went to a distant health-resort for nervous intestinal catarrh. I shall not continue the history of the illness; it developed into an ordinary hysteria.

387 In the analysis of this case great resistance was found to the sexual problem. The resistance was due to numerous perverse fantasies whose existence the patient would not admit. The question as to where these perverse fantasies, so unexpected in a young girl, could come from led to the discovery that once, as a child of eight years old, she had found herself suddenly confronted in the street by an exhibitionist. She was rooted to the spot by fright, and for a long time afterwards the ugly image pursued her in her dreams. Her younger sister had been with her at the time. The night after the patient told me about this, she dreamt of a man in a grey suit, who started to do in front of

her what the exhibitionist had done. She awoke with a cry of terror.

388 Her first association to the grey suit was a suit of her father's, which he had been wearing on an excursion she had made with him when she was about six years old. This dream, without any doubt, connects the father with the exhibitionist. There must be some reason for this. Did something happen with the father that might possibly call forth such an association? This question met with violent resistance from the patient, but it would not let her alone. At the next interview she reproduced some very early reminiscences, in which she had watched her father undressing; and one day she came, terribly embarrassed and shaken, to tell me that she had had an abominable vision, absolutely distinct. In bed at night, she suddenly felt herself once again a child of two or three years old, and she saw her father standing by her bed in an obscene attitude. The story was gasped out bit by bit, obviously with the greatest internal struggle. Then followed wild lamentations about how dreadful it was that a father should do such a terrible thing to his child.

389 Nothing is less probable than that the father really did this. It is only a fantasy, presumably constructed in the course of the analysis from that same need for causality which once misled the analysts into supposing that hysteria was caused merely by such impressions.

390 This case seems to me perfectly designed to demonstrate the importance of the regression theory, and to show at the same time the sources of the previous theoretical errors. Originally, as we saw, there was only a slight difference between the two sisters, but from the moment of their engagement their ways became totally divided. They now seemed to have two entirely different characters. The one, vigorous in health, and enjoying life, was a fine courageous girl, willing to submit to the natural demands of womanhood; the other was gloomy, ill-tempered, full of bitterness and malice, unwilling to make any effort to lead a reasonable life, egotistical, quarrelsome, and a nuisance to all around her. This striking difference was brought out only when one of the sisters successfully got over the difficulties of the engagement period, while the other did not. For both, it hung by a hair whether the affair would be broken off. The younger, somewhat more placid, was the more decided, and she

was able to find the right word at the right moment. The elder was more spoiled and more sensitive, consequently more influenced by her emotions, so that she could not find the right word, nor had she the courage to sacrifice her pride to put things straight afterwards. This little cause had a great effect, as we shall see. Originally the conditions were exactly the same for both sisters. It was the greater sensitiveness of the elder that made all the difference.

### SENSITIVENESS AND REGRESSION

391 The question now is, whence came this sensitiveness which had such unfortunate results? Analysis demonstrated the existence of an extraordinarily well-developed sexuality with an infantile, fantastic character; further, of an incestuous fantasy about the father. Assuming that these fantasies had long been alive and active in the patient, we have here a quick and very simple solution of the problem of sensitiveness. We can easily understand why the girl was so sensitive: she was completely shut up in her fantasies and had a secret attachment to her father. In these circumstances it would have been a miracle if she had been willing to love and marry another man.

392 The further we pursue the development of these fantasies back to their source, following our need for causality, the greater become the difficulties of analysis, that is, the greater become the "resistances," as we called them. Finally we reach that impressive scene, that obscene act, whose improbability has already been established. This scene has exactly the character of a later fantasy-formation. Therefore, we have to conceive these difficulties, these "resistances," not—at least in this stage of the analysis—as defences against the conscious realization of a painful memory, but as a struggle against the construction of this fantasy.

393 You will ask in astonishment: But what is it that compels the patient to weave such a fantasy? You will even be inclined to suggest that the analyst forced the patient to invent it, otherwise she would never have produced such an absurd idea. I do not venture to doubt that there have been cases where the analyst's need to find a cause, especially under the influence of the

trauma theory, forced the patient to invent a fantasy of this kind. But the analyst, in his turn, would never have arrived at this theory had he not followed the patient's line of thought, thus taking part in that retrograde movement of libido which we call regression. He is simply carrying out to its logical conclusion what the patient is afraid to carry out, that is, a regression, a retreat of libido with all the consequences that this entails.

394 Hence, in tracing the libido regression, the analysis does not always follow the exact path marked out by the historical development, but often that of a subsequently formed fantasy, based only in part on former realities. In our case, too, the events were only partly real, and they got their enormous significance only afterwards, when the libido regressed. Whenever the libido seizes upon a certain reminiscence, we may expect it to be elaborated and transformed, for everything that is touched by the libido revives, takes on dramatic form, and becomes systematized. We have to admit that by far the greater part of the material became significant only later, when the regressing libido, seizing hold of anything suitable that lay in its path, had turned all this into a fantasy. Then that fantasy, keeping pace with the regressive movement of libido, came back at last to the father and put upon him all the infantile sexual wishes. Even so has it ever been thought that the golden age of Paradise lay in the past!

395 As we know that the fantasy material brought out by analysis became significant only afterwards, we are not in a position to use this material to explain the onset of the neurosis; we should be constantly moving in a circle. The critical moment for the neurosis was the one when the girl and the man were both ready to be reconciled, but when the inopportune sensitiveness of the patient, and perhaps also of her partner, allowed the opportunity to slip by.

### IS SENSITIVENESS PRIMARY?

396 It might be said—and the psychoanalytic school inclines to this view—that the critical sensitiveness arose from a special psychological history which made this outcome a foregone conclu-

sion. We know that in psychogenic neuroses sensitiveness is always a symptom of disunion with oneself, a symptom of the struggle between two divergent tendencies. Each of these tendencies has its psychological prehistory, and in our case it can clearly be shown that the peculiar resistance at the bottom of the patient's critical sensitiveness was in fact bound up historically with certain infantile sexual activities, and also with that so-called traumatic experience—things which may very well cast a shadow on sexuality. This would be plausible enough, were it not that the patient's sister had experienced pretty much the same things—including the exhibitionist—without suffering the same consequences, and without becoming neurotic.

397 We would therefore have to assume that the patient experienced these things in a special way, perhaps more intensely and enduringly than her sister, and that the events of early childhood would have been more significant to her in the long run. If that had been true in so marked a degree, some violent effect would surely have been noticed even at the time. But in later youth the events of early childhood were as much over and done with for the patient as they were for her sister. Therefore, yet another conjecture is conceivable with regard to that critical sensitiveness, namely, that it did not come from her peculiar prehistory but had existed all along. An attentive observer of small children can detect, even in early infancy, any unusual sensitiveness. I once analysed a hysterical patient who showed me a letter written by her mother when the patient was two years old. Her mother wrote about her and her sister: she—the patient—was always a friendly and enterprising child, but her sister had difficulties in getting along with people and things. The first one in later life became hysterical, the other catatonic. These far-reaching differences, which go back into earliest childhood, cannot be due to accidental events but must be regarded as innate. From this standpoint we cannot assert that our patient's peculiar prehistory was to blame for her sensitiveness at the critical moment; it would be more correct to say that this sensitiveness was inborn and naturally manifested itself most strongly in any unusual situation.

398 This excessive sensitiveness very often brings an enrichment of the personality and contributes more to its charm than to the undoing of a person's character. Only, when difficult and un-

usual situations arise, the advantage frequently turns into a very great disadvantage, since calm consideration is then disturbed by untimely affects. Nothing could be more mistaken, though, than to regard this excessive sensitiveness as in itself a pathological character component. If that were really so, we should have to rate about one quarter of humanity as pathological. Yet if this sensitiveness has such destructive consequences for the individual, we must admit that it can no longer be considered quite normal.

399 We are driven to this contradiction when we contrast the two views concerning the significance of the psychological prehistory as sharply as we have done here. In reality, it is not a question of either one or the other. A certain innate sensitiveness produces a special prehistory, a special way of experiencing infantile events, which in their turn are not without influence on the development of the child's view of the world. Events bound up with powerful impressions can never pass off without leaving some trace on sensitive people. Some of them remain effective throughout life, and such events can have a determining influence on a person's whole mental development. Dirty and disillusioning experiences in the realm of sexuality are especially apt to frighten off a sensitive person for years afterwards, so that the mere thought of sex arouses the greatest resistances.

400 As the trauma theory shows, we are too much inclined, knowing of such cases, to attribute the emotional development of a person wholly, or at least very largely, to accidents. The old trauma theory went too far in this respect. We must never forget that the world is, in the first place, a subjective phenomenon. *The impressions we receive from these accidental happenings are also our own doing.* It is not true that the impressions are forced on us unconditionally; our own predisposition conditions the impression. A man whose libido is blocked will have, as a rule, quite different and very much more vivid impressions than one whose libido is organized in a wealth of activities. A person who is sensitive in one way or another will receive a deep impression from an event which would leave a less sensitive person cold.

401 Therefore, in addition to the accidental impression, we have to consider the subjective conditions seriously. Our previous

reflections, and in particular our discussion of an actual case, have shown that the most important subjective condition is regression. The effect of regression, as practical experience shows, is so great and so impressive that one might be inclined to attribute the effect of accidental occurrences solely to the mechanism of regression. Without any doubt, there are many cases where everything is dramatized, where even the traumatic experiences are pure figments of the imagination, and the few real events among them are afterwards completely distorted by fantastic elaboration. We can safely say that there is not a single case of neurosis in which the emotional value of the antecedent experience is not intensified by libido regression, and even when large tracts of infantile development seem to be extraordinarily significant (as for instance the relationship to the parents), it is almost always a regression that gives them this value.

402 The truth, as always, lies in the middle. The previous history certainly has a determining value, and this is intensified by regression. Sometimes the traumatic significance of the previous history comes more to the forefront, sometimes only its regressive meaning. These considerations naturally have to be applied to infantile sexual experiences as well. Obviously there are cases where brutal sexual experiences justify the shadow thrown on sexuality and make the later resistance to sex thoroughly comprehensible. (I would mention, by the way, that frightful impressions other than sexual can leave behind a permanent feeling of insecurity which may give the individual a hesitating attitude to reality.) Where real events of undoubted traumatic potency are absent—as is the case in most neuroses—the mechanism of regression predominates.

403 It might be objected that we have no criterion by which to judge the potential effect of a trauma, since this is an extremely relative concept. That is not altogether true; we have such a criterion in the average normal person. Something that is likely to make a strong and abiding impression on a normal person must be considered as having a determining influence for neurotics also. But we cannot attribute determining importance, in neurosis either, to impressions which normally would disappear and be forgotten. In most cases where some event has had an unexpected traumatic effect, we shall in all probability find a regression, that is to say, a secondary fantastic dramatization.

*The earlier in childhood an impression is said to have arisen, the more suspect is its reality.* Primitive people and animals have nothing like that capacity for reviving memories of unique impressions which we find among civilized people. Very young children are not nearly as impressionable as older children. The higher development of the mental faculties is an indispensable prerequisite for impressionability. We can therefore safely assume that the earlier a patient places some impressive experience in his childhood, the more likely it is to be a fantastic and regressive one. Deeper impressions are to be expected only from experiences in late childhood. At any rate, we generally have to attribute only regressive significance to the events of early infancy, that is, from the fifth year back. In later years, too, regression can sometimes play an overwhelming role, but even so one must not attribute too little importance to accidental events. In the later course of a neurosis, accidental events and regression together form a vicious circle: retreat from life leads to regression, and regression heightens resistance to life.

## THE TELEOLOGICAL SIGNIFICANCE OF REGRESSION

404 ⟨Before pursuing our argument further, we must turn to the question of what teleological significance should be attributed to regressive fantasies. We might be satisfied with the hypothesis that these fantasies are simply a substitute for real action and therefore have no further significance. That can hardly be so. Psychoanalytic theory inclines to see the reason for the neurosis in the fantasies (illusions, prejudices, etc.), as their character betrays a tendency which is often directly opposed to reasonable action. Indeed, it often looks as if the patient were really using his previous history only to prove that he cannot act reasonably, whereupon the analyst, who, like everyone else, is easily inclined to sympathize with the patient (i.e., to identify with him unconsciously), gets the impression that the patient's arguments constitute a real aetiology. In other cases the fantasies have more the character of wonderful ideals which put beautiful and airy phantasms in the place of crude reality. Here a more or less obvious megalomania is always present, aptly compensating for the patient's indolence and deliberate incompetence. But the

decidedly sexual fantasies often reveal their purpose quite clearly, which is to accustom the patient to the thought of his sexual destiny, and so help him to overcome his resistance.

405 If we agree with Freud that neurosis is an unsuccessful attempt at self-cure, we must allow the fantasies, too, a double character: on one hand a pathological tendency to resist, on the other a helpful and preparatory tendency. With a normal person the libido, when it is blocked by an obstacle, forces him into a state of introversion and makes him reflect. So, too, with a neurotic under the same conditions: an introversion ensues, with increased fantasy activity. But he gets stuck there, because he prefers the infantile mode of adaptation as being the easier one. He does not see that he is exchanging his momentary advantage for a permanent disadvantage and has thus done himself a bad turn. In the same way, it is much easier and more convenient for the civic authorities to neglect all those troublesome sanitary precautions, but when an epidemic comes the sin of omission takes bitter revenge. If, therefore, the neurotic claims all manner of infantile alleviations, he must also accept the consequences. And if he is not willing to do so, then the consequences will overtake him.

406 It would, in general, be a great mistake to deny any teleological value to the apparently pathological fantasies of a neurotic. They are, as a matter of fact, the first beginnings of spiritualization, the first groping attempts to find new ways of adapting. His retreat to the infantile level does not mean only regression and stagnation, but also the possibility of discovering a new life-plan. Regression is thus in very truth the basic condition for the act of creation. Once again I must refer you to my oft-cited book *Symbols of Transformation.*〉

## 8. THERAPEUTIC PRINCIPLES OF PSYCHOANALYSIS

407 With the concept of regression, psychoanalysis made probably one of the most important discoveries in this field. Not only were the earlier formulations of the genesis of neurosis overthrown or at least considerably modified, but the *actual conflict* received, for the first time, its proper valuation.

408 In our earlier case of the lady and the horses, we saw that the symptomatological dramatization could only be understood when it was seen as an expression of the actual conflict. Here psychoanalytic theory joins hands with the results of the association experiments, of which I spoke in my lectures at Clark University. The association experiment, when conducted on a neurotic person, gives us a number of pointers to definite conflicts in his actual life, which we call complexes. These complexes contain just those problems and difficulties which have brought the patient into disharmony with himself. Generally we find a love-conflict of a quite obvious character. From the standpoint of the association experiment, neurosis appears as something quite different from what it seemed to be from the standpoint of earlier psychoanalytic theory. From that standpoint, neurosis seemed to be a formation having its roots in earliest infancy and overgrowing the normal psychic structure; considered from the standpoint of the association experiment, neurosis appears as a reaction to an actual conflict, which naturally is found just as often among normal people but is solved by them without too much difficulty. The neurotic, however, remains in the grip of the conflict, and his neurosis seems to be more or less the consequence of his having got stuck. We can say, therefore, that the results of the association experiment argue strongly in favour of the regression theory.

## THE EVALUATION OF NEUROTIC FANTASIES

409 With the help of the earlier, "historical" conception of neurosis, we thought we could understand why a neurotic with a powerful parental complex has such great difficulties in adapting himself to life. But now that we know that normal persons have exactly the same complexes and, in principle, go through the same psychological development as a neurotic, we can no longer explain neurosis by the development of certain fantasy systems. The really explanatory approach now is a prospective one. We no longer ask whether the patient has a father or mother complex, or unconscious incest fantasies which tie him to his parents, for we know today that everybody has them. It was a mistake to believe that only neurotics have such things. We ask rather: What is the task which the patient does not want to fulfil? What difficulty is he trying to avoid?

410 If a person tried always to adapt himself fully to the conditions of life, his libido would always be employed correctly and adequately. When that does not happen, it gets blocked and produces regressive symptoms. The non-fulfilment of the demands of adaptation, or the shrinking of the neurotic from difficulties, is, at bottom, the hesitation of every organism in the face of a new effort to adapt. (The training of animals provides instructive examples in this respect, and in many cases such an explanation is, in principle, sufficient. From this standpoint the earlier mode of explanation, which maintained that the resistance of the neurotic was due to his bondage to fantasies, appears incorrect. But it would be very one-sided to take our stand solely on a point of principle. There is *also* a bondage to fantasies, even though the fantasies are, as a rule, secondary. The neurotic's bondage to fantasies (illusions, prejudices, etc.) develops gradually, as a habit, out of innumerable regressions from obstacles since earliest childhood. All this grows into a regular habit familiar to every student of neurosis; we all know those patients who use their neurosis as an excuse for running away from difficulties and shirking their duty. Their habitual evasion produces a habit of mind which makes them take it for granted that they should live out their fantasies instead of fulfilling disagreeable obligations. And this bondage to fantasy

makes reality seem less real to the neurotic, less valuable and less interesting, than it does to the normal person. As I explained earlier, the fantastic prejudices and resistances may also arise, sometimes, from experiences that were not intended at all; in other words, were not deliberately sought disappointments and suchlike.⟩

411 The ultimate and deepest root of neurosis appears to be the innate sensitiveness,[1] which causes difficulties even to the infant at the mother's breast, in the form of unnecessary excitement and resistance. The apparent aetiology of neurosis elicited by psychoanalysis is actually, in very many cases, only an inventory of carefully selected fantasies, reminiscences, etc., aiming in a definite direction and created by the patient out of the libido he did not use for biological adaptation. Those allegedly aetiological fantasies thus appear to be nothing but substitute formations, disguises, artificial explanations for the failure to adapt to reality. The aforementioned vicious circle of flight from reality and regression into fantasy is naturally very apt to give the illusion of seemingly decisive causal relationships, which the analyst as well as the patient believes in. Accidental occurrences intervene in this mechanism only as "mitigating circumstances." Their real and effective existence must, however, be acknowledged.

412 I must admit that those critics are partly right who get the impression, from their reading of psychoanalytic case histories, that it is all fantastic and artificial. Only, they make the mistake of attributing the fantastic artefacts and lurid, far-fetched symbolisms to the suggestion and fertile imagination of the analyst, and not to the incomparably more fertile fantasy of his patients. In the fantasy material of a psychoanalytic case history there is, indeed, very much that is artificial. But the most striking thing is the active inventiveness of the patient. And the critics are not so wrong, either, when they say that their neurotic patients have no such fantasies. I do not doubt that most of their patients are totally unconscious of having any fantasies at all. When it is in the unconscious, a fantasy is "real" only when it has some demonstrable effect on consciousness, for instance in the form of a dream. Otherwise we can say with a clear conscience that it is

1 ⟨Sensitiveness is naturally only one word for it. We could also say "reactivity" or "lability." As we know, there are many other words in circulation.⟩

not real. So anyone who overlooks the almost imperceptible effects of unconscious fantasies on consciousness, or dispenses with a thorough and technically irreproachable analysis of dreams, can easily overlook the fantasies of his patients altogether. We are therefore inclined to smile when we hear this oft-repeated objection.

413 Nevertheless, we must admit that there is some truth in it. The regressive tendency of the patient, reinforced by the attentions of the psychoanalyst in his examination of the unconscious fantasy activity, goes on inventing and creating even during the analysis. One could even say that this activity is greatly increased in the analytical situation, since the patient feels his regressive tendency strengthened by the interest of the analyst and produces even more fantasies than before. For this reason our critics have often remarked that a conscientious therapy of the neurosis should go in exactly the opposite direction to that taken by psychoanalysis; in other words, that it is the first task of therapy to extricate the patient from his unhealthy fantasies and bring him back again to real life.

414 The psychoanalyst, of course, is well aware of this, but he knows just how far one can go with this extricating of neurotics from their fantasies. As medical men, we should naturally never dream of preferring a difficult and complicated method, assailed by all the authorities, to a simple, clear, and easy one unless for a very good reason. I am perfectly well acquainted with hypnotic suggestion and Dubois' method of persuasion, but I do not use them because they are comparatively ineffective. For the same reason, I do not use "rééducation de la volonté" directly, as psychoanalysis gives me better results.

## ACTIVE PARTICIPATION IN THE FANTASY

415 But, if we do use psychoanalysis, we must go along with the regressive fantasies of our patients. Psychoanalysis has a much broader outlook as regards the evaluation of symptoms than have the usual psychotherapeutic procedures. These all start from the assumption that neurosis is an entirely pathological formation. In the whole of neurology hitherto, no one has ever thought of seeing in the neurosis an attempt at healing, or, con-

sequently, of attributing to the neurotic formations a quite special teleological significance. But, like every illness, neurosis is only a compromise between the pathogenic causes and the normal function. Modern medicine no longer considers fever as the illness itself but as a purposive reaction of the organism. Similarly, psychoanalysis does not conceive the neurosis as antinatural and in itself pathological, but as having a meaning and a purpose.

416 From this follows the inquiring and expectant attitude of psychoanalysis towards neurosis. In all cases it refrains from judging the value of a symptom, and tries instead to understand what tendencies lie beneath that symptom. If we were able to destroy a neurosis in the same way, for instance, as a cancer is destroyed, we would be destroying at the same time a large amount of useful energy. We save this energy, that is, we make it serve the purposes of the drive for recuperation, by pursuing the meaning of the symptoms and going along with the regressive movement of the patient. Those unfamiliar with the essentials of psychoanalysis will certainly have some difficulty in understanding how a therapeutic effect can be achieved when the analyst enters into the "harmful" fantasies of his patients. Not only the opponents of psychoanalysis but the patients themselves doubt the therapeutic value of such a method, which concentrates attention on the very things that the patient condemns as worthless and reprehensible, namely his fantasies. Patients will often tell you that their former doctors forbade them to have any concern with their fantasies, explaining that they could only consider themselves well when they were free, if only temporarily, from this terrible scourge. Naturally they wonder what good it will do when the treatment leads them back to the very place from which they consistently tried to escape.

417 This objection can be answered as follows: it all depends on the attitude the patient takes towards his fantasies. Hitherto, the patient's fantasying was a completely passive and involuntary activity. He was lost in his dreams, as we say. Even his so-called "brooding" was nothing but an involuntary fantasy. What psychoanalysis demands of the patient is apparently the same thing, but only a person with a very superficial knowledge of psychoanalysis could confuse this passive dreaming with the

attitude now required. What psychoanalysis asks of the patient is the exact opposite of what the patient has always done. He is like a man who has unintentionally fallen into the water and sunk, whereas psychoanalysis wants him to act like a diver. It was no mere chance which led him to fall in just at that spot. There lies the sunken treasure, but only a diver can bring it to the surface.

418 That is to say, when the patient judges them from a rational standpoint, he regards his fantasies as worthless and meaningless. In reality, however, they exert their great influence just because they are of such great importance. They are sunken treasures which can only be recovered by a diver; in other words the patient, contrary to his wont, must now deliberately turn his attention to his inner life. Where formerly he dreamed, he must now think, consciously and intentionally. This new way of thinking about himself has about as much resemblance to his former state of mind as a diver has to a drowning man. His former compulsion now has a meaning and a purpose, it has become *work*. The patient, assisted by the analyst, immerses himself in his fantasies, not in order to lose himself in them, but to salvage them, piece by piece, and bring them into the light of day. He thus acquires an objective vantage-point from which to view his inner life, and can now tackle the very thing he feared and hated. Here we have the basic principle of all psychoanalytic treatment.

### THE TASK OF ADAPTATION

419 Previously, because of his illness, the patient stood partly or wholly outside life. Consequently he neglected many of his duties, either in regard to social achievement or in regard to his purely human tasks. He must get back to fulfilling these duties if he wants to become well again. By way of caution, I would remark that "duties" are not to be understood here as general ethical postulates, but as duties to himself, by which again I do not mean egocentric interests—for a human being is also a social being, a fact too easily forgotten by individualists. A normal person feels very much more comfortable sharing a common virtue than possessing an individual vice, no matter how seduc-

tive it may be. He must already be a neurotic, or an otherwise unusual person, if he lets himself be deluded by special interests of this kind.

420 The neurotic shrank from his duties and his libido turned away, at least partly, from the tasks imposed by reality. Consequently it became introverted, directed towards his inner life. Because no attempt was made to master any real difficulties, his libido followed the path of regression, so that fantasy largely took the place of reality. Unconsciously—and very often consciously—the neurotic prefers to live in his dreams and fantasies. In order to bring him back to reality and to the fulfilment of his necessary tasks, psychoanalysis proceeds along the same "false" track of regression which was taken by the libido of the patient, so that at the beginning the analysis looks as if it were supporting his morbid proclivities. But psychoanalysis follows the false tracks of fantasy in order to restore the libido, the valuable part of the fantasies, to consciousness and apply it to the duties of the present. This can only be done by bringing up the unconscious fantasies, together with the libido attached to them. Were there no libido attached, we could safely leave these unconscious fantasies to their own shadowy existence. Unavoidably the patient, feeling confirmed in his regressive tendency by the mere fact of having started the analysis, will, amid increasing resistances, lead the analyst's interest down to the depths of his unconscious shadow-world.

421 It will readily be understood that every analyst, as a normal person, will feel in himself the greatest resistances to the regressive tendency of the patient, as he is quite convinced that this tendency is pathological. As a doctor, he believes he is acting quite rightly not to enter into his patient's fantasies. He is understandably repelled by this tendency, for it is indeed repulsive to see somebody completely given up to such fantasies, finding only himself important and admiring himself unceasingly. Moreover, for the aesthetic sensibilities of the normal person, the average run of neurotic fantasies is exceedingly disagreeable, if not downright disgusting. The psychoanalyst, of course, must put aside all aesthetic value-judgments, just like every other doctor who really wants to help his patient. He must not shudder at dirty work. Naturally there are a great many patients who are physically ill and who do recover through

the application of ordinary physical methods, dietetic or suggestive, without closer exploration and radical treatment. But severe cases can be helped only by a therapy based on an exact investigation and thorough knowledge of the illness. Our psychotherapeutic methods hitherto were general measures of this kind; in mild cases they do no harm, on the contrary they are often of real use. But a great many patients prove inaccessible to these methods. If anything helps here, it is psychoanalysis, which is not to say that psychoanalysis is a cure-all. This is a sneer that comes only from ill-natured criticism. We know very well that psychoanalysis fails in certain cases. As everybody knows, we shall never be able to cure all illnesses.

422 The "diving" work of analysis brings up dirty material, piece by piece, out of the slime, but it must first be cleaned before we can recognize its value. The dirty fantasies are valueless and are thrown aside, but the libido attached to them is of value and this, after the work of cleaning, becomes serviceable again. To the professional psychoanalyst, as to every specialist, it will sometimes seem that the fantasies have a value of their own, and not just the libido. But their value is no concern of the patient's. For the analyst these fantasies have only a scientific value, just as it may be of special interest to the surgeon to know whether the pus contains staphylococci or streptococci. To the patient it is all the same, and so far as he is concerned it is better for the analyst to conceal his scientific interest, lest the patient be tempted to take more pleasure than necessary in his fantasies. The aetiological significance which is attributed to these fantasies—incorrectly, to my mind—explains why so much space is given up to the extensive discussion of all forms of fantasy in the psychoanalytic literature. Once one knows that in this sphere absolutely nothing is impossible, the initial estimation of fantasies will gradually wear itself out, and with it the attempt to discover in them an aetiological significance. Nor will the most exhaustive discussion of case histories ever succeed in emptying this ocean. Theoretically the fantasies in each case are inexhaustible.

423 In most cases, however, the production of fantasies ceases after a time, from which one must not conclude that the possibilities of fantasy are exhausted; the cessation only means that no more libido is regressing. The end of the regressive move-

ment is reached when the libido seizes hold of the actualities of life and is used for the solution of necessary tasks. There are cases, and not a few of them, where the patient continues to produce endless fantasies, whether for his own pleasure or because of the mistaken expectations of the analyst. Such a mistake is especially easy for beginners, since, blinded by psychoanalytic case histories, they keep their interest fixed on the alleged aetiological significance of the fantasies, and are constantly endeavouring to fish up more fantasies from the infantile past, vainly hoping to find there the solution of the neurotic difficulties. They do not see that the solution lies in action, in the fulfilment of certain necessary obligations to life. It will be objected that the neurosis is entirely due to the incapacity of the patient to carry out these tasks, and that, by analysing the unconscious, the therapist ought to enable him to do so, or at least give him the means of doing so.

424 Put in this way, the objection is perfectly true, but we have to add that it is valid only when the patient is really conscious of the task he has to fulfil—conscious of it not only academically, in general theoretical outline, but also in detail. It is characteristic of neurotics to be wanting in this knowledge, although, because of their intelligence, they are well aware of the general duties of life, and struggle perhaps only too hard to fulfil the precepts of current morality. But for that very reason they know all the less, sometimes nothing at all, about the incomparably more important duties to themselves. It is not enough, therefore, to follow the patient blindfold on the path of regression, and to push him back into his infantile fantasies by an untimely aetiological interest. I often hear from patients who have got stuck in a psychoanalytic treatment: "My analyst thinks I must have an infantile trauma somewhere, or a fantasy I am still repressing." Apart from cases where this conjecture happened to be true, I have seen others in which the stoppage was caused by the fact that the libido, hauled up by the analysis, sank back again into the depths for want of employment. This was due to the analyst directing his attention entirely to the infantile fantasies and his failure to see what task of adaptation the patient had to fulfil. The consequence was that the libido always sank back again, as it was given no opportunity for further activity.

425 There are many patients who, quite on their own account, discover their life-tasks and stop the production of regressive fantasies fairly soon, because they prefer to live in reality rather than in fantasy. It is a pity that this cannot be said of all patients. A good many of them postpone the fulfilment of their life-tasks indefinitely, perhaps for ever, and prefer their idle neurotic dreaming. I must emphasize yet again that by "dreaming" we do not mean a conscious phenomenon.

426 In consequence of these facts and insights, the character of psychoanalysis has changed in the course of the years. If in its first stage psychoanalysis was a kind of surgery, which removed the foreign body, the blocked affect, from the psyche, in its later form it was a kind of historical method, which tried to investigate the genesis of the neurosis in all its details and to trace it back to its earliest beginnings.

## THE TRANSFERENCE

427 There is no doubt that this method owed its existence not only to a strong scientific interest but also to the personal "empathy" of the analyst, traces of which can clearly be seen in the psychoanalytic case material. Thanks to this personal feeling, Freud was able to discover wherein lay the therapeutic effect of psychoanalysis. While this was formerly sought in the discharge of the traumatic affect, it was now found that the fantasies brought out by analysis were all associated with the person of the analyst. Freud called this process the *transference,* because the patient transferred to the analyst the fantasies that were formerly attached to the memory-images of the parents. The transference is not limited to the purely intellectual sphere; rather, the libido that is invested in the fantasies precipitates itself, together with the fantasies, upon the analyst. All those sexual fantasies which cluster round the imago of the parents now cluster round him, and the less the patient realizes this, the stronger will be his unconscious tie to the analyst.

428 This discovery is of fundamental importance in several ways. Above all, the transference is of great biological value to the patient. The less libido he gives to reality, the more exaggerated will be his fantasies and the more he will be cut off from the

world. Typical of neurotics is their disturbed relationship to reality—that is to say, their reduced adaptation. The transference to the analyst builds a bridge across which the patient can get away from his family into reality. He can now emerge from his infantile milieu into the world of adults, since the analyst represents for him a part of the world outside the family.

429 On the other hand, the transference is a powerful hindrance to the progress of the treatment, because the patient assimilates the analyst, who should stand for a part of the extrafamilial world, to his father and mother, so that the whole advantage of his new acquisition is jeopardized. The more he is able to see the analyst objectively, to regard him as he does any other individual, the greater becomes the advantage of the transference. The less he is able to see the analyst in this way, and the more he assimilates him to the father imago, the less advantageous the transference will be and the greater the harm it will do. The patient has merely widened the scope of his family by the addition of a quasi-parental personality. He himself is, as before, still in the infantile milieu and therefore maintains his infantile constellation. In this manner all the advantages of the transference can be lost.

430 There are patients who follow the analysis with the greatest interest without making the slightest improvement, remaining extraordinarily productive in their fantasies although the whole previous history of their neurosis, even its darkest corners, seems to have been brought to light. An analyst under the influence of the historical view might easily be thrown into confusion, and would have to ask himself: What is there in this case still to be analysed? These are just the cases I had in mind before, when I said it is no longer a matter of analysing the historical material, but of action, of overcoming the infantile attitude. The historical analysis would show over and over again that the patient has an infantile attitude to the analyst, but it would not tell us how to alter it. Up to a certain point, this serious disadvantage of the transference applies to every case. It has gradually proved, even, that the part of psychoanalysis so far discussed, extraordinarily interesting and valuable though it may be from a scientific point of view, is in practice far less important than what now has to follow, namely, the analysis of the transference itself.

## CONFESSION AND PSYCHOANALYSIS

431 Before I discuss in detail this especially important part of the analysis, I should like to draw attention to a parallel between the first stage of psychoanalysis and a certain cultural institution. By this I mean the religious institution of confession.

432 Nothing makes people more lonely, and more cut off from the fellowship of others, than the possession of an anxiously hidden and jealously guarded personal secret. Very often it is "sinful" thoughts and deeds that keep them apart and estrange them from one another. Here confession sometimes has a truly redeeming effect. The tremendous feeling of relief which usually follows a confession can be ascribed to the readmission of the lost sheep into the human community. His moral isolation and seclusion, which were so difficult to bear, cease. Herein lies the chief psychological value of confession.

433 Besides that, however, it has other consequences: through the transference of his secret and all the unconscious fantasies underlying it, a moral bond is formed between the patient and his father confessor. We call this a "transference relationship." Anyone with psychoanalytic experience knows how much the personal significance of the analyst is enhanced when the patient is able to confess his secrets to him. The change this induces in the patient's behaviour is often amazing. This, too, is an effect probably intended by the Church. The fact that by far the greater part of humanity not only needs guidance, but wishes for nothing better than to be guided and held in tutelage, justifies, in a sense, the moral value which the Church sets on confession. The priest, equipped with all the insignia of paternal authority, becomes the responsible leader and shepherd of his flock. He is the father confessor and the members of his parish are his penitent children.

434 Thus priest and Church replace the parents, and to that extent they free the individual from the bonds of the family. In so far as the priest is a morally elevated personality with a natural nobility of soul and a mental culture to match, the institution of confession may be commended as a brilliant method of social guidance and education, which did in fact perform a tre-

mendous educative task for more than fifteen hundred years. So long as the medieval Church knew how to be the guardian of art and science—a role in which her success was due, in part, to her wide tolerance of worldly interests—confession was an admirable instrument of education. But it lost its educative value, at least for more highly developed people, as soon as the Church proved incapable of maintaining her leadership in the intellectual sphere—the inevitable consequence of spiritual rigidity. The more highly developed men of our time do not want to be guided by a creed or a dogma; they want to understand. So it is not surprising if they throw aside everything they do not understand; and religious symbols, being the least intelligible of all, are generally the first to go overboard. The sacrifice of the intellect demanded by a positive belief is a violation against which the conscience of the more highly developed individual rebels.

435 So far as analysis is concerned, in perhaps the majority of cases the transference to and dependence on the analyst could be regarded as a sufficient end with a definite therapeutic effect, provided that the analyst was a commanding personality and in every way capable of guiding his patients responsibly and being a "father to his people." But a modern, mentally developed person strives, consciously or unconsciously, to govern himself and stand morally on his own feet. He wants to take the helm in his own hands; the steering has too long been done by others. He wants to understand; in other words, he wants to be an adult. It is much easier to be guided, but this no longer suits intelligent people today, for they feel that the spirit of the age requires them to exercise moral autonomy. Psychoanalysis has to reckon with this requirement, and has therefore to reject the demand of the patient for constant guidance and instruction. The analyst knows his own shortcomings too well to believe that he could play the role of father and guide. His highest ambition must consist only in educating his patients to become independent personalities, and in freeing them from their unconscious bondage to infantile limitations. He must therefore analyse the transference, a task left untouched by the priest. Through the analysis the unconscious—and sometimes conscious—tie to the analyst is cut, and the patient is set upon his own feet. That, at least, is the aim of the treatment.[2]

2 [Cf. the "Psychology of the Transference" for a more detailed study.]

## ANALYSIS OF THE TRANSFERENCE

436 The transference introduces all sorts of difficulties into the relationship between analyst and patient because, as we have seen, the analyst is always more or less assimilated to the family. The first part of the analysis, the discovery of complexes, is fairly easy, thanks to the fact that everyone likes to unburden himself of his painful secrets. Also, he experiences a particular satisfaction in at last finding someone who has an understanding ear for all those things to which nobody would listen before. For the patient it is a singularly agreeable sensation to be understood and to have a doctor who is determined to understand him at all costs, and is willing to follow him, apparently, through all his devious ways. There are patients who even have a special "test" for this, a special question which the analyst has to go into; if he cannot or will not do this, or if he overlooks it, then he is no good. The feeling of being understood is especially sweet to all those lonely souls who are insatiable in their demand for "understanding."

437 For patients with such an obliging disposition, the beginning of the analysis is, as a rule, fairly simple. The therapeutic effects, often considerable, which may appear about this time are easy to obtain, and for that reason they may seduce the beginner into a therapeutic optimism and analytical superficiality which bear no relation to the seriousness and peculiar difficulties of his task. The trumpeting of therapeutic successes is nowhere more contemptible than in psychoanalysis, for no one should know better than the psychoanalyst that the therapeutic result ultimately depends far more on the co-operation of nature and of the patient himself. The psychoanalyst may legitimately pride himself on his increased insight into the essence and structure of neurosis, an insight that greatly exceeds all previous knowledge in this field. But psychoanalytic publications to date cannot be acquitted of the charge of sometimes showing psychoanalysis in a false light. There are technical publications which give the uninitiated person the impression that psychoanalysis is a more or less clever trick, productive of astonishing results.

438 The first stage of the analysis, when we try to understand, and in this way often relieve, the patient's feelings, is responsi-

ble for these therapeutic illusions. The improvements that may appear at the beginning of an analysis are naturally not really results of the treatment, but are generally only passing alleviations which greatly assist the process of transference. After the initial resistances to the transference have been overcome, it turns out to be an ideal situation for a neurotic. He does not need to make any effort himself, and yet someone comes to meet him more than halfway, someone with an unwonted and peculiar wish to understand, who does not allow himself to get bored and is not put off by anything, although the patient sometimes does his utmost to rile him with his wilfulness and childish defiance. This forbearance is enough to melt the strongest resistances, so that the patient no longer hesitates to set the analyst among his family gods, i.e., to assimilate him to the infantile milieu.

439 At the same time, the patient satisfies another need, that is, he achieves a relationship outside the family and thus fulfils a biological demand. Hence the patient obtains a double advantage from the transference relationship: a personality who on the one hand is expected to bestow on him a loving attention in all his concerns, and to that extent is equated with father and mother, but who, on the other hand, is outside the family and thus helps him to fulfil a vitally important and difficult duty without the least danger to himself. When, on top of that, this acquisition is coupled with a marked therapeutic effect, as not infrequently happens, the patient is fortified in his belief that his new-found situation is an excellent one. We can readily appreciate that he is not in the least inclined to give up all these advantages. If it were left to him, he would prefer to remain united with the analyst for ever. Accordingly, he now starts to produce numerous fantasies showing how this goal might be attained. Eroticism plays a large role here, and is exploited and exaggerated in order to demonstrate the impossibility of separation. The patient, understandably enough, puts up the most obstinate resistance when the analyst tries to break the transference relationship.

440 We must not forget, however, that for a neurotic the acquisition of an extrafamilial relationship is one of life's duties, as it is for everyone, and a duty which till then he has either not fulfilled at all or fulfilled in a very limited way. At this point I

must energetically oppose the view one so often hears that an extrafamilial relationship always means a sexual relationship. ⟨In many cases one would like to say: it is precisely not that. It is a favourite neurotic misunderstanding that the right attitude to the world is found by indulgence in sex. In this respect, too, the literature of psychoanalysis is not free from misrepresentations; indeed there are publications from which no other conclusions can be drawn. This misunderstanding is far older than psychoanalysis, however, and so cannot be laid altogether at its door. The experienced medical man knows this advice very well, and I have had more than one patient who has acted according to this prescription. But when a psychoanalyst recommends it, he is making the same mistake as his patient, who believes that his sexual fantasies come from pent-up ("repressed") sexuality. If that were so, this recipe would naturally be a salutary one. It is not a question of that at all, but of regressive libido which exaggerates the fantasies because it evades the real task and strives back to the infantile level.⟩ If we support this regressive tendency at all points we simply reinforce the infantile attitude from which the neurotic is suffering. He has to learn the higher adaptation which life demands from mature and civilized people. Those who have a decided tendency to sink lower will proceed to do so; they need no psychoanalysis for that.

441 At the same time, we must be careful that we do not fall into the opposite extreme of thinking that psychoanalysis creates nothing but quite exceptional personalities. Psychoanalysis stands outside traditional morality; for the present it should adhere to no general moral standard. It is, and should be, only a means for giving the individual trends breathing-space, for developing them and bringing them into harmony with the rest of the personality. It should be a biological method, whose aim is to combine the highest subjective well-being with the most valuable biological performance. As man is not only an individual but also a member of society, these two tendencies inherent in human nature can never be separated, or the one subordinated to the other, without doing him serious injury.

442 The best result for a person who undergoes an analysis is that he shall become in the end what he really is, in harmony with himself, neither good nor bad, just as he is in his natural state. Psychoanalysis cannot be considered a method of educa-

tion, if by education we mean the topiary art of clipping a tree into a beautiful artificial shape. But those who have a higher conception of education will prize most the method of cultivating a tree so that it fulfils to perfection its own natural conditions of growth. We yield too much to the ridiculous fear that we are at bottom quite impossible beings, that if everyone were to appear as he really is a frightful social catastrophe would ensue. Many people today take "man as he really is" to mean merely the eternally discontented, anarchic, rapacious element in human beings, quite forgetting that these same human beings have also erected those firmly established forms of civilization which possess greater strength and stability than all the anarchic undercurrents. ⟨The strengthening of his social personality is one of the essential conditions for man's existence. Were it not so, humanity would cease to be. The selfishness and rebelliousness we meet in the neurotic's psychology are not "man as he really is" but an infantile distortion. In reality the normal man is "civic-minded and moral"; he created his laws and observes them, not because they are imposed on him from without—that is a childish delusion—but because he loves law and order more than he loves disorder and lawlessness.⟩

### RESOLUTION OF THE TRANSFERENCE

443 In order to resolve the transference, we have to fight against forces which are not merely neurotic but have a general significance for normal human beings. In trying to get the patient to break the transference relationship, we are asking of him something that is seldom, or never, demanded of the average person, namely, *that he should conquer himself completely.* Only certain religions demanded this of the individual, and it is this that makes the second stage of analysis so very difficult.

444 ⟨As you know, it is an habitual prejudice of children to think that love gives them the right to make demands. The infantile conception of loving is getting presents from others. Patients make demands in accordance with this definition, and thus behave no differently from most normal people, whose infantile cupidity is only prevented from reaching too high a pitch by their fulfilling their duties to life and by the satisfaction this

affords the libido, and also because a certain lack of temperament does not incline them from the start to passionate behaviour. The basic trouble with the neurotic is that, instead of adapting himself to life in his own special way, which would require a high degree of self-discipline, he makes infantile demands and then begins to bargain. The analyst will hardly be disposed to comply with the demands the patient makes on him personally, but circumstances may arise in which he will seek to buy his freedom with compromises. For instance, he might throw out hints of moral liberties which, if turned into a maxim, would bring about a general lowering of the cultural level. But in that way the patient merely sinks to the lower level and becomes inferior. Nor is it, in the end, a question of culture at all, but simply of the analyst buying his way out of the constricting transference situation by offering other, alleged advantages. It goes against the real interests of the patient to hold out these compensating advantages so enticingly; at that rate he will never be freed from his infantile cupidity and indolence. Only self-conquest can free him from these.

445 The neurotic has to prove that he, just as much as a normal person, can live reasonably. Indeed, he must do more than a normal person, he must give up a large slice of his infantilism, which nobody asks a normal person to do.

446 Patients often try to convince themselves, by seeking out special adventures, that it is possible to go on living in an infantile way. It would be a great mistake if the analyst tried to stop them. There are experiences which one must go through and for which reason is no substitute. Such experiences are often of inestimable value to the patient.

447 Nowhere more clearly than at this stage of the analysis will everything depend on how far the analyst has been analysed himself. If he himself has an infantile type of desire of which he is still unconscious, he will never be able to open his patient's eyes to this danger. It is an open secret that all through the analysis intelligent patients are looking beyond it into the soul of the analyst, in order to find there the confirmation of the healing formulae—or its opposite. It is quite impossible, even by the subtlest analysis, to prevent the patient from taking over instinctively the way in which his analyst deals with the problems of life. Nothing can stop this, for personality teaches more

than thick tomes full of wisdom. All the disguises in which he wraps himself in order to conceal his own personality avail him nothing; sooner or later he will come across a patient who calls his bluff. An analyst who from the first takes his profession seriously is faced with the inexorable necessity of testing out the principles of psychoanalysis on himself as well. He will be astonished to see how many apparently technical difficulties vanish in this way. Note that I am not speaking of the initial stage of analysis, which might be called the stage of unearthing the complexes, but of this final, extraordinarily tricky stage which is concerned with the resolution of the transference.

448 I have frequently found that beginners look upon the transference as an entirely abnormal phenomenon that has to be "fought against." Nothing could be more mistaken. To begin with we have to regard the transference merely as a falsification, a sexualized caricature, of the social bond which holds human society together and which also produces close ties between people of like mind. This bond is one of the most valuable social factors imaginable, and it would be a cruel mistake to reject absolutely these social overtures on the part of the patient. It is only necessary to purge them of their regressive components, their infantile sexualism. If that is done, the transference becomes a most convenient instrument of adaptation.

449 The only danger—and it is a great one—is that the unacknowledged infantile demands of the analyst may identify themselves with the parallel demands of the patient. The analyst can avoid this only by submitting to a rigorous analysis at the hands of another. He then learns to understand what analysis really means and how it feels to experience it on your own psyche. Every intelligent analyst will at once see how much this must redound to the benefit of his patients. There are analysts who believe that they can get along with a self-analysis. This is Munchausen psychology, and they will certainly remain stuck. They forget that one of the most important therapeutically effective factors is subjecting yourself to the objective judgment of another. As regards ourselves we remain blind, despite everything and everybody. The analyst, of all people, must give up all isolationist tactics and autoerotic mystification if he wants to help his patients to become socially mature and independent personalities.

450 I know that I am also at one with Freud when I set it up as a self-evident requirement that a psychoanalyst must discharge his own duties to life in the proper way. If he does not, nothing can stop his unutilized libido from automatically descending on his patients and in the end falsifying the whole analysis. Immature and incompetent persons who are themselves neurotic and stand with only one foot in reality generally make nothing but nonsense out of analysis. *Exempla sunt odiosa!* Medicine in the hand of a fool was ever poison and death. Just as we demand from a surgeon, besides his technical knowledge, a skilled hand, courage, presence of mind, and power of decision, so we must expect from an analyst a very serious and thorough psychoanalytic training of his own personality before we are willing to entrust a patient to him. I would even go so far as to say that the acquisition and practice of the psychoanalytic technique presuppose not only a specific psychological gift but in the very first place a serious concern with the moulding of one's own character.⟩

451 The technique for resolving the transference is the same as the one we have already described. The problem of what the patient is to do with the libido he has withdrawn from the person of the analyst naturally occupies a large place. Here too the danger for the beginner is great, as he will be inclined to suggest or to give advice. For the patient the analyst's efforts in this respect are extremely convenient, and therefore fatal. At this important juncture, as everywhere in psychoanalysis, we have to let the patient and his impulses take the lead, even if the path seems a wrong one. Error is just as important a condition of life's progress as truth.

## THE PROSPECTIVE FUNCTION OF DREAMS

452 In this second stage of analysis, with its hidden reefs and shoals, we owe an enormous amount to dreams. At the beginning of the analysis, dreams helped us chiefly to discover the fantasies; but here they are often extremely valuable guides to the use of libido. Freud's work laid the foundation for an immense increase in our knowledge in regard to the determination of the manifest dream content by historical material and wish-

ful tendencies. He showed how dreams give access to a mass of subliminal material, mostly memories that have sunk below the threshold. In keeping with his genius for the purely historical method, Freud's procedure is predominantly analytical. Although this method is incontestably of great value we ought not to adopt this standpoint exclusively, as a one-sided historical view does not take sufficient account of the teleological significance of dreams (stressed in particular by Maeder[3]). Unconscious thinking would be quite inadequately characterized if we considered it only from the standpoint of its historical determinants. For a complete evaluation we have unquestionably to consider its teleological or prospective significance as well. If we pursued the history of the English Parliament back to its earliest beginnings, we should undoubtedly arrive at an excellent understanding of its development and the way its present form was determined. But that would tell us nothing about its prospective function, that is, about the tasks it has to accomplish now and in the future.

453 The same is true of dreams, whose prospective function alone was valued in the superstitions of all times and races. There may well be a good deal of truth in this view. Without presuming to say that dreams have prophetic foresight, it is nevertheless possible that we might find, in this subliminal material, combinations of future events which are subliminal simply because they have not yet attained the degree of clarity necessary for them to become conscious. Here I am thinking of those dim presentiments we sometimes have of the future, which are nothing but very faint, subliminal combinations of events whose objective value we are not yet able to apperceive.

454 The future tendencies of the patient are elaborated with the help of these teleological components of the dream. If this work is successful, the patient passes out of the treatment and out of the semi-infantile transference relationship into a life which has been carefully prepared within him, which he has chosen himself, and to which, after mature deliberation, he can declare himself committed.

3 ["Die Symbolik in den Legenden, Märchen, Gebräuchen und Träumen" (1908). —EDITORS.]

## FUTURE USES OF PSYCHOANALYSIS

455 As will readily be understood, psychoanalysis can never be used for polyclinical work. It must always remain in the hands of the few who, because of their innate educative and psychological capacities, have a particular aptitude and a special liking for this profession. Just as not every doctor makes a good surgeon, not everyone is fitted to be a psychoanalyst. The predominantly psychological nature of the work will make it difficult for the medical profession to monopolize it. Sooner or later other branches of science will master the method, either for practical reasons or out of theoretical interest. So long as orthodox science excludes psychoanalysis from general discussion as sheer nonsense, we cannot be surprised if other departments learn to master the material before the medical profession does. This is all the more likely as psychoanalysis is a general method of psychological research and a heuristic principle of the first rank in the domain of the humane sciences.

456 It is chiefly the work of the Zurich school that has demonstrated the applicability of psychoanalysis as a method of investigation in mental disease. Psychoanalytic investigation of dementia praecox, for instance, has given us most valuable insights into the psychological structure of this remarkable disease. It would lead me too far afield to go at all deeply into the results of these investigations. The theory of the psychological determinants of this disease is a sufficiently vast territory in itself, and if I were to discuss the symbolistic problems of dementia praecox I would have to put before you a mass of material which I could not hope to deploy within the framework of these lectures, whose purpose is to provide a general survey.

457 The question of dementia praecox has become so extraordinarily complicated because the recent incursion of psychoanalysis into the domains of mythology and comparative religion has afforded us deep insight into ethnological symbolism. Those who were familiar with the symbolism of dreams and of dementia praecox were astounded by the parallelism between the symbols found in modern individuals and those found in the history of the human race. Most startling of all is the parallelism between ethnic and schizophrenic symbols. The complicated

relations between psychology and mythology make it impossible for me to discuss in detail my views on dementia praecox. For the same reason I must refrain from discussing the results of the psychoanalytic investigation of mythology and comparative religion. The principal result of these investigations at present is the discovery of far-reaching parallels between ethnic and individual symbolisms. We cannot yet see what vast perspectives this ethnopsychology may open out. But, from all we know at present, we may expect that psychoanalytic research into the nature of subliminal processes will be enormously enriched and deepened by a study of mythology.

## 9. A CASE OF NEUROSIS IN A CHILD

458 In these lectures I have had to confine myself to giving you a general account of the nature of psychoanalysis. Detailed discussion of the method and theory would have required a mass of case material, exposition of which would have detracted from a comprehensive view of the whole. But, in order to give you some idea of the actual process of psychoanalytic treatment, I have decided to present a fairly short analysis of an eleven-year-old girl. The case was analysed by my assistant, Miss Mary Moltzer. I must preface my remarks by saying that this case is no more typical of the length or course of an ordinary psychoanalysis than one individual is typical of all others. Nowhere is the abstraction of generally valid rules so difficult as in psychoanalysis, for which reason it is better not to make too many formulations. We must not forget that, notwithstanding the great uniformity of conflicts and complexes, every case is unique, because every individual is unique. Every case demands the analyst's individual interest, and in every case the course of analysis is different.

459 In presenting this case, therefore, I am offering but a small section of the infinitely varied world of the psyche, showing all those apparently bizarre and arbitrary peculiarities which the whim of so-called chance scatters into a human life. It is not my intention to withhold any of the more interesting psychoanalytic details, as I do not want to evoke the impression that psychoanalysis is a rigidly formalistic method. The scientific needs of the investigator prompt him always to look for rules and categories in which the most alive of all living things can be captured. The analyst and observer, on the other hand, must eschew formulas and let the living reality work upon him in all its lawless profusion. Thus I shall try to present this case in its natural setting, and I hope I shall succeed in showing you how differently an analysis develops from what might have been expected on purely theoretical grounds.

460 The case in question is that of an intelligent eleven-year-old girl of good family.

## ANAMNESIS

461 The clinical history is as follows: She had to leave school several times on account of sudden nausea and headaches, and was obliged to go to bed. In the morning she sometimes refused to get up and go to school. She suffered from bad dreams, was moody and unreliable. I informed the mother, who came to consult me, that these might be the signs of a neurosis, and that something special might be hidden behind them about which one would have to ask the child. This conjecture was not an arbitrary one, for every attentive observer knows that if children are so restless and bad-tempered something is worrying them.

462 The child now confessed to her mother the following story. She had a favourite teacher, on whom she had a crush. During this last term she had fallen behind with her work, and she thought she had sunk in her teacher's estimation. She then began to feel sick during his lessons. She felt not only estranged from her teacher, but even rather hostile to him. She directed all her friendly feelings to a poor boy with whom she usually shared the bread she took to school. She now gave him money as well, so that he could buy bread for himself. Once, in conversation with this boy, she made fun of her teacher and called him a goat. The boy attached himself to her more and more, and considered that he had the right to levy an occasional tribute from her in the form of a little present of money. Then she became afraid that the boy would tell the teacher she had called him a goat, and she promised him two francs if he would give her his solemn word never to say anything to the teacher. From that moment the boy began to blackmail her; he demanded money with threats, and persecuted her with his demands on the way to school. She was in despair. Her attacks of sickness were closely connected with this story; yet, after the affair had been settled as a result of this confession, her peace of mind was not restored as we would have expected.

463 Very often, as I mentioned in the previous lecture, the mere relation of a painful episode has a favourable therapeutic effect.

Generally this does not last very long, although on occasion it may be maintained for a long time. Such a confession is naturally a long way from being an analysis, despite the fact that there are many nerve specialists nowadays who believe that an analysis is only a somewhat more extensive anamnesis or confession.

464 Not long afterwards, the child had a violent attack of coughing and missed school for one day. After that she went back to school for one day and felt perfectly well. On the third day a renewed attack of coughing came on, with pains on the left side, fever and vomiting. She had a temperature of 103° F. The doctor feared pneumonia. But the next day everything had disappeared again. She felt quite well, and there was no trace of fever or nausea.

465 But still our little patient wept the whole time and did not wish to get up. From this strange course of events I suspected a serious neurosis, and I therefore advised analytical treatment.

### FIRST INTERVIEW

466 The little girl seemed nervous and constrained, now and then giving a disagreeable forced laugh. She was first of all given an opportunity to talk about what it felt like to be allowed to stay in bed. We learn that it was especially nice then, as she always had company. Everybody came to see her; best of all, she could get herself read to by Mama, from a book with the story in it of a *prince who was ill and only got well again when his wish was fulfilled, the wish being that his little friend, a poor boy, might be allowed to stay with him.*

467 The obvious relation between this story and her own little love-story, as well as its connection with her sickness, was pointed out to her, whereupon she began to weep, saying that she would rather go with the other children and play with them, or they would run away. This was at once allowed, and away she ran, but came back again in no time, somewhat crestfallen. It was explained to her that she had not run away because she was afraid her playmates would run away, but that she herself wanted to run away because of resistances.

SECOND INTERVIEW

468 At the second interview she was less anxious and inhibited. The conversation was led round to the teacher, but she was too embarrassed to speak about him. Finally came the shamefaced admission that she liked him very much. It was explained to her that she need not be ashamed of that; on the contrary, her love was a guarantee that she would do her very best in his lessons. "So then I may like him?" asked the little patient with a happier face.

469 This explanation justified the child in her choice of a love-object. She had, it seemed, been afraid to admit to herself her feelings for the teacher. It is not easy to explain why this should be so. It was previously assumed that the libido has great difficulty in seizing upon a person outside the family because it still finds itself caught in the incestuous bond—a very plausible view indeed, from which it is difficult to withdraw. On the other hand, it must be emphasized that her libido had taken vehement possession of the poor boy, and he too was someone outside the family, so that the difficulty cannot lie in transferring libido to an extra-familial object, but in some other circumstance. Her love for the teacher was for her a more difficult task, it demanded much more from her than her love for the boy, which did not require any moral effort on her part. The hint dropped in the analysis that love would enable her to do her best brought the child back to her real task, which was to adapt to the teacher.

470 Now if the libido draws back from a necessary task, it does so for the very human reason of indolence, which is particularly marked not only in children but also in primitives and animals. Primitive inertia and laziness are the primary reason for not making the effort to adapt. The libido which is not used for this purpose stagnates, and will then make the inevitable regression to former objects or modes of adaptation. The result is a striking activation of the incest complex. The libido withdraws from the object which is so difficult to attain and which demands such great efforts, and turns instead to the easier ones, and finally to the easiest of all, the infantile fantasies, which are then elaborated into real incest fantasies. The fact that, whenever there is a disturbance of psychological adaptation, we always find an

excessive development of these fantasies must likewise be conceived, as I pointed out before, as a regressive phenomenon. That is to say, the incest fantasy is of secondary and not of causal significance, while the primary cause is the resistance of human nature to any kind of exertion. Accordingly, drawing back from certain tasks cannot be explained by saying that man prefers the incestuous relationship, rather he falls back into it because he shuns exertion. Otherwise we would have to say that resistance to conscious effort is identical with preference for the incestuous relationship. This would be obvious nonsense, since not only primitive man but animals too have a mighty dislike of all intentional effort, and are addicted to absolute laziness until circumstances prod them into action. Neither of primitive people nor of animals can it be asserted that preference for incestuous relationships is the cause of their aversion to efforts at adaptation, for, especially in the case of animals, there can be absolutely no question of an incestuous relationship.

471 Characteristically, the child expressed joy not at the prospect of doing her best for the teacher but at being allowed to love him. That was the thing she heard first, because it suited her best. Her relief came from the confirmation that she was justified in loving him—even without making any special effort first.

472 The conversation then went on to the story of the blackmail, which she told again in detail. We learn, furthermore, that she tried to force open her money-box, and when she did not succeed she tried to steal the key from her mother. She also made a clean breast of the other matter: she had made fun of the teacher because he was much nicer to the other girls than to her. But it was true that she had got worse at his lessons, especially in arithmetic. Once she did not understand something, but had not dared to ask for fear of losing the teacher's esteem. Consequently she made mistakes, fell behind, and really did lose it. As a result, she got into a very unsatisfactory position with her teacher.

473 About this time it happened that a girl in her class was sent home because she felt sick. Soon after, the same thing happened to her. In this way, she tried to get away from school, which she no longer liked. The loss of her teacher's esteem led her, on the one hand, to insult him and, on the other, into the affair with the little boy, obviously as a compensation for her lost relation-

ship with the teacher. The explanation she was now given was a simple hint: she would be doing her teacher a good turn if she took pains to understand his lessons by asking questions in time. I may add that this hint had good results; from that moment the little girl became the best pupil and missed no more arithmetic lessons.

474 A point worth stressing in the story of the blackmail is its compulsive character and the lack of freedom it shows in the girl. This is a quite regular phenomenon. As soon as anyone permits his libido to draw back from a necessary task, it becomes autonomous and, regardless of the protests of the subject, chooses its own goals and pursues them obstinately. It is therefore quite common for a person leading a lazy and inactive life to be peculiarly prone to the compulsion of libido, that is, to all kinds of fears and involuntary constraints. The fears and superstitions of primitives furnish the best proof of this, but the history of our own civilization, especially the civilization of antiquity, provides ample confirmation as well. Non-employment of the libido makes it ungovernable. But we must not believe that we can save ourselves permanently from the compulsion of libido by forced efforts. Only to a very limited extent can we consciously set tasks for the libido; other natural tasks are chosen by the libido itself because it is destined for them. If these tasks are avoided, even the most industrious life avails nothing, for we have to consider all the conditions of human nature. Innumerable neurasthenias from overwork can be traced back to this cause, for work done amid internal conflicts creates nervous exhaustion.

## THIRD INTERVIEW

475 The girl related a dream she had had when she was five years old, which made an unforgettable impression on her. "I'll never forget the dream as long as I live," she said. I would like to add here that such dreams are of quite special interest. The longer a dream remains spontaneously in the memory, the greater is the importance to be attributed to it. This is the dream: *"I was in a wood with my little brother, looking for strawberries. Then a wolf came and jumped at me. I fled up a staircase, the wolf*

*after me. I fell down and the wolf bit me in the leg. I awoke in deadly fear."*

476 Before we take up the associations given us by the little girl, I will try to form an arbitrary opinion as to the possible content of the dream, and then see how our results compare with the associations given by the child. The beginning of the dream reminds us of the well-known fairytale of Little Red Ridinghood, which is, of course, known to every child. The wolf ate the grandmother first, then took her shape, and afterwards ate Little Red Ridinghood. But the hunter killed the wolf, cut open the belly, and Little Red Ridinghood sprang out safe and sound.

477 This motif is found in countless myths all over the world, and is the motif of the Bible story of Jonah. The meaning immediately lying behind it is astro-mythological: the sun is swallowed by the sea monster and is born again in the morning. Of course, the whole of astro-mythology is at bottom nothing but psychology—unconscious psychology—projected into the heavens; for myths never were and never are made consciously, they arise from man's unconscious. This is the reason for the sometimes miraculous similarity or identity of myth-forms among races that have been separated from each other in space ever since time began. It explains, for instance, the extraordinary distribution of the cross symbol, quite independently of Christianity, of which America offers specially remarkable examples. It is not possible to suppose that myths were created merely in order to explain meteorological or astronomical processes; they are, in the first instance, manifestations of unconscious impulses, comparable to dreams. These impulses were actuated by the regressive libido in the unconscious. The material which comes to light is naturally infantile material—fantasies connected with the incest complex. Thus, in all these so-called solar myths, we can easily recognize infantile theories about procreation, birth, and incestuous relations. In the fairytale of Little Red Ridinghood it is the fantasy that the mother has to eat something which is like a child, and that the child is born by cutting open the mother's body. This fantasy is one of the commonest and can be found everywhere.

478 From these general psychological considerations we can conclude that the child, in this dream, was elaborating the problem

of procreation and birth. As to the wolf, we must probably put him in the father's place, for the child unconsciously attributed to the father any act of violence towards the mother. This motif, too, is based on countless myths dealing with the violation of the mother. With regard to the mythological parallels, I would like to call your attention to the work of Boas,[1] which includes a magnificent collection of American Indian sagas; then the book by Frobenius, *Das Zeitalter des Sonnengottes;* and finally the works of Abraham, Rank, Riklin, Jones, Freud, Maeder, Silberer, and Spielrein,[2] and my own investigations in *Symbols of Transformation.*

479 After these general reflections, which I give here for theoretical reasons but which naturally formed no part of the treatment, we will go on to see what the child has to tell us about her dream. Needless to say, she was allowed to speak about her dream just as she liked, without being influenced in any way. She picked first on the bite in the leg, and explained that *she had once been told by a woman who had had a baby that she could still show the place where the stork had bitten her.* This expression is, in Switzerland, a variant of the widespread symbolism of copulation and birth. Here we have a perfect parallelism between our interpretation and the association process of the child. For the first association she produced, quite uninfluenced, goes back to the problem we conjectured above on theoretical grounds. I know that the innumerable cases published in the psychoanalytic literature, which were definitely not influenced, have not been able to quash our critics' contention that we suggest our interpretations to the patients. This case, too, will convince no one who is determined to impute to us the crude mistakes of beginners—or, what is worse, falsification.

480 After this first association the little patient was asked what the wolf made her think of. She answered, "I think of my father when he is angry." This, too, coincides absolutely with our theoretical considerations. It might be objected that these considerations were made expressly for this purpose and therefore lack general validity. I think this objection vanishes of itself as soon as one has the requisite psychoanalytic and mythological

1 [The anthropologist Franz Boas (1858–1942); see especially his *Indianische Sagen* (1895).—EDITORS.] 2 [See Bibliography.]

knowledge. The validity of a hypothesis can be seen only on the basis of the right knowledge, otherwise not at all.

481 The first association put the stork in the place of the wolf; the association to the wolf now brings us to the father. In the popular myth the stork stands for the father, for he brings the children. The apparent contradiction between the fairytale, where the wolf is the mother, and the dream, where the wolf is the father, is of no importance for the dream or the dreamer. We can therefore dispense with a detailed explanation. I have dealt with this problem of bisexual symbols in my book.[3] As you know, in the legend of Romulus and Remus both animals, the bird Picus and the wolf, were raised to the rank of parents.

482 Her fear of the wolf in the dream is therefore her fear of the father. The dreamer explained that she was afraid of her father because he was very strict with her. He had also told her that we have bad dreams only when we have done something wrong. She then asked her father, "But what does Mama do wrong? She always has bad dreams."

483 Once her father slapped her because she was sucking her finger. She kept on doing this despite his prohibition. Was this, perhaps, the wrong she had done? Hardly, because sucking the finger was simply a rather anachronistic infantile habit, of little real interest at her age, and serving more to irritate her father so that he would punish her by slapping. In this way she relieved her conscience of an unconfessed and much more serious "sin": *it came out that she had induced a number of girls of her own age to perform mutual masturbation.*

484 It was because of these sexual interests that she was afraid of her father. But we must not forget that she had the wolf dream in her fifth year. At that time these sexual acts had not been committed. Hence we must regard the affair with the other girls at most as a reason for her present fear of her father, but that does not explain her earlier fear. Nevertheless, we may expect that it was something similar, some unconscious sexual wish in keeping with the psychology of the forbidden act just mentioned. The character and moral evaluation of this act are naturally far more unconscious to a child than to an adult. In order to understand what could have made an impression on

3 [Cf. *Symbols of Transformation*, particularly par. 547.]

the child so early, we have to ask what happened in her fifth year. *That was the year in which her younger brother was born.* So even then she was afraid of her father. The associations already discussed show us the unmistakable connection between her sexual interests and her fear.

485 The problem of sex, which nature connects with positive feelings of pleasure, appears in the wolf dream in the form of fear, apparently on account of the bad father, who stands for moral education. The dream was therefore the first impressive manifestation of the sexual problem, obviously stimulated by the recent birth of a younger brother, when as we know all these questions become aired. But because the sexual problem was connected at all points with the history of certain pleasurable physical sensations which education devalues as "bad habits," it could apparently manifest itself only in the guise of moral guilt and fear.

486 This explanation, plausible though it is, seems to me superficial and inadequate. We then attribute the whole difficulty to moral education, on the unproven assumption that education can cause a neurosis. This is to disregard the fact that even people with no trace of moral education become neurotic and suffer from morbid fears. Furthermore, moral law is not just an evil that has to be resisted, but a necessity born from the innermost needs of man. Moral law is nothing other than an outward manifestation of man's innate urge to dominate and control himself. This impulse to domestication and civilization is lost in the dim, unfathomable depths of man's evolutionary history and can never be conceived as the consequence of laws imposed from without. Man himself, obeying his instincts, created his laws. We shall never understand the reasons for the fear and suppression of the sexual problem in a child if we take into account only the moral influences of education. The real reasons lie much deeper, in human nature itself, perhaps in that tragic conflict between nature and culture, or between individual consciousness and collective feeling.

487 Naturally, it would have been pointless to give the child a notion of the higher philosophical aspects of the problem; it would certainly have had not the slightest effect. It was sufficient to remove the idea that she was doing something wrong in being interested in the procreation of life. So it was made clear to her

how much pleasure and curiosity she was bringing to bear on the problem of generation, and how her groundless fear was only pleasure turned into its opposite. The affair of her masturbation met with tolerant understanding, and the discussion was limited to drawing the child's attention to the aimlessness of her action. At the same time, it was explained to her that her sexual actions were mainly an outlet for her curiosity, which she might satisfy in a better way. Her great fear of her father expressed an equally great expectation, which because of the birth of her little brother was closely connected with the problem of generation. These explanations justified the child in her curiosity. With that, a large part of the moral conflict was removed.

### FOURTH INTERVIEW

488 The little girl was now much nicer and much more confiding. Her former constrained and unnatural manner had quite disappeared. She brought a dream which she dreamt after the last interview. It ran: *"I am as tall as a church-spire and can see into every house. At my feet are very small children, as small as flowers are. A policeman comes. I say to him, 'If you dare to make any remark, I shall take your sword and cut off your head.'"*

489 In the analysis of the dream she made the following remark: "I would like to be taller than my father, because then he would have to obey me." She at once associated the policeman with her father, who was a military man and had, of course, a sword. The dream clearly fulfils her wish. As a church-spire, she is much bigger than her father, and if he dares to make a remark he will be decapitated. The dream also fulfils the natural wish of the child to be "big," i.e., grown-up, and to have children playing at her feet. In this dream she got over her fear of her father, and from this we may expect a significant increase in her personal freedom and feeling of security.

490 On the theoretical side, we may regard this dream as a clear example of the compensatory significance and teleological function of dreams. Such a dream must leave the dreamer with a heightened sense of the value of her own personality, and this is of great importance for her personal well-being. It does not

matter that the symbolism was not clear to the consciousness of the child, for the emotional effect of symbols does not depend on conscious understanding. It is more a matter of intuitive knowledge, the source from which all religious symbols derive their efficacy. Here no conscious understanding is needed; they influence the psyche of the believer through intuition.

### FIFTH AND SIXTH INTERVIEWS

491 The child related the following dream which she had dreamt in the meantime: *"I was standing with my whole family on the roof. The windows of the houses on the other side of the valley shone like fire. The rising sun was reflected in them. Suddenly I saw that the house at the corner of our street was really on fire. The fire came nearer and nearer and took hold of our house. I ran into the street, and my mother threw all sorts of things after me. I held out my apron, and among other things she threw me a doll. I saw that the stones of our house were burning, but the wood remained untouched."*

492 The analysis of this dream presented peculiar difficulties and had to be extended over two sittings. It would lead me too far to describe the whole of the material this dream brought forth; I shall have to limit myself to what is most essential. The salient associations began with the peculiar image of the stones of the house burning but not the wood. It is sometimes worth while, especially with longer dreams, to take the most striking images and analyse them first. This is not the general rule but it may be excused here by the practical need for abbreviation.

493 "It is queer, like in a fairytale," said the little patient about this image. She was shown, with the help of examples, that fairytales always have a meaning. "But not all fairytales," she objected. "For instance, the tale of Sleeping Beauty. What could that mean?" It was explained to her that Sleeping Beauty had to wait for a hundred years in an enchanted sleep until she could be set free. Only the hero whose love overcame all difficulties and who boldly broke through the thorny hedge could rescue her. Thus one often has to wait for a long time before one obtains one's heart's desire.

494 This explanation was suited to the child's understanding,

and on the other hand was perfectly in accord with the history of this fairytale motif. The tale of Sleeping Beauty has obvious connections with an ancient spring and fertility myth, and at the same time contains a problem which has a remarkably close affinity with the psychological situation of a rather precocious little girl of eleven. It belongs to a whole cycle of legends in which a virgin, guarded by a dragon, is rescued by a hero. Without wishing to embark on an interpretation of this myth, I would like to emphasize its astronomical or meteorological components, clearly brought out in the Edda. The earth, in the form of a maiden, is held prisoner by the winter, and is covered with ice and snow. The young spring sun, the fiery hero, melts her out of her frosty prison, where she had long awaited her deliverer.

495 The association given by the little girl was chosen by her simply as an example of a fairytale without a meaning, and not as a direct association to the dream-image of the burning house. About this she only made the remark, "It is queer, like in a fairytale," by which she meant impossible; for to say that stones burn is something completely impossible, nonsensical, and like a fairytale. The explanation she was given showed her that "impossible" and "like a fairytale" are only partly identical, since fairytales do have a great deal of meaning. Although this particular fairytale, from the casual way it was mentioned, seems to have nothing to do with the dream, it deserves special attention because it appeared, as though by chance, while the dream was being analysed. The unconscious came out with just this example, and this cannot be mere chance but is somehow characteristic of the situation at that moment. In analysing dreams we have to look out for these seeming accidents, for in psychology there are no blind accidents, much as we are inclined to assume that these things are pure chance. You can hear this objection as often as you like from our critics, but for a really scientific mind there are only causal relationships and no accidents. From the fact that the little girl chose Sleeping Beauty as an example we must conclude that there was some fundamental reason for this in the psychology of the child. This reason was the comparison or partial identification of herself with Sleeping Beauty; in other words, in the psyche of the child there was a complex which found expression in the Sleeping Beauty motif.

The explanation given to the child took account of this inference.

496 Nevertheless, she was not quite satisfied, and still doubted that fairytales have a meaning. As a further example of an incomprehensible fairytale she cited Snow White, who lay enclosed in a glass coffin, in the sleep of death. It is not difficult to see that Snow White belongs to the same cycle of myths as Sleeping Beauty. It contains even clearer indications of the myth of the seasons. The myth material chosen by the child points to an intuitive comparison with the earth, held fast by the winter's cold, awaiting the liberating sun of spring.

497 This second example confirms the first one and the explanation we have given. It would be difficult to maintain that the second example, accentuating as it does the meaning of the first, was suggested by the explanation. The fact that the little girl gave Snow White as another example of a meaningless fairytale proves that she did not realize the identity of Snow White and Sleeping Beauty. We may therefore conjecture that Snow White arose from the same unconscious source as Sleeping Beauty, namely, from a complex concerned with the expectation of coming events. These events may be compared exactly with the deliverance of the earth from the prison of winter and its fertilization by the rays of the spring sun. As you know, from ancient times the fertilizing spring sun was associated with the symbol of the bull, the animal embodying the mightiest procreative power. Although we cannot yet see the connection between these insights and the dream, we will hold fast to what we have gained and proceed with our analysis.

498 The next dream-image shows the little girl catching the doll in her apron. Her first association tells us that her attitude and the whole situation in the dream reminded her of *a picture she knew, showing a stork flying over a village, with little girls standing in the street holding out their aprons and shouting to the stork to bring them a baby*. She added that she herself had long wanted a baby brother or sister. This material, given spontaneously, is clearly related to the myth-motifs already discussed. It is evident that the dream was in fact concerned with the same problem of the awakening reproductive instinct. Of course, nothing of these connections was mentioned to the child.

499 Then, abruptly, after a pause, came the next association:

"Once, when I was five years old, I lay down in the street and a bicycle passed over my stomach." This highly improbable story proved to be, as might be expected, a fantasy, which had become a paramnesia. Nothing of the kind had ever happened, but on the other hand we learn that at school *the little girls used to lie crosswise over each other's bodies and trample with their legs.*

500 Anyone who has read the analyses of children published by Freud and myself [4] will recognize in this childish game the same basic motif of trampling, which we considered must have a sexual undercurrent. This view, demonstrated by our earlier work, was borne out by the next association of our little patient: "I would much rather have a real baby than a doll."

501 All this highly remarkable material brought out by the stork fantasy suggests the typical beginnings of an infantile sexual theory, and at the same time shows us the point round which the little girl's fantasies were revolving.

502 It may be of interest to know that the motif of treading or trampling can be found in mythology. I have documented this in my book on libido.[5] The use of these infantile fantasies in the dream, the paramnesia about the bicyclist, and the tense expectation expressed in the Sleeping Beauty motif all show that the child's inner interest was dwelling on certain problems that had to be solved. Probably the fact that her libido was attracted by the problem of generation was the reason why her interest flagged at school, so that she fell behind in her work. How very much this problem fascinates girls of twelve and thirteen I was able to show in a special case, published in "A Contribution to the Psychology of Rumour." [6] It is the cause of all that smutty talk among children, and of mutual attempts at enlightenment which naturally turn out to be very nasty and often ruin the child's imagination for good. Even the most careful protection cannot prevent them from one day discovering the great secret, and then probably in the dirtiest way. It would be far better for children to learn the facts of life cleanly and in good time, so that they would not need to be enlightened in ugly ways by their playmates.

4 [Cf. "Psychic Conflicts in a Child," pars. 47ff.]

5 [*Symbols of Transformation*, pars. 370, 480.]

6 [Cf. *Freud and Psychoanalysis*, pars. 95ff., and *The Psychoanalytic Years.*]

503 These and other indications showed that the moment had come for a certain amount of sexual enlightenment. The little girl listened attentively to the talk that followed, and then asked very seriously: "So then I really can't have a child?" This question led to an explanation about sexual maturity.

### SEVENTH INTERVIEW

504 The little girl began by remarking that she perfectly understood why it was not yet possible for her to have a child; she had therefore renounced all idea of it. But this time she did not make a good impression. It turned out that she had lied to her teacher. She had been late to school, and told the teacher that she had had to go somewhere with her father and had therefore arrived late. In reality, she had been too lazy to get up in time. She told a lie because she was afraid of losing the teacher's favour by confessing the truth. This sudden moral defeat requires an explanation. According to the principles of psychoanalysis, a sudden and striking weakness can only come about when the analysand does not draw from the analysis the conclusions that are necessary at the moment, but still keeps the door open to other possibilities. This means, in our case, that though the analysis had apparently brought the libido to the surface, so that an improvement of personality could occur, for some reason or other the adaptation was not made, and the libido slipped back along its old regressive path.

### EIGHTH INTERVIEW

505 The eighth interview proved that this was indeed the case. Our patient had withheld an important piece of evidence in regard to her ideas of sex, and one which contradicted the analyst's explanation of sexual maturity. *She had not mentioned a rumour current in the school that a girl of eleven had got a baby from a boy of the same age.* This rumour was proved to be groundless; it was a fantasy, fulfilling the secret wishes of girls of this age. Rumours often start in this way, as I have tried to show in my paper on the psychology of rumour. They air the

unconscious fantasies, and in this function they correspond to dreams and myths. This rumour kept another way open: she need not wait, she could have a child already at eleven. The contradiction between the accepted rumour and the analyst's explanation created resistances against the latter, as a result of which it was immediately devalued. All the other information and instruction fell to the ground at the same time, giving rise to momentary doubt and uncertainty. The libido then took to its former path and became regressive. This moment was the moment of the relapse.

NINTH INTERVIEW

506 This interview contributed some important details to the history of her sexual problem. First came a significant dream fragment: *"I was with other children in a clearing in a wood, surrounded by beautiful fir-trees. It began to rain, there was thunder and lightning, and it grew dark. Then I suddenly saw a stork in the air."*

507 Before we start analysing this dream, I must mention its parallels with certain mythological ideas. To anyone familiar with the works of Adalbert Kuhn and Steinthal, to which Abraham [7] has recently drawn attention, the curious combination of thunderstorm and stork is not at all surprising. Since ancient times the thunderstorm has had the meaning of an earth-fecundating act, it is the cohabitation of Father Heaven and Mother Earth, where the lightning takes over the role of the winged phallus. The stork in flight is just the same thing, a winged phallus, and its psychosexual meaning is known to every child. But the psychosexual meaning of the thunderstorm is not known to everyone, and certainly not to our little patient. In view of the whole psychological constellation previously described, the stork must unquestionably be given a psychosexual interpretation. The fact that the thunderstorm is connected with the stork and, like it, has a psychosexual meaning seems difficult to accept at first. But when we remember that psychoanalytic research has already discovered a vast number of purely mytholog-

7 [See *Symbols of Transformation*, index, s.vv.—EDITORS.]

ical connections in the unconscious psychic products, we may conclude that the psychosexual link between the two images is present also in this case. We know from other experiences that those unconscious strata which once produced mythological formations are still active in modern individuals and are unceasingly productive. Only, the production is limited to dreams and to the symptomatology of the neuroses and psychoses, as the correction by reality is so strong in the modern mind that it prevents them from being projected upon the real world.

508 To return to the analysis of the dream: the associations that led to the heart of this image began with the idea of *rain during a thunderstorm*. Her actual words were: "I think of water—my uncle was drowned in the water—it must be awful to be stuck in the water like that, in the dark—but wouldn't the baby drown in the water, too? Does it drink the water that is in the stomach? Queer, when I was ill Mama sent my water to the doctor. I thought he was going to mix something with it like syrup, which babies grow from, and Mama would have to drink it."

509 We see with unquestionable clearness from this string of associations that the child connected psychosexual ideas specifically relating to fertilization with the rain during the thunderstorm.

510 Here again we see that remarkable parallelism between mythology and the individual fantasies of our own day. This series of associations is so rich in symbolical connections that a whole dissertation could be written about them. The symbolism of drowning was brilliantly interpreted by the child herself as a pregnancy fantasy, an explanation given in the psychoanalytic literature long ago.

## TENTH INTERVIEW

511 The tenth interview was taken up with the child's spontaneous description of infantile theories about fertilization and birth, which could now be dismissed as settled. The child had always thought that the urine of the man went into the body of the woman, and that from this the embryo would grow. Hence the child was in the water, i.e., urine, from the beginning. Another version was that the urine was drunk with the

doctor's syrup, the child grew in the head, the head was then split open to help the child grow, and one wore hats to cover this up. She illustrated this by a little drawing, showing a childbirth through the head. This idea is archaic and highly mythological. I need only remind you of the birth of Pallas Athene, who came out of her father's head. The fertilizing significance of urine is also mythological; we find excellent proofs of this in the Rudra songs of the Rig-veda.[8] I should also mention something which the mother corroborated, that once the little girl, long before the analysis, declared that she saw a jack-in-a-box dancing on her younger brother's head—a fantasy which may well be the origin of this birth-theory.

512 The drawing had a remarkable affinity with certain artefacts found among the Bataks of Sumatra. They are called magic wands or ancestor-columns, and consist of a number of figures standing one on top of another. The explanation given by the Bataks themselves of these columns, and generally regarded as nonsense, is in remarkable agreement with the mentality of a child, still caught in the infantile bonds. They assert that these superimposed figures are members of a family who, because they committed incest, were entwined by a snake while being bitten to death by another snake. This explanation runs parallel with the assumptions of our little patient, for her sexual fantasies, too, as we saw from the first dream, revolved round her father. Here, as with the Bataks, the primary condition is the incest relationship.

513 A third version was the theory that the child grew in the intestinal canal. This version had its own symptomatic phenomenology thoroughly in accord with Freudian theory. The girl, acting on her fantasy that children were "sicked up," frequently tried to induce nausea and vomiting. She also performed regular pushing-exercises in the water-closet, in order to push the child out. In this situation it was not surprising that the first and most important symptoms in the manifest neurosis were those of nausea.

514 We have now got so far with our analysis that we can cast a glance back at the case as a whole. We found, behind the neurotic symptoms, complicated emotional processes that were un-

[8] [Cf. *Symbols of Transformation*, par. 322f.]

doubtedly connected with these symptoms. If we may venture to draw general conclusions from such limited material, we can reconstruct the course of the neurosis somewhat as follows.

515 At the gradual approach of puberty, the libido of the child produced in her an emotional rather than an objective attitude to reality. She developed a crush on her teacher, and this sentimental indulgence in starry-eyed fantasies obviously played a greater role than the thought of the increased efforts which such a love really demanded. Consequently, her attention fell off, and her work suffered. This upset her former good relationship with the teacher. He became impatient, and the girl, who had been made over-demanding by conditions at home, grew resentful instead of trying to improve her work. As a result, her libido turned away from the teacher as well as from her work and fell into that characteristically compulsive dependence on the poor young boy, who exploited the situation as much as he could. For when an individual consciously or unconsciously lets his libido draw back from a necessary task, the unutilized (so-called "repressed") libido provokes all sorts of accidents, within and without—symptoms of every description which force themselves on him in a disagreeable way. Under these conditions the girl's resistance to going to school seized on the first available opportunity, which soon presented itself in the form of the other girl who was sent home because she felt sick. Our patient duly copied this.

516 Once out of school, the way was open to her fantasies. Owing to the libido regression, the symptom-creating fantasies were aroused in real earnest and acquired an influence which they never had before, for previously they had never played such an important role. But now they took on a highly significant content and seemed themselves to be the real reason why the libido regressed to them. It might be said that the child, with her fantasy-spinning nature, saw her father *too much in the teacher*, and consequently developed incestuous resistances against him. As I explained earlier, I think it is simpler and more probable to assume that it was temporarily convenient for her to see her teacher as the father. Since she preferred to follow the secret promptings of puberty rather than her obligations to the school and her teacher, she allowed her libido to pick on the little boy, from whom, as we saw in the analysis, she promised herself

certain secret advantages. Even if the analysis had proved she really did have incestuous resistances against her teacher owing to the transference of the father-imago, these resistances would only have been secondarily blown-up fantasies. The prime mover would in any case be laziness or convenience, or, to put it in more scientific language, the principle of least resistance.

517 ⟨I think there are cogent reasons for assuming—I mention this only in passing—that it is not always a perfectly legitimate interest in sexual processes and their unknown nature that accounts for the regression to infantile fantasies. For we find the same regressive fantasies even in adults who have long known all about sex, and here there is no legitimate reason. It is also my impression that young people in analysis often try to keep up their alleged ignorance, despite enlightenment, in order to direct attention there rather than to the task of adaptation. Although there is no doubt in my mind that children do exploit their real or pretended ignorance, it must on the other hand be stressed that young people have a right to be sexually enlightened. As I said before, for many children it would be a distinct advantage if this were decently done at home.

518 Through the analysis it became clear that independently of the progressive development of the child's life a regressive movement had set in, which caused the neurosis, the disunion with herself.⟩ By following this regressive tendency, the analysis discovered a keen sexual curiosity, circling round quite certain definite problems. The libido, caught in this labyrinth of fantasies, was made serviceable again as soon as the child was freed from the burden of mistaken infantile fantasies by being enlightened. This also opened her eyes to her own attitude to reality and gave her an insight into her true potentialities. The result was that she was able to look at her immature, adolescent fantasies in an objective and critical way, and to give up these and all other impossible desires, using her libido instead for a positive purpose, in her work and in obtaining the goodwill of her teacher. The analysis brought her great peace of mind, as well as marked intellectual improvement in school; for the teacher himself confirmed that the little girl soon became the best pupil in his class.

519 ⟨In principle, this analysis is no different from that of an adult. Only the sexual enlightenment would be dropped, but its

place would be taken by something very similar, namely, enlightenment concerning the infantilism of his previous attitude to reality and how to acquire a more reasonable one. Analysis is a refined technique of Socratic maieutics, and it is not afraid to tread the darkest paths of neurotic fantasy.⟩

520 I hope that with the help of this very condensed example I may have succeeded in giving you some insight not only into the actual course of treatment, and into the difficulties of technique, but no less into the beauty of the human psyche and its endless problems. I have deliberately stressed certain parallels with mythology in order to indicate some of the uses to which psychoanalytic insights may be put. At the same time, I would like to point out the implications of this discovery. The marked predominance of mythological elements in the psyche of the child gives us a clear hint of the way the individual mind gradually develops out of the "collective mind" of early childhood, thus giving rise to the old theory of a state of perfect knowledge before and after individual existence.

521 ⟨These mythological references which we find in children are also met with in dementia praecox and in dreams. They offer a broad and fertile field of work for comparative psychological research. The distant goal to which these investigations lead is a phylogeny of the mind, which, like the body, has attained its present form through endless transformations. The rudimentary organs, as it were, which the mind still possesses can be found in full activity in other mental variants and in certain pathological conditions.⟩

522 With these hints I have now reached the present position of our research, and have sketched out at least those insights and working hypotheses which define the nature of my present and future work. ⟨I have endeavoured to propound certain views, which deviate from the hypotheses of Freud, not as contrary assertions but as illustrations of the organic development of the basic ideas Freud has introduced into science. It would not be fitting to disturb the progress of science by adopting the most contradictory standpoint possible and by making use of an entirely different nomenclature—that is the privilege of the very few; but even they find themselves obliged to descend from their lonely eminence after a time and once more take part in the slow progress of average experience by which ideas are

evaluated. I hope, also, that my critics will not again accuse me of having contrived my hypotheses out of thin air. I would never have ventured to override the existing ones had not hundreds of experiences shown me that my views fully stand the test in practice. No great hopes should be set on the results of any scientific work; yet if it should find a circle of readers, I hope it will serve to clear up various misunderstandings and remove a number of obstacles which bar the way to a better comprehension of psychoanalysis. Naturally my work is no substitute for lack of psychoanalytic experience. Anyone who wishes to have his say in these matters will have, now as then, to investigate his cases as thoroughly as was done by the psychoanalytic school.⟩

# SHORTER PAPERS

# GENERAL ASPECTS OF PSYCHOANALYSIS[1]

523 Psychoanalysis today is as much a science as a technique. From the results of the technique there has grown up, in the course of the years, a new psychological science which could be called "analytical psychology." I would willingly use Bleuler's expression "depth psychology" instead, if this kind of psychology were concerned only with the unconscious.

524 Psychologists and doctors in general are by no means conversant with this particular branch of psychology, owing to the fact that its technical foundations are as yet comparatively unknown to them. The main reason for this is that the new method is of an essentially psychological nature, and therefore belongs neither to the realm of medicine nor to that of philosophy. The medical man has, as a rule, but little knowledge of psychology, and the philosopher has no medical knowledge. Consequently, there is a lack of suitable soil in which to plant the spirit of this new method. Furthermore, the method itself appears to many persons so arbitrary that they cannot reconcile its use with their scientific conscience. The formulations of Freud, the founder of the method, laid great stress on the sexual factors; this aroused strong prejudice and repelled many scientific men. I need hardly remark that such an antipathy is not a logical reason for rejecting a new method. In psychoanalysis, moreover, there is much discussion of case-histories, but little discussion of principle. This, too, has naturally led to the method being little understood and therefore to its being regarded as unscientific. For if we do not acknowledge the scientific character of the method, we cannot acknowledge the scientific character of its results.

1 [Originally written in German with the title "Allgemeine Aspekte der Psychoanalyse," translated (anonymously) into English, and read before the Psycho-Medical Society, London, Aug. 5, 1913. With the title "Psycho-Analysis," the translation was published in the *Transactions of the Psycho-Medical Society* (Cockermouth), 1913, and reprinted in *Collected Papers on Analytical Psychology* (London and New York, 1916; 2nd edn., 1917). The present translation is made in consultation with the original German manuscript.—EDITORS.]

525 Before discussing the principles of the psychoanalytic method, I must mention two common prejudices against it. The first is that psychoanalysis is nothing but a rather deep and complicated form of *anamnesis*. Now it is well known that an anamnesis is based on the statements made by the patient's family, and on his own conscious self-knowledge in reply to direct questions. The psychoanalyst naturally makes his anamnesis as carefully as any other specialist. But this is merely the patient's history and must not be confused with analysis. Analysis is the reduction of actual contents of consciousness, ostensibly of a fortuitous nature, to their psychological determinants. This process has nothing to do with the anamnestic reconstruction of the history of the illness.

526 The second prejudice, which is based, as a rule, on a superficial knowledge of psychoanalytic literature, is that psychoanalysis is a *method of suggestion*, by which some kind of systematic teaching is instilled into the patient, thereby effecting a cure in the manner of mental healing or Christian Science. Many analysts, especially those who have practised psychoanalysis for a long time, previously used suggestion therapy, and therefore know very well what suggestion is and what it is not. They know that the psychoanalyst's method of working is diametrically opposed to that of the hypnotist. In direct contrast with suggestion therapy, the psychoanalyst does not attempt to force anything on his patient which the latter does not see for himself and find plausible with his own understanding. Faced with the constant demand of the neurotic for suggestions and advice, the analyst just as constantly endeavours to get him out of this passive attitude and make him use his common sense and powers of criticism in order to equip him for an independent life. We have often been accused of forcing interpretations upon patients, interpretations that are often quite arbitrary. I wish one of these critics would try forcing arbitrary interpretations on my patients, who are very often persons of great intelligence and highly cultured—indeed, not infrequently my own colleagues. The impossibility of such an undertaking would quickly be demonstrated. In psychoanalysis we are entirely dependent on the patient and on his powers of judgment, for the reason that the very nature of analysis consists in leading him to a knowledge of himself. The principles of psycho-

analysis are so utterly different from those of suggestion therapy that on this point the two methods cannot be compared.

527 An attempt has also been made to compare psychoanalysis with the ratiocinative method of Dubois,[2] which is an essentially rational procedure. But this comparison does not hold good, for the psychoanalyst strictly avoids reasoning and arguing with his patients. Naturally he has to listen to their conscious problems and conflicts and take note of them, but not for the purpose of fulfilling their desire to obtain advice or instruction with regard to the conduct of their lives. The problems of a neurotic cannot be solved by advice and conscious reasoning. I do not doubt that good advice at the right time can produce good results, but I do not know how anyone can believe that the psychoanalyst can always give the right advice at the right moment. The neurotic conflict is frequently, indeed usually, of such a nature that advice cannot possibly be given. Furthermore, it is well known that the patient only wants authoritative advice in order to shuffle off the burden of responsibility, referring himself and others to the opinion of a higher authority. So far as reasoning and persuasion are concerned, their effect as a method of therapy is as little to be doubted as that of hypnosis. What I would like to stress here is simply its difference in principle from psychoanalysis.

528 In contradistinction to all previous methods, psychoanalysis endeavours to overcome the disorders of the neurotic psyche through the unconscious, and not from the conscious side. In this work we naturally have need of the patient's conscious contents, for only in this way can we reach the unconscious. The conscious content from which our work starts is the material supplied by the anamnesis. In many cases the anamnesis provides useful clues which make the psychic origin of his symptoms clear to the patient. This, of course, is necessary only when he is convinced that his neurosis is organic in origin. But even in those cases where the patient is convinced from the start of the psychic nature of his illness, a critical survey of the anamnesis can be of advantage, for it discloses a psychological context of which he was unaware before. In this way problems that need special discussion are frequently brought to the surface. This work may occupy many sittings. Finally, the elucidation of the

2 [Paul Dubois (1848–1918), of Bern, treated neuroses by "persuasion."]

conscious material comes to an end when neither the analyst nor the patient can contribute anything further of decisive importance. In the most favourable cases the end comes with the formulation of the problem which, very often, proves insoluble.

529 Let us take the case of a man who was once healthy but developed a neurosis between the ages of thirty-five and forty. His position in life was secure, and he had a wife and children. Parallel with his neurosis he developed an intense resistance to his professional work. He observed that the first symptoms of neurosis became noticeable when he had to overcome a particular difficulty in his career. Later they got worse with each successive difficulty that arose. Passing ameliorations occurred whenever fortune favoured him in his work. The problem that presented itself after a critical discussion of the anamnesis was as follows: the patient knew that he could improve his work and that the satisfaction resulting from this would bring about the much-desired improvement in his neurotic condition. But he was unable to do his work more efficiently because of his great resistance to it. This problem is rationally insoluble. Psychoanalytic treatment must therefore start at the critical point, his resistance to his work.

530 Let us take another case. A woman of forty, mother of four children, became neurotic four years ago after the death of one of them. A new pregnancy, followed by the birth of another child, brought a great improvement in her condition. She now thought that if she could have yet another child she would be helped still further. She knew, however, that she could not have any more children, so she tried to devote her energies to philanthropic interests. But she failed to obtain the least satisfaction from this work. She noticed a distinct alleviation whenever she succeeded in giving real interest to something, however fleetingly, but she felt quite incapable of discovering anything that would bring her lasting interest and satisfaction. The rational insolubility of the problem is clear. Psychoanalytic work must begin with the question of what prevented the patient from developing any interest beyond her longing for a child.

531 Since we cannot pretend that we know from the outset what the solution of such problems is, we have to rely on the clues furnished by the individuality of the patient. Neither conscious questioning nor rational advice can aid us in the discovery of

these clues, for the obstacles which prevent us from finding them are hidden from the patient's consciousness. There is, therefore, no clearly prescribed way of getting at the unconscious obstacles. The only rule that psychoanalysis lays down in this respect is: let the patient talk about anything that comes into his head. The analyst must observe carefully what the patient says and, to begin with, simply take note of it without attempting to force his own opinions upon him. We notice, for instance, that the first-named patient began by talking about his marriage, which we had been told was normal. We now learn that he has difficulties with his wife and does not understand her in the least. This prompts the analyst to remark that evidently the patient's professional work is not his only problem, and that his relation to his wife also needs reviewing. This starts a train of associations all relating to the marriage. Then follow associations about the love-affairs he had before he was married. These experiences, recounted in detail, show that the patient was always rather peculiar in his more intimate relations with women, and that his peculiarity took the form of a childish egoism. This is a new and surprising point of view for him, and explains to him many of his misfortunes with women.

532 We cannot in every case get as far as this on the principle of simply letting the patient talk; few patients have their psychic material so much on the surface. Furthermore, many patients have a real resistance against speaking freely about what occurs to them on the spur of the moment, some because it is too painful for them to tell it to an analyst whom they may not entirely trust, others because apparently nothing occurs to them and they force themselves to talk of things about which they are more or less indifferent. This trick of not talking to the point does not prove that the patient is *consciously* concealing certain painful contents; it can also occur quite unconsciously. In such cases it sometimes helps the patient to tell him that he need not force himself, but need only seize on the very first thoughts that come to him, no matter how unimportant or ridiculous they may seem. In certain cases even these instructions are of no use, and then the analyst has to resort to other measures. One of these is the association experiment, which usually gives apt information concerning the main tendencies of the patient at that moment.

533 A second expedient is the analysis of dreams; this is the real instrument of psychoanalysis. We have already experienced so much opposition to dream analysis that a brief exposition of its principles may not be out of place. The interpretation of dreams, as well as the meaning given to them, is, as we know, in bad odour. It is not long since oneiromancy was practised and believed in; nor is the time long past when even the most enlightened persons were still under the spell of superstition. It is therefore comprehensible that our age should still entertain a lively fear of superstitions that have been only partially overcome. This nervousness in regard to superstition is largely responsible for the opposition to dream-interpretation, but psychoanalysis is in no way to blame for this. We select the dream as an object not because we pay it the homage of superstitious admiration, but because it is a psychic product that is independent of consciousness. We ask for the patient's free associations, but he gives us little or nothing, or else something forced or irrelevant. A dream is a free association, a free fantasy, it is not forced, and is just as much a psychic phenomenon as an association.[3]

534 I cannot disguise the fact that in practice, especially at the beginning of an analysis, we do not under all circumstances make complete and ideal analyses of the dreams. Usually we gather the dream-associations together until the problem which the patient is hiding from us becomes so clear that he can recognize it himself. This problem is then worked through consciously until it is cleared up as far as possible and we are once again confronted with an unanswerable question.

535 You will now ask what is to be done when the patient does not dream at all. I can assure you that hitherto all patients, even those who claimed never to have dreamed before, began to dream when they went through analysis. On the other hand it frequently happens that patients who began by dreaming vividly are suddenly no longer able to remember their dreams. The empirical and practical rule which I have adopted is that the patient, if he does not dream, still has sufficient conscious material which he is keeping back for certain reasons. A common reason is: "I am in the analyst's hands and am quite willing

[3] [The passage which here follows in the original is identical with "The Theory of Psychoanalysis," supra, pars. 324–31.—EDITORS.]

to be treated by him. But the analyst must do the work, I shall remain passive in the matter." Sometimes there are resistances of a more serious nature. For instance, patients who cannot admit certain moral defects in themselves project them upon the analyst, calmly assuming that since he is more or less deficient morally they cannot communicate certain unpleasant things to him.

536 If, then, a patient does not dream from the beginning or ceases to dream, he is keeping back material which would be capable of conscious elaboration. Here the relationship between analyst and patient may be considered one of the chief obstacles. It can prevent them both, the analyst as well as the patient, from seeing the situation clearly. We must not forget that as the analyst shows, and must show, a searching interest in the psychology of his patient, so the patient, if he has an active mind, feels his way into the psychology of the analyst and adopts a corresponding attitude towards him. The analyst is blind to the attitude of his patient to the exact extent that he does not see himself and his own unconscious problems. For this reason I maintain that a doctor must himself be analysed before he practises analysis. Otherwise analysis may easily be a great disappointment to him, because he can, under certain circumstances, get absolutely stuck and then lose his head. He is then readily inclined to assume that psychoanalysis is nonsense, so as to avoid having to admit that he has run his vessel aground. If you are sure of your own psychology you can confidently tell your patient that he does not dream because there is conscious material still to be dealt with. I say you must be sure of yourself at such moments, for the criticisms and unsparing judgments to which you sometimes have to submit can be excessively disturbing to one who is unprepared to meet them. The immediate consequence of the analyst's losing his balance is that he begins to argue with his patient in order to maintain his influence over him. This, of course, renders all further analysis impossible.

537 I have told you that, in the first instance, dreams need be used only as a source of material for analysis. At the beginning of an analysis it is not only unnecessary, but at times unwise, to give a so-called complete interpretation of a dream. A complete and really exhaustive interpretation is very difficult indeed. The interpretations you sometimes come across in the psychoanalytic

literature are very often one-sided and, not infrequently, contestable formulations. I include among these the one-sided sexual reductions of the Viennese school. In view of the myriad-sidedness of the dream-material one must beware of all one-sided formulations. The many-sided meaning of a dream, rather than its singleness of meaning, is of the utmost value especially at the beginning of the treatment. Thus, a patient had the following dream not long after her treatment had begun. *She was in a hotel in a strange city. Suddenly a fire broke out. Her husband and her father, who were with her, helped her in the rescue work.*

538 The patient was intelligent, extraordinarily sceptical, and absolutely convinced that dream-analysis was nonsense. I had the greatest difficulty in inducing her to give it even one trial. I selected the fire, the most conspicuous event in the dream, as the starting-point for associations. The patient informed me that she had recently read in the newspapers that a certain hotel in Zurich had been burnt down; that she remembered the hotel because she had once stayed there. At the hotel she had made the acquaintance of a man, and from this a somewhat questionable love-affair developed. In connection with this story the fact came out that she had already had quite a number of similar adventures, all of them decidedly frivolous. This important bit of past history was brought out by the very first association. In her case it would have been pointless to make clear to her the very obvious meaning of the dream. With her frivolous attitude, of which her scepticism was only a special instance, she would have coldly repelled such an attempt. But after the frivolity of her attitude had been recognized and demonstrated to her from the material she herself had furnished, it was possible to analyse the dreams which followed much more thoroughly.

539 It is, therefore, advisable in the beginning to use dreams for getting at the critical material through their associations. This is the best and most cautious procedure, especially for the beginner in psychoanalysis. An arbitrary translation of the dreams is exceedingly inadvisable. That would be a superstitious practice based on the assumption that dreams have well-established symbolic meanings. But there are no fixed symbolic meanings. There are certain symbols that recur frequently, but we are not in a position to get beyond very general statements. For in-

stance, it is quite incorrect to assume that a snake, when it appears in dreams, always has a merely phallic meaning; just as incorrect as it is to deny that it may have a phallic meaning in some cases. Every symbol has at least two meanings. The very frequent sexual meaning of dream-symbols is at most one of them. I cannot, therefore, accept the exclusively sexual interpretations which appear in certain psychoanalytic publications, as little as I can accept the interpretation of dreams as wish-fulfilments, for my experience has led me to regard these formulations as one-sided and inadequate. As an example I will tell you a very simple dream of a young man, a patient of mine. It was as follows: *I was going up a flight of stairs with my mother and sister. When we reached the top I was told that my sister was going to have a baby.*

540 First I will show how, in accordance with the hitherto prevailing point of view, this dream may be translated sexually. We know that incest fantasies play a prominent role in the life of a neurotic, hence the image "with my mother and sister" could be understood as a hint in this direction. "Stairs" are alleged to have a well-established sexual meaning: they represent the sexual act because of the rhythmic climbing. The baby the sister is expecting is nothing but the logical consequence of these premises. Thus translated, the dream would be a clear fulfilment of so-called infantile wishes, which, as you know, are an important part of Freud's dream-theory.

541 I have analysed this dream on the basis of the following reasoning. If I say that stairs are a *symbol* for the sexual act, by what right do I take the mother and sister and baby as *real*, that is, not symbolically? If, on the strength of the assertion that dream-images are symbolic, I assign a symbolic value to certain of these images, what right have I to exempt certain others? If I attach a symbolic value to the ascent of the stairs, I must also attach a symbolic value to the images called mother, sister, and baby. I therefore did not "translate" the dream but really analysed it. The result was surprising. I will give you the patient's associations to the individual dream-images word for word, so that you can form your own opinion of the material. I should say in advance that the young man had finished his studies at the university a few months previously, that he had found the choice of a profession too difficult to make, and that he there-

upon became neurotic. In consequence of this he gave up his work. His neurosis took, among other things, a manifestly homosexual form.

542 His associations to *mother* were as follows: "I have not seen her for a long time, a very long time. I must really reproach myself for this, it is wrong of me to neglect her so."

543 *Mother,* then, stands for something that is neglected in an irresponsible manner. I asked the patient: "What is that?" and he replied, with considerable embarrassment: "My work."

544 Associations to *sister:* "It is years since I have seen her. I long to see her again. Whenever I think of her I always remember the moment I said good-bye. I kissed her with real affection, and at that moment I understood for the first time what love for a woman can mean." It was at once clear to the patient that "sister" stood for "love for a woman."

545 Associations to *stairs:* "Climbing up—getting to the top—making a career—growing up, becoming great."

546 Associations to *baby:* "Newborn—renewal—rebirth—becoming a new man."

547 One has only to hear this material to understand at once that the dream represents not so much the fulfilment of infantile wishes as the fulfilment of biological duties which the patient has neglected because of his neurotic infantilism. Biological justice, which is inexorable, often compels us to make up in dreams for the duties we have neglected in real life.

548 This dream is a typical example of the prospective and finally-oriented function of dreams in general, especially stressed by my colleague Maeder. If we adhered to a one-sided sexual interpretation the real meaning of the dream would escape us. Sexuality in dreams is, in the first instance, a means of expression and by no means always the meaning and aim of the dream. The discovery of its prospective or final meaning is particularly important when the analysis is so far advanced that the eyes of the patient are turned more readily to the future than to his inner world and the past.

549 As regards the handling of the symbolism, we learn from this example that there can be no dream-symbols whose meanings are fixed in every detail, but, at most, a frequent occurrence of symbols with fairly general meanings. So far as the

specifically sexual meaning of dreams is concerned, experience has led me to lay down the following practical rules:

550 If dream-analysis at the beginning of the treatment shows that the dreams have an undoubtedly sexual meaning, this meaning is to be taken realistically; that is, it proves that the sexual problems of the patient need to be subjected to a careful review. For instance, if an incest fantasy is clearly shown to be a latent content of the dream, one must subject the patient's infantile relations with his parents and brothers and sisters, as well as his relations with other persons who are fitted to play the role of father or mother, to a thorough investigation. But if a dream that comes at a later stage of the analysis has, let us say, an incest fantasy as its essential content—a fantasy that we have reason to consider disposed of—concrete value should not under all circumstances be attached to it; it should be regarded as symbolic. The formula for interpretation is: the unknown meaning of the dream is expressed, by analogy, through a fantasy of incest. In this case symbolic and not real value must be attached to the sexual fantasy. If we did not get beyond the real value we should keep reducing the patient to sexuality, and this would arrest the progress of the development of his personality. The patient's salvation does not lie in thrusting him back again and again into primitive sexuality; this would leave him on a low cultural level whence he could never obtain freedom and complete restoration to health. Retrogression to a state of barbarism is no advantage at all for a civilized human being.

551 The above-mentioned formula, according to which the sexuality of a dream is a symbolic or analogical expression of its meaning, naturally applies also to dreams occurring at the beginning of an analysis. But the practical reasons that have impelled us not to take the symbolic value of these sexual fantasies into consideration arise from the fact that a genuine realistic value must be attached to the abnormal sexual fantasies of a neurotic in so far as he allows his actions to be influenced by them. The fantasies not only hinder him in adapting better to his situation, they also lead him to all manner of real sexual acts, and occasionally even to incest, as experience shows. Under these circumstances, it would be of little use to consider the symbolic content only; the concrete aspect must be first dealt with.

552 These statements are based, as you will have observed, on a

different conception of the dream from that put forward by Freud. Indeed, experience has forced a different conception upon me. For Freud, the dream is essentially a symbolic disguise for repressed wishes which would come into conflict with the aims of the personality. I am obliged to regard the structure of a dream from a different point of view. For me the dream is, in the first instance, a subliminal picture of the actual psychological situation of the individual in his waking state. It gives us a résumé of the subliminal associative material constellated by the psychological situation of the moment. The volitional content of the dream, which Freud calls the repressed wish, is for me essentially a means of expression.

553 The activity of consciousness represents, biologically speaking, the individual's struggle for psychological adaptation. Consciousness tries to adjust itself to the necessities of the moment, or, to put it differently: there are tasks ahead which the individual must overcome. In many cases the solution is, in the nature of things, unknown, for which reason consciousness always tries to find the solution by way of analogous experiences. We try to grasp the unknown future on the model of our experience in the past. We have no reason to suppose that the subliminal psychic material obeys other laws than the "supraliminal" material. The unconscious, like the conscious, mobilizes itself round the biological tasks and seeks solutions on the analogy of what has gone before, just as consciousness does. Whenever we wish to assimilate something unknown, we do so by means of analogy. A simple example of this is the well-known fact that when America was discovered by the Spaniards the Indians took the horses of the conquerors, which were unknown to them, for large pigs, because only pigs were familiar in their experience. This is the way we always recognize things, and it is also the essential reason for the existence of symbolism: it is a process of comprehension by means of analogy. The dream is a *subliminal* process of comprehension by analogy. The apparently repressed wishes are volitional tendencies which supply the unconscious dream-thought with a verbal means of expression. On this particular point I find myself in entire agreement with the views of Adler, another pupil of Freud's. As to the fact that the unconscious expresses itself by means of volitional elements or

tendencies, this is due to the archaic nature of dream-thinking, a problem I have discussed elsewhere.[4]

554 Owing to our different conception of the structure of dreams, the further course of analysis assumes a rather different aspect. The symbolic evaluation of sexual fantasies in the later stages necessarily leads, not to a reduction of the personality to primitive tendencies, but to a broadening and continuous development of the patient's attitude; that is, it tends to make his thinking richer and deeper, thus giving him what has always been one of man's most powerful weapons in the struggle for adaptation. By following this new course consistently, I have come to the realization that the religious and philosophical driving forces—what Schopenhauer calls the "metaphysical need" of man—must receive positive consideration during the analytical work. They must not be destroyed by reducing them to their primitive sexual roots, but made to serve biological ends as psychologically valuable factors. In this way these driving forces assume once more the function that has been theirs from time immemorial.

555 Just as primitive man was able, with the help of religious and philosophical symbols, to free himself from his original condition, so too the neurotic can free himself from his illness. It is hardly necessary for me to remark that I do not mean inoculating him with belief in a religious or philosophical dogma; I mean simply that there must be built up in him that same psychological attitude which was characterized by the living belief in a religious or philosophical dogma on earlier levels of culture. A religious or philosophical attitude is not the same thing as belief in a dogma. A dogma is a temporary intellectual formulation, the outcome of a religious and philosophical attitude conditioned by time and circumstances. But the attitude itself is a cultural achievement; it is a function that is exceedingly valuable from a biological point of view, for it gives rise to incentives that drive human beings to do creative work for the benefit of a future age and, if necessary, to sacrifice themselves for the welfare of the species.

556 Thus man attains the same sense of unity and wholeness, the same confidence, the same capacity for self-sacrifice in his

[4] [Cf. *Symbols of Transformation*, pars. 25ff.—EDITORS.]

conscious existence that belong unconsciously and instinctively to wild animals. Every reduction, every digression from the path that has been laid down for the development of civilization, does nothing more than turn the human being into a crippled animal; it never makes a so-called natural man of him. I have had numerous successes and failures in the course of my analytical practice which have convinced me of the inexorable rightness of this kind of psychological orientation. We do not help the neurotic by relieving him of the demands made by civilization; we can help him only by inducing him to take an active part in the strenuous work of carrying on its development. The suffering he undergoes in performing this service takes the place of his neurosis. But whereas the neurosis and the troubles that attend it are never followed by the pleasant feeling of good work well done, of duty fearlessly performed, the suffering that comes from useful work and from victory over real difficulties brings with it those moments of peace and satisfaction which give the human being the priceless feeling that he has really lived his life.

## PSYCHOANALYSIS AND NEUROSIS[1]

After many years' experience I now know that it is extremely difficult to discuss psychoanalysis at public meetings and at congresses. There are so many misconceptions of the matter, so many prejudices against certain psychoanalytic views, that it is an almost impossible task to reach mutual understanding in a public discussion. I have always found a quiet conversation on the subject much more useful and fruitful than heated arguments *coram publico*. However, having been honoured by an invitation from the Committee of this Congress to speak as a representative of the psychoanalytic movement, I will do my best to discuss some of the fundamental theoretical problems of psychoanalysis. I must limit myself to this aspect of the subject because I am quite unable to put before my audience all that psychoanalysis means and strives for, and its various applications in the fields of mythology, comparative religion, philosophy, etc. But if I am to discuss certain theoretical problems fundamental to psychoanalysis, I must presuppose that my audience is familiar with the development and the main results of psychoanalytic research. Unfortunately, it often happens that people think themselves entitled to judge psychoanalysis who have not even read the literature. It is my firm conviction that no one is competent to form an opinion on this matter until he has studied the basic writings of the psychoanalytic school.

In spite of the fact that Freud's theory of neurosis has been worked out in great detail, it cannot be said to be, on the whole, very clear or easy to understand. This justifies my giving you a short abstract of his fundamental views on the theory of neurosis.

You are aware that the original theory that hysteria and the related neuroses have their origin in a trauma or sexual shock

1 [Originally written in English and read before the New York Academy of Medicine, 8 Oct. 1912. Revised and read before the 17th International Medical Congress, London, 1913, under the title "On Psychoanalysis." First published in *Collected Papers on Analytical Psychology* (London and New York, 1916; 2nd edn., 1917), pp. 226–35. The present version is a stylistic revision of this.—EDITORS.]

in early childhood was given up about fifteen years ago. It soon became evident that the sexual trauma could not be the real cause of the neurosis, for the simple reason that the trauma was found to be almost universal. There is scarcely a human being who has not had some sexual shock in early youth, and yet comparatively few develop a neurosis in later life. Freud himself soon realized that many of the patients who related an early traumatic experience had only invented the story of the so-called trauma; it had never occurred in reality, but was a mere creation of fantasy. Moreover, on further investigation it became quite obvious that even if a trauma had actually occurred it was not always responsible for the whole of the neurosis, although it does sometimes look as if the structure of the neurosis depended entirely on the trauma. If a neurosis were the inevitable consequence of the trauma it would be quite incomprehensible why neurotics are not incomparably more numerous than they are.

560 The apparently heightened effect of the shock was clearly due to the exaggerated and morbid fantasy of the patient. Freud also saw that this same fantasy activity manifested itself relatively early in bad habits, which he called infantile perversions. His new conception of the aetiology of neurosis was based on this insight, and he traced the neurosis back to some sexual activity in early infancy. This conception led to his recent view that the neurotic is "fixated" to a certain period of his early infancy, because he seems to preserve some trace of it, direct or indirect, in his mental attitude. Freud also makes the attempt to classify or to differentiate the neuroses, as well as dementia praecox, according to the stage of infantile development in which the fixation took place. From the standpoint of this theory, the neurotic appears to be entirely dependent on his infantile past, and all his troubles in later life, his moral conflicts and his deficiencies, seem to be derived from the powerful influences of that period. Accordingly, the main task of the treatment is to resolve this infantile fixation, which is conceived as an unconscious attachment of the sexual libido to certain infantile fantasies and habits.

561 This, so far as I can see, is the essence of Freud's theory of neurosis. But it overlooks the following important question: What is the cause of this fixation of libido to the old infantile

fantasies and habits? We have to remember that almost everyone has at some time had infantile fantasies and habits exactly corresponding to those of a neurotic, yet he does not become fixated to them; consequently, he does not become neurotic later on. The aetiological secret of the neurosis, therefore, does not lie in the mere *existence* of infantile fantasies but in the so-called *fixation*. The numerous statements of neurotics affirming the existence of infantile sexual fantasies are worthless in so far as they attribute an aetiological significance to them, for the same fantasies can be found in normal individuals as well, a fact which I have often proved. It is only the fixation which seems to be characteristic.

562 It is therefore necessary to demand proof of the reality of this infantile fixation. Freud, an absolutely sincere and painstaking empiricist, would never have evolved this hypothesis had he not had sufficient grounds for it. These grounds are furnished by the results of psychoanalytic investigations of the unconscious. Psychoanalysis reveals the unconscious presence of numerous fantasies which have their roots in the infantile past and are grouped round the so-called "nuclear complex," which in men may be designated as the Oedipus complex, in women as the Electra complex. These terms convey their own meaning exactly. The whole tragic fate of Oedipus and Electra was acted out within the narrow confines of the family, just as a child's fate lies wholly within the family boundaries. Hence the Oedipus complex, like the Electra complex, is very characteristic of an infantile conflict. The existence of these conflicts in infancy has been proved by means of psychoanalytic research. It is in the realm of this complex that the fixation is supposed to have taken place. The extremely potent and effective existence of the nuclear complex in the unconscious of neurotics led Freud to the hypothesis that the neurotic has a peculiar fixation or attachment to it. Not the mere existence of this complex—for everybody has it in the unconscious—but the very strong attachment to it is what is typical of the neurotic. He is far more influenced by this complex than the normal person; many examples in confirmation of this can be found in every one of the recent psychoanalytic histories of neurotic cases.

63 We must admit that this view is a very plausible one, because the hypothesis of fixation is based on the well-known fact that

certain periods of human life, and particularly infancy, do sometimes leave determining traces behind them which are permanent. The only question is whether this is a sufficient explanation or not. If we examine persons who have been neurotic from infancy it seems to be confirmed, for we see the nuclear complex as a permanent and powerful agent throughout life. But if we take cases which never show any noticeable trace of neurosis except at the particular time when they break down, and there are many such, this explanation becomes doubtful. If there is such a thing as fixation, it is not permissible to erect upon it a new hypothesis, claiming that at times during certain periods of life the fixation becomes loosened and ineffective, while at others it suddenly becomes strengthened. In these cases we find that the nuclear complex is as active and potent as in those which apparently support the theory of fixation. Here a critical attitude is justifiable, especially when we consider the oft-repeated observation that the moment of the outbreak of neurosis is not just a matter of chance; as a rule it is most critical. It is usually *the moment when a new psychological adjustment, that is, a new adaptation, is demanded.* Such moments facilitate the outbreak of a neurosis, as every experienced neurologist knows.

564 This fact seems to me extremely significant. If the fixation were indeed real we should expect to find its influence constant; in other words, a neurosis lasting throughout life. This is obviously not the case. The psychological determination of a neurosis is only partly due to an early infantile predisposition; it must be due to some cause in the present as well. And if we carefully examine the kind of infantile fantasies and occurrences to which the neurotic is attached, we shall be obliged to agree that there is nothing in them that is specifically neurotic. Normal individuals have pretty much the same inner and outer experiences, and may be attached to them to an astonishing degree without developing a neurosis. Primitive people, especially, are very much bound to their infantility. It now begins to look as if this so-called fixation were a normal phenomenon, and that the importance of infancy for the later mental attitude is natural and prevails everywhere. The fact that the neurotic seems to be markedly influenced by his infantile conflicts shows that it is less a matter of fixation than of the peculiar use which

he makes of his infantile past. It looks as if he exaggerated its importance and attributed to it a wholly artificial value. Adler, a pupil of Freud's, expresses a very similar view.

565 It would be unjust to say that Freud limited himself to the hypothesis of fixation; he was also aware of the problem I have just discussed. He called this phenomenon of reactivation or secondary exaggeration of infantile reminiscences "regression." But in Freud's view it appears as if the incestuous desires of the Oedipus complex were the real cause of the regression to infantile fantasies. If this were the case, we should have to postulate an unexpected intensity of the primary incestuous tendencies. This view led Freud to his recent comparison between what he calls the psychological "incest barrier" in children and the "incest taboo" in primitive man. He supposes that a desire for real incest led primitive man to frame laws against it; while to me it looks as if the incest taboo were only one among numerous taboos of all kinds, and were due to the typical superstitious fear of primitive man—a fear existing independently of incest and its prohibition. I am able to attribute as little strength to incestuous desires in childhood as in primitive humanity. I do not even seek the reason for regression in primary incestuous or any other sexual desires. I must admit that a purely sexual aetiology of neurosis seems to me much too narrow. I base this criticism not on any prejudice against sexuality but on an intimate acquaintance with the whole problem.

566 I therefore suggest that psychoanalytic theory should be freed from the purely sexual standpoint. In place of it I should like to introduce an *energic viewpoint* into the psychology of neurosis.

567 All psychological phenomena can be considered as manifestations of energy, in the same way that all physical phenomena have been understood as energic manifestations ever since Robert Mayer discovered the law of the conservation of energy. Subjectively and psychologically, this energy is conceived as *desire*. I call it *libido*, using the word in its original sense, which is by no means only sexual. Sallust uses it exactly as we do here when he says: "They took more pleasure in handsome arms and war horses than in harlots and revelry." [2]

2 "Magis in armis et militaribus equis quam in scortis et conviviis libidinem habebant." *Catilina*, 7, trans. by Rolfe, pp.14–15.

568 From a broader standpoint libido can be understood as vital energy in general, or as Bergson's *élan vital*. The first manifestation of this energy in the infant is the nutritive instinct. From this stage the libido slowly develops through numerous variants of the act of sucking into the sexual function. Hence I do not consider the act of sucking a sexual act. The pleasure in sucking can certainly not be considered as sexual pleasure, but as pleasure in nutrition, for it is nowhere proved that pleasure is sexual in itself. This process of development is continued into adult life and is accompanied by constantly increasing adaptation to the external world. Whenever the libido, in the process of adaptation, meets an obstacle, an accumulation takes place which normally gives rise to an increased effort to overcome the obstacle. But if the obstacle seems to be insurmountable, and the individual abandons the task of overcoming it, the stored-up libido makes a regression. Instead of being employed for an increased effort, the libido gives up its present task and reverts to an earlier and more primitive mode of adaptation.

569 The best examples of such regressions are found in hysterical cases where a disappointment in love or marriage has precipitated a neurosis. There we find those well-known digestive disorders, loss of appetite, dyspeptic symptoms of all sorts, etc. In these cases the regressive libido, turning back from the task of adaptation, gains power over the nutritive function and produces marked disturbances. Similar effects can be observed in cases where there is no disturbance of the nutritive function but, instead, a regressive revival of reminiscences from the distant past. We then find a reactivation of the parental imagos, of the Oedipus complex. Here the events of early infancy—never before important—suddenly become so. They have been regressively reactivated. Remove the obstacle from the path of life and this whole system of infantile fantasies at once breaks down and becomes as inactive and ineffective as before. But let us not forget that, to a certain extent, it is at work all the time, influencing us in unseen ways. This view, incidentally, comes very close to Janet's hypothesis that the "parties supérieures" of a function are replaced by its "parties inférieures." I would also remind you of Claparède's conception of neurotic symptoms as emotional reflexes of a primitive nature.

570 For these reasons I no longer seek the cause of a neurosis in

the past, but in the present. I ask, what is the necessary task which the patient will not accomplish? The long list of his infantile fantasies does not give me any sufficient aetiological explanation, because I know that these fantasies are only puffed up by the regressive libido, which has not found its natural outlet in a new form of adaptation to the demands of life.

571 You may ask why the neurotic has a special tendency not to accomplish his necessary tasks. Here let me point out that no living creature adjusts itself easily and smoothly to new conditions. The law of inertia is valid everywhere.

572 A sensitive and somewhat unbalanced person, as a neurotic always is, will meet with special difficulties and perhaps with more unusual tasks in life than a normal individual, who as a rule has only to follow the well-worn path of an ordinary existence. For the neurotic there is no established way of life, because his aims and tasks are apt to be of a highly individual character. He tries to go the more or less uncontrolled and half-conscious way of normal people, not realizing that his own critical and very different nature demands of him more effort than the normal person is required to exert. There are neurotics who have shown their heightened sensitiveness and their resistance to adaptation in the very first weeks of life, in the difficulty they have in taking the mother's breast and in their exaggerated nervous reactions, etc. For this peculiarity in the neurotic predisposition it will always be impossible to find a psychological aetiology, because it is anterior to all psychology. This predisposition—you can call it "congenital sensitiveness" or what you like—is the cause of the first resistances to adaptation. As the way to adaptation is blocked, the biological energy we call libido does not find its appropriate outlet or activity, with the result that a suitable form of adaptation is replaced by an abnormal or primitive one.

573 In neurosis we speak of an infantile attitude or of the predominance of infantile fantasies and wishes. In so far as infantile impressions are of obvious importance in normal people they will be equally influential in neurosis, but they have no aetiological significance; they are reactions merely, being chiefly secondary and regressive phenomena. It is perfectly true, as Freud says, that infantile fantasies determine the form and the subsequent development of neurosis, but this is not an aetiology.

Even when we find perverted sexual fantasies whose existence can be demonstrated in childhood, we cannot consider them of aetiological significance. A neurosis is not really caused by infantile sexual fantasies, and the same must be said of the sexualism of neurotic fantasy in general. It is not a primary phenomenon based on a perverted sexual disposition, but merely secondary and a consequence of the failure to apply the stored-up libido in a suitable way. I realize that this is a very old view, but this does not prevent it from being true. The fact that the patient himself very often believes that his infantile fantasies are the real cause of his neurosis does not prove that he is right in his belief, or that a theory based on this belief is right either. It may look as if it were so, and I must admit that very many cases do have that appearance. At all events, it is perfectly easy to understand how Freud arrived at this view. Everyone who has any psychoanalytic experience will agree with me here.

574 To sum up: I cannot see the real aetiology of neurosis in the various manifestations of infantile sexual development and the fantasies to which they give rise. The fact that these fantasies are exaggerated in neurosis and occupy the foreground is a consequence of the stored-up energy or libido. The psychological trouble in neurosis, and the neurosis itself, can be formulated as *an act of adaptation that has failed.* This formulation might reconcile certain views of Janet's with Freud's view that a neurosis is, in a sense, an attempt at self-cure—a view which can be and has been applied to many other illnesses.

575 Here the question arises as to whether it is still advisable to bring to light all the patient's fantasies by analysis, if we now consider them of no aetiological significance. Hitherto psychoanalysis has set about unravelling these fantasies because they were considered aetiologically important. My altered view of the theory of neurosis does not affect the psychoanalytic procedure. The technique remains the same. Though we no longer imagine we are unearthing the ultimate root of the illness, we have to pull up the sexual fantasies because the energy which the patient needs for his health, that is, for adaptation, is attached to them. By means of psychoanalysis the connection between his conscious mind and the libido in the unconscious is re-established. Thus the unconscious libido is brought under the control of the will. Only in this way can the split-off energy

become available again for the accomplishment of the necessary tasks of life. Considered from this standpoint, psychoanalysis no longer appears as a mere reduction of the individual to his primitive sexual wishes, but, if rightly understood, as a highly moral task of immense educational value.

# SOME CRUCIAL POINTS IN PSYCHOANALYSIS

## A Correspondence between Dr. Jung and Dr. Loÿ[1]

### *Foreword*

A few words may suffice to explain the reasons which led to this correspondence, and the purpose in publishing it.

After being introduced to the theory and practice of suggestion therapy by Professor Forel, I practised it for many years and still use it in suitable cases. When I became aware of the great significance of Freud's psychoanalytic works, I studied them and gradually began to take up analysis myself. I made contact with the nearest centre of psychoanalytic research, which was Zurich. Yet in technical matters I had, in the main, to rely on myself. Hence, when I met with failures, I had to ask myself who or what was to blame, I alone, because I did not know how to apply the "correct psychoanalytic method," or perhaps the method itself, which might not be suitable in all cases. A special stumbling-block for me was the interpretation of dreams: I could not convince myself that there was a generally valid symbolism, and that this symbolism was exclusively sexual, as many psychoanalysts declared. Their interpretations often seemed to me to bear the stamp of arbitrariness.

And so, when I read the following statement by Freud in the *Zentralblatt für Psychoanalyse,* in June 1912, the words seemed to come from my own heart: "Some years ago I gave as an answer to the question of how one can become an analyst: 'By analysing one's own dreams.' This preparation is no doubt enough for many people, but not for everyone who wishes to learn analysis. Nor can everyone succeed in interpreting his own dreams without outside help. I count it as one of the many merits of the Zurich school of analysis that they

1 [Originally published as *Psychotherapeutische Zeitfragen; Ein Briefwechsel mit Dr. C. G. Jung,* edited by Dr. R. Loÿ (Leipzig and Vienna, 1914). Translated (except for Dr. Loÿ's foreword) by Mrs. Edith Eder as "On Some Crucial Points in Psychoanalysis," in *Collected Papers on Analytical Psychology* (London and New York, 1916; 2nd edn., 1917). The present translation is based on this. —Editors.]

have laid increased emphasis on this requirement, and have embodied it in the demand that everyone who wishes to carry out analyses on other people shall first himself undergo an analysis by someone with expert knowledge. Anyone who takes up the work seriously should choose this course, which offers more than one advantage; the sacrifice involved in laying oneself open to another person without being driven to it by illness is amply rewarded. Not only is one's aim of learning to know what is hidden in one's own mind far more rapidly attained and with less expense of affect, but impressions and convictions will be gained in relation to oneself which will be sought in vain from studying books and attending lectures." [2]

Dr. Jung declared himself ready to undertake my analysis. A great obstacle arose, however: the distance between us. Thus, many questions which had come up in the analytical interviews and could not be discussed sufficiently thoroughly were settled by correspondence.

When the correspondence reached its present proportions I asked myself whether other colleagues might not find it as stimulating as I had done: psychoanalysts who were just beginning and who needed a guiding thread through the mounting tangle of psychoanalytic literature, practising physicians who perhaps knew of psychoanalysis only through the violent attacks it has had to endure (often from quite unqualified persons who have no experience of it).

I could only answer this question in the affirmative. I asked Dr. Jung to give his consent to my publishing the correspondence, which he readily did.

I do not doubt that the reader will, like me, give him the thanks that are his due; for a more concise and easily understandable account of the psychoanalytic method and of some of the problems it raises does not, to my knowledge, exist.

DR. R. LOŸ

*Sanatorium L'Abri, Montreux-Territet,*
*14 December 1913*

## *From Dr. Loÿ*

12 January 1913

576 What you said at our last interview was extraordinarily stimulating. I was expecting you to throw light on the interpretation of my own and my patients' dreams from the standpoint

2 "Recommendations to Physicians Practising Psycho-Analysis" (orig. 1912), pp. 116f.

of Freud's dream interpretation. Instead, you put before me an entirely new conception: the dream as a means, produced by the subconscious, of restoring the moral balance. That is certainly a fruitful thought. But still more fruitful, it seems to me, is your other suggestion. You conceive the tasks of psychoanalysis to be much deeper than I had ever imagined: it is no longer a question of getting rid of troublesome pathological symptoms, but of the analysand learning to know himself completely—not just his anxiety experiences—and on the basis of this knowledge building up and shaping his life anew. But he himself must be the builder; the analyst only furnishes him with the necessary tools.

577 To begin with, I would ask you to consider what justification there is for the original procedure of Breuer and Freud, now entirely given up both by Freud himself and by you, but practised by Frank, for instance, as his only method: the "abreaction of inhibited affects under light hypnosis." Why did you give up the cathartic method? Please explain. More particularly, has light hypnosis in psychocatharsis a different value from suggestion during sleep, long practised in suggestion therapy? That is, has it only the value which the doctor attributes, or says he attributes to it, the value which the patient's faith gives it? In other words, is suggestion in the waking state equivalent to suggestion in the hypnoid state, as Bernheim now asserts, after having used suggestion for many years in hypnosis? You will tell me that we must talk of psychoanalysis, not of suggestion. What I really mean is this: is not the *suggestion* that psychocatharsis in the hypnoid state will produce a therapeutic effect (with limitations, naturally, the age of the patient, etc.) the main factor in the therapeutic effects of psychocatharsis? Frank says in his *Affektstörungen:* "These one-sided attitudes, suggestibility and suggestion, are almost entirely in abeyance in psychocatharsis under light sleep, so far as the content of the ideas reproduced is concerned." [3] Is that really true? Frank himself adds: "How can ruminating on the dreams of youth *in itself* lead to discharge of the stored-up anxiety, whether in the hypnoid state or any other? Must we not rather suppose that ruminating on them would make the anxiety states even

[3] Ludwig Frank, *Affektstörungen: Studien über ihre Aetiologie und Therapie* (1913).

greater?" (I have noticed this myself, far more than I liked.) Of course one says to the patient, "First we must stir up, then afterwards comes peace." And it does come. But does it not come *in spite of the stirring-up process,* because gradually, by means of frequent talks *apart from* light hypnosis, the patient gains such confidence in the analyst that he becomes susceptible to the direct suggestion that an improvement and then a cure will follow? I go still further: in an analysis in the waking state, is not the patient's faith that the method employed will cure him, coupled with his growing confidence in the analyst, a main cause of his cure? And I go still further: in every therapeutic method systematically carried out is not faith in it, confidence in the doctor, a main cause of its success? I won't say the only cause, for one cannot deny that physical, dietetic, and chemical procedures, when properly selected, have their own effect in bringing about a cure, over and above the striking effects produced by indirect suggestion.

### *From Dr. Jung*

28 January 1913

578 With regard to your question concerning the applicability of the cathartic procedure, I can say that I adopt the following standpoint: every procedure is good if it helps. I therefore acknowledge every method of suggestion including Christian Science, mental healing, etc. "A truth is a truth, when it works." It is another question, though, whether a scientifically trained doctor can square it with his conscience to sell little bottles of Lourdes water because this suggestion is at times very helpful. Even the so-called highly scientific suggestion therapy employs the wares of the medicine-man and the exorcising shaman. And why not? The public is not much more advanced either and continues to expect miraculous cures from the doctor. And indeed, we must rate those doctors wise—worldly-wise in every sense—who know how to surround themselves with the aura of a medicine-man. They have not only the biggest practices but also get the best results. This is because, apart from the neuroses, countless physical illnesses are tainted and complicated with psychic material to an unsuspected degree. The medical exorcist betrays by his whole demeanour his full appreciation of

that psychic component when he gives the patient the opportunity of fixing his faith firmly on the mysterious personality of the doctor. In this way he wins the sick man's mind, which from then on helps him to restore his body to health. The cure works best when the doctor himself believes in his own formulae, otherwise he may be overcome by scientific doubt and so lose the proper convincing tone. I myself practised hypnotic suggestion-therapy for a time with enthusiasm. But then there befell me three dubious incidents which I would like to bring to your attention.

579 One day a withered old peasant woman of about 56 came to me to be hypnotized for various neurotic troubles. She was not easy to hypnotize, was very restless, and kept opening her eyes —but at last I did succeed. When I woke her up again after about half an hour she seized my hand and with many words testified to her overflowing gratitude. I told her, "You are by no means cured yet, so keep your thanks till the end of the treatment." "I'm not thanking you for that," she whispered, blushing, "but because you were so *decent*." She looked at me with a sort of tender admiration and departed. I gazed for a long time at the spot where she had stood. So decent? I asked myself, flabbergasted—good heavens, surely she hadn't imagined . . . ? This glimpse made me suspect for the first time that possibly the old reprobate, with the atrocious directness of feminine (at the time I called it "animal") instinct, understood more about the essence of hypnosis than I did with all my knowledge of the scientific profundity of the text-books. My innocence was gone.

580 Next came a pretty, coquettish, seventeen-year-old girl with a very harassed-looking mama. She had suffered since early childhood from *enuresis nocturna* (which she used, among other things, to stop herself being sent to a finishing school in Italy). At once I thought of the old woman and her wisdom. I tried to hypnotize the girl; she went into fits of laughter and held up the hypnosis for twenty minutes. I kept my temper and thought: I know why you laugh, you have already fallen in love with me, but I will give you proof of my decency as a reward for wasting my time with your provocative laughter. At last I put her under. The effect was immediate. The enuresis stopped, and I thereupon informed the young lady that, instead of Wednesday, I would not see her again for hypnosis till the following Satur-

day. On Saturday she arrived with a cross face, boding disaster. The enuresis had come back again. I thought of my wise old woman and asked, "When did it come back?" She (unsuspecting): "Wednesday night." I thought to myself: There we have it, she wants to prove to me that I absolutely must see her on Wednesdays too; not to see me for a whole long week is too much for a tender loving heart. But I did not intend to pander to this annoying romance, so I said, "It would be quite wrong to continue the treatment under these circumstances. We must drop it altogether for three weeks, to give the enuresis a chance to stop. Then come again for treatment." In my malicious heart I knew that I would be away on holiday and the course for hypnotic treatment would be finished. After the holiday my *locum tenens* told me that the young lady had been there with the news that the enuresis had vanished, but her disappointment at not seeing me was very keen. The old woman was right, I thought.

581 The third case gave my joy in suggestion therapy its deathblow. This case really was the limit. A 65-year-old lady came hobbling into the consulting-room on a crutch. She had suffered from pain in the knee-joint for seventeen years, and this at times kept her chained to her bed for many weeks. No doctor had been able to cure her, and she had run through all the cures of present-day medicine. After letting the stream of her narrative pour over me for ten minutes, I said, "I will try to hypnotize you, perhaps that will do you good." "Oh yes, please do!" she said, then leaned her head to one side and fell asleep before ever I said or did a thing. She passed into somnambulism and showed every form of hypnosis you could possibly desire. After half an hour I had the greatest difficulty in waking her; when at last she was awake she jumped up: "I am well, I am all right, you have cured me!" I tried to raise timid objections, but her praises drowned me. She could really walk. I blushed, and said embarrassed to my colleagues: "Behold the marvels of hypnotic therapy!" That day saw the death of my connection with therapy by suggestion; the notoriety aroused by this case shamed and depressed me. When, a year later, the good old lady returned, this time with a pain in her back, I was already sunk in hopeless cynicism; I saw written on her brow that she had just

read in the paper the notice of the reopening of my course on hypnotism. That tiresome romanticism had provided her with a convenient pain in the back so that she might have a pretext for seeing me, and again let herself be cured in the same spectacular fashion. This proved true in every particular.

582 As you will understand, a man possessed of a scientific conscience cannot digest such cases with impunity. I was resolved to abandon suggestion altogether rather than allow myself to be passively transformed into a miracle-worker. I wanted to understand what really goes on in people's minds. It suddenly seemed to me incredibly childish to think of dispelling an illness with magical incantations, and that this should be the sole result of our efforts to create a psychotherapy. Thus the discovery of Breuer and Freud came as a veritable life-saver. I took up their method with unalloyed enthusiasm and soon recognized how right Freud was when, at a very early date, indeed as far back as *Studies on Hysteria,* he began to direct a searchlight on the circumstances of the so-called trauma. I soon discovered that, though traumata of clearly aetiological significance were occasionally present, the majority of them appeared very improbable. Many traumata were so unimportant, even so normal, that they could be regarded at most as a pretext for the neurosis. But what especially aroused my criticism was the fact that not a few traumata were simply inventions of fantasy and had never happened at all. This realization was enough to make me sceptical about the whole trauma theory. (I have discussed these matters in detail in my lectures on the theory of psychoanalysis.) I could no longer imagine that repeated experiences of a fantastically exaggerated or entirely fictitious trauma had a different therapeutic value from a suggestion procedure. It is good if it helps. If only one did not have a scientific conscience and that hankering after the truth! I recognized in many cases, particularly with intelligent patients, the therapeutic limitations of this method. It is merely a rule of thumb, convenient for the analyst because it makes no particular demands on his intellect or his capacity to adapt. The theory and practice are delightfully simple: "The neurosis comes from a trauma. The trauma is abreacted." If the abreacting takes place under hypnotism or with other magical accessories (dark room, special

lighting, etc.), I think at once of my clever old woman, who opened my eyes not only to the magical influence of the mesmeric passes but to the nature of hypnotism itself.

583 What alienated me once and for all from this comparatively effective, indirect method of suggestion, based as it is on an equally effective false theory, was the simultaneous recognition that behind the bewildering and deceptive maze of neurotic fantasies there is a *conflict* which may best be described as a moral one. With this there began for me a new era of understanding. Research and therapy now joined hands in the effort to discover the causes and the *rational* solution of the conflict. For me this meant psychoanalysis. While I was arriving at this insight, Freud had built up his sexual theory of neurosis, thus posing a mass of questions for discussion, all of which seemed worthy of the deepest consideration. I had the good fortune to collaborate with Freud for a long time, and to work with him on the problem of sexuality in neurosis. You know perhaps from some of my earlier works that I was always rather dubious about the significance of sexuality. This has now become the point on which I am no longer altogether of Freud's opinion.

584 I have preferred to answer your questions in a somewhat inconsequential fashion. I will now catch up on the rest: light hypnosis and total hypnosis are simply varying degrees of intensity of unconscious susceptibility to the hypnotist. Who can draw sharp distinctions here? To a critical intelligence it is unthinkable that suggestibility and suggestion can be avoided in the cathartic method. They are present everywhere as general human attributes, even with Dubois [4] and the psychoanalysts, who all think they are working on purely rational lines. No technique and no self-effacement avails here; the analyst works willy-nilly, and perhaps most of all, through his personality, i.e., through suggestion. In the cathartic method, what is of far more importance to the patient than the conjuring up of old fantasies is the experience of being together so often with the analyst, his trust and belief in him personally and in his method. The belief, the self-confidence, perhaps also the devotion with which the analyst does his work, are far more important to the

[4] [See supra, par. 527, n. 2.]

patient (imponderabilia though they may be) than the rehearsing of old traumata.[5]

585 It is time we learnt from the history of medicine everything that has ever been of help, then perhaps we shall discover the really necessary therapy—that is, psychotherapy. Did not even the old apothecaries' messes achieve brilliant cures, cures which faded only with the belief in their efficacy?!

586 Because I know that, despite all rational safeguards, the patient does attempt to assimilate the analyst's personality, I have laid it down as a requirement that the psychotherapist must be just as responsible for the cleanness of his hands as the surgeon. I even hold it to be an indispensable prerequisite that the psychoanalyst should first submit himself to the analytical process, as his personality is one of the main factors in the cure.

587 Patients read the analyst's character intuitively, and they should find in him a man with failings, admittedly, but also a man who strives at every point to fulfil his human duties in the fullest sense. Many times I have had the opportunity of seeing that the analyst is successful with his treatment just so far as he has succeeded in his own moral development. I think this answer will satisfy your question.

## *From Dr. Loÿ*

2 February 1913

588 You answer several of my questions in a decidedly affirmative tone, taking it as proved that in cures by the cathartic method the main role is played by faith in the analyst and his method and not by "abreacting" the real or imaginary traumata. I think so too. Equally I agree with your view that the old "apothecaries' messes," as well as the Lourdes cures or those of the mental healers, Christian Scientists, and persuasionists, are to be attributed to faith in the miracle-worker rather than to any of the methods employed.

589 But now comes the ticklish point: the augur can remain an

[5] Thus a woman patient, who had been treated by a young colleague without entire success, once said to me: "Certainly I made great progress with him and I am much better than I was. He tried to analyse my dreams. It's true he never understood them, but he took *so much trouble* over them. He is really a good doctor."

augur so long as he himself believes that the will of the gods is made manifest by the entrails of the sacrificial beast. When he no longer believes, he can ask himself: Shall I continue to use my augur's authority to promote the welfare of the State, or shall I make use of my newer, and I hope truer, convictions of today? Both ways are possible. The first is called opportunism, the second the pursuit of truth and scientific honesty. For the doctor, the first way perhaps brings therapeutic success and fame, the second brings the reproach that such a man is not to be taken seriously. What I esteem most highly in Freud and his school is just this passionate desire for truth. On the other hand some people pronounce a different verdict: "It is impossible for a busy practitioner to keep pace with the development of the views of this investigator and his initiates" (Frank, *Affektstörungen,* Introduction, p. 2).

590 One can easily disregard this little quip, but self-criticism needs to be taken more seriously. One can after all ask oneself: Since science is in continual flux, have I the right to ignore on principle any method or combination of methods by which I know I can get therapeutic results?

591 Looking more closely at the fundamental reason for your aversion to the ancillary use of hypnosis (or semi-hypnosis; the degree matters nothing) in treatment by suggestion (which as you say every doctor and every therapeutic method makes use of willy-nilly, no matter what it is called), one must say that what has disgusted you with hypnotism is at bottom nothing but the so-called "transference" to the doctor, which you, with your purely psychoanalytic procedure, can eliminate as little as anybody else, and which actually plays an essential part in the success of the treatment. Your requirement that the psychoanalyst must be responsible for the cleanness of his hands—here I agree unreservedly—is the logical conclusion. But is the possible recourse to hypnosis in a psychotherapeutic procedure any more "augurish" than the unavoidable use of the "transference to the analyst" for therapeutic purposes? In either case we bank on faith as the healing agent. As for the feeling which the patient—whether man or woman—entertains for the analyst, is there never anything in the background save a conscious or unconscious sexual wish? In many cases your impression is certainly correct, and more than one woman has been frank enough

to confess that the beginning of hypnosis was accompanied by a voluptuous sensation. But it is not true in all instances—or how would you explain the underlying feeling in the hypnotizing of one animal by another, e.g., snake and bird? Surely you would say that here the feeling of *fear* prevails, which is an inversion of libido, whereas in the hypnoid state that comes over the female before she succumbs to the male it is the pure *libido sexualis* that predominates, though possibly still mixed with fear.

592 However that may be, from your three cases I cannot draw any ethical distinction between "susceptibility to the hypnotist" and "transference to the analyst" that would condemn a possible combination of hypnosis with psychoanalysis, as an auxiliary. You will ask why I cling so much to the use of hypnosis, or rather of the hypnoid state. It is because I think there are cases that can be cured much more quickly in this way than by a purely psychoanalytic procedure. For example, in no more than five or six interviews I completely cured a fifteen-year-old girl who had suffered from *enuresis nocturna* even since infancy, but was otherwise perfectly sound, gifted, first in her class, etc. Previously she had tried all sorts of treatment without any result.

593 Perhaps I ought to have sought out the psychoanalytic connections between the enuresis and her psychosexual disposition, explained it to her, etc., but I couldn't, the girl had only the short Easter holidays for treatment: so I just hypnotized her and the trouble vanished.

594 In psychoanalysis I use hypnosis to help the patient overcome "resistance."

595 Further, I use semi-hypnosis in conjunction with psychoanalysis to accelerate the "reconstruction" stage.

596 To take an example, a patient afflicted with a washing mania was sent to me after a year's psychocathartic treatment with Dr. X. The symbolic meaning of her washing ceremonies had previously been explained to her, but she became more and more agitated during the "abreaction" of alleged traumata in childhood, because she had persuaded herself by auto-suggestion that she was too old to be cured, that she saw no "images," etc. So I used hypnosis to help her reduce the number of washings—"so that the anxiety feeling would stay away"—and to

train her to throw things on the floor and pick them up again without washing her hands afterwards, etc.

597 In view of these considerations I should, if you feel disposed to go further into the matter, be grateful if you would furnish me with more convincing reasons why the hypnotic procedure is to be condemned, and explain how to do without it, or what to replace it with in such cases. Were I convinced, I would give it up as you have done; but what convinced you has not, so far, convinced me. *Si duo faciunt idem, non est idem.*

598 I would now like to go on to another important matter to which you alluded, but only cursorily, and to put one question: Behind the neurotic fantasies there is almost always (or always) a moral conflict belonging to the present. That is perfectly clear to me. Research and therapy coincide; their task is: to seek the causes and the rational solution of the conflict.

599 Good.—But can the rational solution always be found? "Reasons of expediency" so often bar the way, varying with the type of patient (children, young girls and women, from "pious"—hypocritical!—Catholic or Protestant families). Again that accursed opportunism!—A colleague of mine was perfectly right when he began to give sexual enlightenment to a young French boy who was indulging in masturbation. Whereupon, like one possessed, in rushed a bigoted grandmother, and a disagreeable scene ensued. How to act in these and similar cases? What to do in cases where there is a moral conflict between love and duty (conflicts in marriage)—or in general between instinct and moral duty? What to do in the case of a girl afflicted with hysterical or anxiety symptoms, who is in need of love and has no chance to marry, or cannot find a suitable man, and, because she comes of "good family," wants to remain chaste? Simply try to get rid of the symptoms by suggestion? But that is wrong as soon as one knows of a better way.

600 How is one to reconcile one's two consciences: that of the man who does not want to confine his fidelity to truth *intra muros,* and that of the doctor who *must* cure, or if he dares not cure according to his real convictions (owing to opportunist motives), must at least provide some alleviation? We live in the present, but with the ideas and the ideals of the future. That is *our* conflict. How to resolve it?

*From Dr. Jung*

4 February 1913

601 . . . You have put me in a somewhat embarrassing position with your question in yesterday's letter. You have rightly guessed the spirit which dictated my last. I am glad you, too, acknowledge this spirit. There are not very many who can boast of such liberalism. I should deceive myself if I thought I was a practising physician. I am above all an investigator, and this naturally gives me a different attitude to many problems. In my last letter I purposely left the practical needs of the doctor out of account, chiefly in order to show you on what grounds one might be moved to give up hypnotic therapy. To anticipate a possible objection, let me say at once that I did not give up hypnosis because I wanted to avoid dealing with the basic forces of the human psyche, but because I wanted to battle with them directly and openly. When once I understood what kind of forces play a part in hypnotism I gave it up, simply to get rid of all the indirect advantages of this method. As we psychoanalysts find to our cost every day—and our patients also—we do not work *with* the "transference to the analyst," [6] but *against it and in spite of it.* Hence we do not bank on the faith of the patient, but on his *criticism.* So much I would say for now about this delicate question.

602 As your letter shows, we are at one in regard to the theoretical aspect of treatment by suggestion. We can therefore apply ourselves to the further task of reaching agreement on practical questions. Your remarks on the doctor's dilemma—whether to be a magician or a scientist—bring us to the heart of the matter. I strive not to be a fanatic—though there are not a few who accuse me of fanaticism. I struggle merely for the recognition of methods of research and their results, not for the application of psychoanalytic methods at all costs. I was a medical practitioner quite long enough to realize that practice obeys, and must obey, other laws than does the search for truth. One might almost say that the practitioner must submit first and foremost

[6] Defined in the Freudian sense as the transference to the analyst of infantile and sexual fantasies. A more advanced conception of the transference perceives in it the important process of *empathy*, which begins by making use of infantile and sexual analogies.

to the law of expediency. The investigator would be doing him a great wrong if he accused him of not using the "one true" scientific method. As I said to you in my last letter: "A truth is a truth, when it works." On the other hand, the practitioner must not reproach the investigator if in his search for truth and for new and perhaps better methods he tries out unusual procedures. After all, it is not the practitioner who will have to bear the brunt, but the investigator and possibly his patient. The practitioner must certainly use those methods which he knows how to apply to the greatest advantage and which give him relatively the best results. My liberalism, as you see, extends even to Christian Science. But I deem it most uncalled for that Frank, a practising doctor, should cast aspersions on research in which he cannot participate—the very line of research to which he owes his own method. It is surely high time to stop this running down of every new idea. No one asks Frank and his confrères to be psychoanalysts. We grant them their right to existence, why should they always seek to curtail ours?

603 As my own "cures" show you, I do not doubt the effect of suggestion. I merely had the feeling that I might be able to discover something still better. This hope has been justified. Not for ever shall it be said:

> *If ever in this world we reach what's good*
> *We call what's better just a plain falsehood!* [7]

604 I frankly confess that if I were doing your work I should often be in difficulties if I relied on psychoanalysis alone. I can scarcely imagine a general practice, especially in a sanatorium, with no other auxiliaries than psychoanalysis. It is true that at Bircher's sanatorium in Zurich the principle of psychoanalysis has been adopted, at least by several of the assistants, but a whole series of other important educative influences are also brought to bear on the patients, without which things would probably go very badly. In my own purely psychoanalytic practice I have often regretted that I could not avail myself of other methods of re-education that are naturally at hand in an institution—but only, of course, in special cases where one is dealing with particularly uncontrolled, untrained patients. Which of us would

7 [*Faust, Part I,* The Night Scene.]

assert that he has discovered the panacea? There are cases where psychoanalysis works worse than any other method. But who has ever claimed that psychoanalysis should be used always and everywhere? Only a fanatic could maintain such a view. Patients for whom psychoanalysis is suitable have to be selected. I unhesitatingly send cases I think unsuitable to other doctors. This does not happen often, as a matter of fact, because patients have a way of sorting themselves out. Those who go to a psychoanalyst usually know quite well why they go to him and not to someone else. Moreover there are very many neurotics excellently suited for psychoanalysis. In these matters all schematism is to be abhorred. It is never quite wise to run your head against a brick wall. Whether simple hypnotism, or cathartic treatment, or psychoanalysis shall be used must be determined by the conditions of the case and the preference of the doctor. Every doctor will obtain the best results with the instrument he knows best.

605 But, barring exceptions, I must say definitely that for me, as well as for my patients, psychoanalysis works better than any other method. This is not merely a matter of feeling; from manifold experiences I know many cases can still be helped by psychoanalysis that are refractory to all other methods of treatment. I know many colleagues whose experience is the same, even men engaged exclusively in practical work. It is scarcely credible that an altogether inferior method would meet with so much support.

606 When once psychoanalysis has been applied in a suitable case, it is *imperative* that rational solutions of the conflicts should be found. The objection is at once advanced that many conflicts are intrinsically insoluble. People sometimes take this view because they think only of external solutions—which at bottom are not solutions at all. If a man cannot get on with his wife, he naturally thinks the conflict would be solved if he married someone else. When such marriages are examined they are seen to be no solution whatever. The old Adam enters upon the new marriage and bungles it just as badly as he did the earlier one. A real solution comes only from within, and then only because the patient has been brought to a different attitude.

607 If an external solution is possible no psychoanalysis is necessary; but if an internal solution is sought, we are faced with the

peculiar task of psychoanalysis. The conflict between "love and duty" must be solved on that level of character where "love and duty" are no longer opposites, which in reality they are not. Similarly, the familiar conflict between "instinct and conventional morality" must be solved in such a way that both factors are taken sufficiently into account, and this again is possible only through a change of character. This change psychoanalysis can bring about. In such cases external solutions are worse than none at all. Naturally, expediency determines which road the doctor must ultimately follow and what is then his duty. I regard the conscience-searching question of whether he should remain true to his scientific convictions as a minor one in comparison with the far weightier question of how he can best help his patient. The doctor *must,* on occasion, be able to play the augur. *Mundus vult decipi*—but the curative effect is no deception. It is true that there is a conflict between ideal conviction and concrete possibility. But we should ill prepare the ground for the seed of the future were we to forget the tasks of the present, and sought only to cultivate ideals. That would be but idle dreaming. Do not forget that Kepler once cast horoscopes for money, and that countless artists are condemned to work for a living wage.

### *From Dr. Loÿ*

9 February 1913

608 The same passion for truth possesses us when we think of pure research, and the same wish to cure when we consider therapy. For the researcher, as for the doctor, we desire the fullest freedom in all directions—complete freedom to choose and practise the methods which promise the best fulfilment of their ends at any moment. On this last point we are at one, but it remains a postulate which we must prove to the satisfaction of others if we want recognition for our views.

609 First and foremost there is one question that must be answered, an old question already asked in the Gospels: "What is truth?" I think clear definitions of fundamental ideas are everywhere necessary. How shall we contrive a working definition of the concept "Truth?" Perhaps an allegory may help us.

610 Imagine a gigantic prism in front of the sun, so that its rays

are broken up, but suppose man entirely ignorant of this fact. (I disregard the chemical, invisible, ultra-violet rays.) Men living in the blue-lit region will say, "The sun sends forth blue light only." They are right and yet they are wrong: from their standpoint they are capable of perceiving only a *fragment* of the truth. And so too with the inhabitants of the red, yellow, and intermediate regions. And they will all scourge and slay one another to force their fragmentary truth on the others—until, grown wiser through travelling in each other's regions, they come to the unanimous view that the sun sends out light of different colours. That is a more comprehensive truth, but it is still not *the* truth. Only when a giant lens has recombined the split-up rays, and when the invisible, chemical, and heat rays have given proof of their specific effects, will a view arise more in accordance with the truth, and men will perceive that the sun emits white light which is split up by the prism into different rays with different qualities, and that these rays are recombined by the lens into a beam of white light.

611 This example serves to show that the road to Truth leads through a series of comparative observations, the results of which must be controlled with the help of freely selected experiments until seemingly well-grounded hypotheses and theories can be put forward; but these hypotheses and theories will fall to the ground as soon as a single new observation or a single new experiment contradicts them.

612 The way is toilsome, and in the end all we ever attain is a *relative* truth. But such relative truth suffices for the time being if it serves to explain the most important concatenations of fact in the past, to light up those of the present, and to predict those of the future, so that we are in a position to adapt through our knowledge. Absolute truth, however, would be accessible only to omniscience, having knowledge of all possible concatenations and combinations; but that is not possible for us, because the number of concatenations and combinations is infinite. Accordingly, we shall never know more than an approximate truth. Should new concatenations be discovered, new combinations be built up, the picture changes and with it the whole range of knowledge and action. To what new revolutions in daily life does not every new scientific discovery lead: how absurdly small

was the beginning of the first theory of electricity, how inconceivably great the results!

613 These are commonplaces, but one must continually repeat them when one sees how life is always made bitter for the innovators in every scientific field, and now especially so for the followers of the psychoanalytic school. Everyone admits these commonplaces so long as it is a matter of "academic" discussion, but only so long; as soon as a concrete case has to be considered, sympathies and antipathies rush to the forefront and darken judgment. Therefore the investigator must fight tirelessly, appealing to logic and honesty, for freedom of research in all fields, and must not allow despots of whatever political or religious persuasion to advance "reasons of expediency" in order to destroy or even restrict this freedom. Reasons of expediency may be and are in place elsewhere, but not here. Finally, we must make an end of the dictum of the Middle Ages, *philosophia ancilla theologiae,* as well as the founding of university chairs in favour of this or that political or religious party. All fanaticism is the enemy of science, which above all things must be independent.

614 And when we turn from the search for Truth back to therapeutics, we see immediately that here again we are in agreement. In practice expediency *must* rule: the doctor from the yellow region must adapt himself to the patients in the yellow region, as must the doctor in the blue region to *his* patients; both have the same object in view. And the doctor who lives in the white light must take into consideration the past experiences of patients from the yellow or blue region, in spite or rather because of his wider knowledge. In such cases the way to healing will be long and difficult, may indeed lead more easily to a *cul-de-sac* than in cases where he has to deal with patients who, like himself, have already attained knowledge of the white light, or, in other words, when his patients have already "sorted themselves out." With these sorted-out patients the psychoanalyst is permitted to work exclusively with the methods of psychoanalysis; he can consider himself lucky that he does not need to "play the augur."

615 Now, these methods of psychoanalysis, what are they? If I understand you aright, it is by and large a question of working directly and openly with the fundamental forces of the human

psyche, to the end that the patient, be he sick or sound or in some stage in between—for sickness and health flow into each other imperceptibly—shall have his mental eyes opened to the drama that is being enacted within him. He must learn to know the automatisms that are hostile to the development of his personality, and through this knowledge he must learn gradually to free himself from them; but he must also learn how to exploit and strengthen the favourable automatisms. He must learn to make his self-knowledge real and to control the workings of his mind so that a balance may be struck between feeling and reason. How large a part is played in all this by *suggestion?* I can hardly believe that suggestion can be avoided altogether till the patient feels really freed. This freedom, it goes without saying, is the main thing to strive for, and it must be an *active* freedom. The patient who simply obeys a suggestion obeys it only so long as the "transference to the analyst" remains in force.

616 But in order to adjust himself to all circumstances the patient must have strengthened himself "from within." He should no longer need the crutches of faith but must be capable of tackling all theoretical and practical problems critically and of solving them himself. That is your view, isn't it, or have I not understood you correctly?

617 I next ask, must not every single case be treated differently—within the limits of the psychoanalytic method? For if every case is a case by itself, it must surely require individual treatment.

618 "Il n'y a pas de maladies, il n'y a que des malades," said a French doctor whose name escapes me. But broadly speaking, what course, from a technical point of view, does analysis take, and what deviations occur most frequently? That I would gladly learn from you. I take it for granted that all "augur's tricks," darkened rooms, masks, chloroform, etc., are out of the question.

619 Psychoanalysis—purged so far as is humanly possible of suggestive influence—appears to have one essential difference from psychotherapy à la Dubois. With Dubois, all talk about the past is prohibited from the outset, and "moral reasons for recovery" are placed in the forefront; whilst psychoanalysis uses the subconscious material from the patient's past and present to promote self-knowledge. Another difference lies in the conception

of morality: morals are above all "relative." But what forms (in broad outline) should one give them at times when suggestion cannot be avoided? Expediency must decide, you will say. Agreed, as regards old people or grown-ups who have to live in a not very enlightened milieu. But if one is dealing with children, the seed of the future, isn't it a sacred duty to enlighten them about the shaky foundations of the so-called moral conceptions of the past, which have only a dogmatic basis, and to educate them to full freedom by courageously unveiling the truth? I ask this not so much with respect to the analysing doctor as with respect to the educator. Should not the founding of *progressive schools* be regarded as a task for the psychoanalyst?

### *From Dr. Jung*

11 February 1913

620 The relativity of "truth" has been known for ages and does not stand in the way of anything, and if it did would merely prevent belief in dogmas and authority. But it does not even do that.

621 You ask me—or rather tell me—what psychoanalysis is. Before considering your views, permit me first to try to mark out the territory and give a definition of psychoanalysis.

622 Psychoanalysis is first of all simply a method—but a method complying with all the rigorous requirements which the concept of a "method" implies today. Let me say at once that psychoanalysis is not an *anamnesis,* as those who know everything without learning it are pleased to believe. It is essentially a way of investigating unconscious associations which cannot be got at by exploring the conscious mind. Again, psychoanalysis is not a method of examination in the nature of an intelligence test, though this mistake is common in certain circles. Nor is it a method of catharsis for abreacting, with or without hypnosis, real or imaginary traumata.

623 Psychoanalysis is a method which makes possible the analytical reduction of psychic contents to their simplest expression, and for discovering the line of least resistance in the development of a harmonious personality. In neurosis there is no uniform direction of life because contrary tendencies frustrate and prevent psychological adaptation. Psychoanalysis, so far as we

can judge at present, seems to be the only rational therapy of the neuroses.

624 No programme can be formulated for the technical application of psychoanalysis. There are only general principles, and working rules for individual analysis. (For the latter I would refer you to Freud's work in Vol. I of the *Internationale Zeitscrift für ärztliche Psychoanalyse.*[8]) My only working rule is to conduct the analysis as a perfectly ordinary, sensible conversation, and to avoid all appearance of medical magic.

625 The main principle of psychoanalytic technique is to analyse the psychic contents that present themselves at a given moment. Any interference on the part of the analyst, with the object of forcing the analysis to follow a systematic course, is a gross mistake in technique. So-called chance is the law and order of psychoanalysis.

626 At the beginning of the analysis the anamnesis and diagnosis naturally come first. The subsequent analytic procedure develops quite differently in every case. To give rules is almost impossible. All one can say is that very frequently, right at the beginning, a number of resistances have to be overcome, resistances against both the method and the analyst. Patients who have no notion of psychoanalysis must first be given some understanding of the method. With those who already know something of it there are very often misconceptions to be set right, and also all those objections to be answered which are levelled by scientific criticism. In either case the misconceptions are due to arbitrary interpretations, superficiality, and gross ignorance of the facts.

627 If the patient is himself a doctor his habit of knowing better may prove extremely tiresome. With intelligent colleagues a thorough theoretical discussion is worth while. With the unintelligent and bigoted ones you begin quietly with the analysis. In the unconscious of such folk you have a confederate who never lets you down. The very first dreams demonstrate the wretched inadequacy of their criticism, so that from the whole beautiful edifice of supposedly scientific scepticism nothing remains over but a little heap of personal vanity. I have had very amusing experiences in this respect.

8 ["On Beginning the Treatment (Further Recommendations on the Technique of Psycho-Analysis I)" (1913).—EDITORS.]

628 It is best to let the patients talk freely and to confine yourself to pointing out a connection here and there. When the conscious material is exhausted you go on to dreams, which give you the subliminal material. If people have no dreams, as they allege, or forget them, there is usually still some conscious material that ought to be produced and discussed, but is kept back owing to resistances. When the conscious is emptied then come the dreams, which as you know are the chief object of analysis.

629 How the analysis is to be conducted and what is to be said to the patient depends, first, on the material to be dealt with; second, on the analyst's skill; and third, on the patient's capacity. I must emphasize that no one should undertake an analysis except on the basis of a sound knowledge of the subject, and this means a thorough knowledge of the existing literature. Without this, the work will only be bungled.

630 I do not know what else to tell you beforehand. I must wait for further questions.

631 As to the question of morality and education, let me say that these things belong to a later stage of the analysis, when they find—or should find—their own solution. You cannot make recipes out of psychoanalysis!

### *From Dr. Loÿ*

16 February 1913

632 You write that a sound knowledge of the literature is necessary for an introduction to psychoanalysis. I agree, but with one reservation: the more one reads of it the more clearly one sees how many contradictions there are among the different writers, and less and less does one know—until one has had sufficient personal experience—to which view to give adherence, since quite frequently assertions are made without any proof. For example, I had thought (strengthened in this view by my own experience of suggestion therapy) that the transference to the analyst might be an essential condition of the patient's cure. But you write: "We psychoanalysts do not bank on the patient's *faith,* but on his *criticism.*" As against this Stekel writes ("Ausgänge der psychoanalytischen Kuren," *Zentralblatt für Psychoanalyse,* III, 1912–13, p. 176): "Love for the analyst can become a force conducive to recovery. Neurotics never get well for love

of themselves, they get well for love of the analyst. They do it to please him . . ." Here again, surely, the accent is on the power of suggestion? And yet Stekel, too, thinks he is a psychoanalyst pure and simple. On the other hand you remark in your letter of January 28: "The personality of the analyst is one of the main factors in the cure." Should not this be translated as: When the analyst inspires respect in the patient and is worthy of his love, the patient will follow his example in order to please him, and will endeavour to get over his neurosis so as to fulfil his human duties in the widest sense of the word?

633 I think one can only emerge from all this uncertainty when one has gained sufficient personal experience, and then one will also know which procedure is best suited to one's own personality and gives the best therapeutic results. This is another reason for submitting to an analysis oneself, to find out what one is. I am very much in agreement with your definition of psychoanalysis in its negative sense: psychoanalysis is neither an anamnesis nor a method of examination like an intelligence test, nor yet a psychocatharsis. But your definition in the positive sense, that "psychoanalysis is a method for discovering the line of least resistance in the development of a harmonious personality," seems to me to apply only to the laziness of the patient, but not to the releasing of sublimated libido for a new aim in life.

634 You say that in neurosis there is no uniform direction because contrary tendencies prevent psychic adaptation. True, but will not psychic adaptation turn out quite differently according to whether the patient, now cured, re-directs his life simply to the avoidance of pain (line of least resistance) or to the attainment of the greatest pleasure? In the first case he would be more passive, and would simply reconcile himself to the "soberness of reality" (Stekel, p. 187). In the second case he would be "filled with enthusiasm" for something or other, or for some person. But what determines whether he will be more active or more passive in his "second" life? In your opinion, does this determining factor appear spontaneously in the course of analysis, and should the analyst carefully avoid tilting the balance to one side or the other by his influence? Or will he, if he does not refrain from canalizing the patient's libido in a definite direction, have to renounce the right to be called a psychoanalyst at all, and is he to be regarded as a "moderate" or a "radical"? (Fürt-

muller, "Wandlungen in der Freud'schen Schule," *Zentralblatt,* III, p. 191.) But I think you have already answered this question in advance when you write in your letter of February 11: "Any interference on the part of the analyst is a gross mistake in technique. So-called chance is the law and order of psychoanalysis." But, torn from its context, perhaps this sentence does not quite give your whole meaning.

635 With regard to enlightening the patient about the psychoanalytic method before beginning the analysis, you appear to be in agreement with Freud and Stekel: better too little than too much. For knowledge pumped into a patient remains half-knowledge anyway, and half-knowledge begets "wanting to know better," which only impedes progress. So, after a brief explanation, first let the patient talk, pointing out a connection here and there, then, after the conscious material is exhausted, go on to the dreams.

636 But here another obstacle stands in my way, which I have already mentioned at our interview: you find the patient adopting the tone, language, or jargon of the analyst (whether from conscious imitation, transference, or plain defiance, so as to fight the analyst with his own weapons)—how then can you prevent his starting to produce all manner of fantasies as supposedly real traumata of early childhood, and *dreams* which are supposedly spontaneous but in reality, whether directly or indirectly, albeit involuntarily, are *suggested*?

637 I told you at the time that Forel (in *Der Hypnotismus*) made his patients dream just what he wanted, and I myself have easily repeated this experiment. But if the analyst wants to *suggest nothing,* must he keep silent most of the time and let the patient talk—except that, when interpreting the dreams, he may put his own interpretation to the patient?

### *From Dr. Jung*

18 February 1913

638 I cannot but agree with your observation that confusion reigns in psychoanalytic literature. Just at this moment different points of view are developing in the theoretical assessment of analytic results, not to mention the many individual deviations. Over against Freud's almost entirely causal conception there

has developed, apparently in absolute contradiction to Freud, Adler's purely finalist view, though in reality it is an essential complement to Freud's theory. I hold rather to a middle course, taking account of both standpoints. It is not surprising that great disagreement prevails with regard to the ultimate questions of psychoanalysis when you consider how difficult they are. In particular, the problem of the therapeutic effect of psychoanalysis is bound up with the most difficult questions of all, so that it would indeed be astonishing if we had already reached final certitude.

639 Stekel's remark is very characteristic. What he says about love for the analyst is obviously true, but it is simply a statement of fact and not a goal or a guiding principle of analytical therapy. If it were the goal, many cures, it is true, would be possible, but also many failures might result which could be avoided. The goal is to educate the patient in such a way that he will get well for his own sake and by reason of his own determination, and not in order to procure his analyst some kind of advantage—though of course it would be absurd from the therapeutic standpoint not to allow the patient to get well because he simply wants to do his analyst a good turn. The patient should know what he is doing, that's all. It is not for us to prescribe for him the ways by which he should get well. Naturally it seems to me (from the psychoanalytic point of view) an illegitimate use of suggestive influence if the patient is forced to get well out of love for his analyst. This kind of coercion sometimes takes a bitter revenge. The "you must and shall be saved" attitude is no more to be commended in the therapy of the neuroses than in any other department of life. Besides, it contradicts the principles of analytic treatment, which shuns all coercion and tries to let everything grow up from within. I am not opposed, as you know, to suggestive influence in general, but merely to doubtful motivations. If the analyst demands that his patient shall get well out of love for him, the patient may easily reckon on reciprocal services, and will without doubt try to extort them. I can only utter a warning against any such practice. A far stronger motive for recovery—also a far healthier and ethically more valuable one—is the patient's thorough insight into the real situation, his recognition of things as they are and how they should be. If he is worth his salt he will then real-

ize that he can hardly remain sitting in the morass of neurosis.

640 I cannot agree with your interpretation of my remarks on the healing effect of the analyst's personality. I wrote [9] that his personality had a healing effect because the patient *reads* the personality of the analyst, and not that he gets well *out of love for* the analyst. The analyst cannot prevent him from beginning to behave towards his conflicts as he himself behaves, for nothing is finer than the empathy of a neurotic. *But every strong transference serves this purpose too.* If the analyst makes himself amiable to the patient, he simply buys off a lot of resistances which the patient ought to have overcome, and which he will quite certainly have to overcome later on. So nothing is gained by this technique; at most the beginning of the analysis is made easier for the patient, though in certain cases this is not without its uses. To have to crawl through a barbed-wire fence without having some enticing end in view testifies to an ascetic strength of will which you can expect neither from the ordinary person nor from the neurotic. Even Christianity, whose moral demands are set very high, has not scorned to dangle before us the kingdom of heaven as the goal and reward of earthly endeavour. In my view the analyst is entitled to speak of the advantages which follow from the ardours of analysis. Only, he should not represent himself or his friendship, by hints or promises, as a reward, unless he is seriously resolved to make it so.

641 As to your criticism of my tentative definition of psychoanalysis, it must be observed that the road over a steep mountain is the line of least resistance when a ferocious bull awaits you in the pleasant valley road. In other words, the line of least resistance is a compromise with *all* eventualities, not just with laziness. It is a prejudice to think that the line of least resistance coincides with the path of inertia. (That's what we thought when we dawdled over our Latin exercises at school.) Laziness is a temporary advantage only and leads to consequences which involve the worst resistances. On the whole, therefore, it does not coincide with the line of least resistance. Nor is life along the line of least resistance synonymous with the ruthless pursuit of selfish desires. Anyone who lived like that would soon realize with sorrow that he was not following the line of least

9 [Presumably a reference to par. 587, or to an unpublished letter.—EDITORS.]

resistance, because man is also a social being and not just a bundle of egoistic instincts, as some people pretend. You can see this best with primitives and domestic animals, who all have a well-developed social sense. Without some such function the herd could not exist at all. Man as a herd-animal, too, has not by any manner of means to subordinate himself to laws imposed from without; he carries his social imperatives within himself, *a priori*, as an inborn necessity. Here, as you see, I place myself in decided opposition to certain views—quite unjustified, in my opinion—which have been expressed here and there inside the psychoanalytic school.

642 Accordingly the line of least resistance does not signify *eo ipso* the avoidance of pain so much as the just balancing of pain and pleasure. Painful activity by itself leads to no result but exhaustion. A man must be able to enjoy life, otherwise the effort of living is not worth while.

643 What direction the patient's life should take in the future is not ours to judge. We must not imagine that we know better than his own nature, or we would prove ourselves educators of the worst kind. (Fundamental ideas of a similar nature have also been worked out by the Montessori school.[10]) Psychoanalysis is only a means for removing the stones from the path of development, and not a method (as hypnotism often claims to be) of putting things into the patient that were not there before. It is better to renounce any attempt to give direction, and simply try to throw into relief everything that the analysis brings to light, so that the patient can see it clearly and be able to draw suitable conclusions. Anything he has not acquired himself he will not believe in the long run, and what he takes over from authority merely keeps him infantile. He should rather be put in a position to take his own life in hand. The art of analysis lies in following the patient on all his erring ways and so gathering his strayed sheep together. Working to programme, on a preconceived system, we spoil the best effects of analysis. I must therefore hold fast to the sentence you object to: "Any interference on the part of the analyst is a gross mistake in technique. So-called chance is the law and order of psychoanalysis."

644 As you must know, we still cannot give up the pedantic preju-

10 [Dr. Maria Montessori (1870–1952) published *The Montessori Method* in 1912. —EDITORS.]

dice of wanting to correct nature and force our limited "truths" on her. But in the therapy of the neuroses we meet with so many strange, unforeseen and unforeseeable experiences that all hope should vanish of our knowing better and being able to prescribe the way. The roundabout way and even the wrong way are necessary. If you deny this you must also deny that the mistakes of history were necessary. That is the pedant's-eye view of the world. This attitude is no good in psychoanalysis.

645 The question as to how much the analyst involuntarily suggests to the patient is a very ticklish one. It certainly plays a much more important role than psychoanalysis has so far admitted. Experience has convinced me that patients rapidly begin to make use of ideas picked up from psychoanalysis, as is also apparent in their dreams. You get many impressions of this sort from Stekel's book *Die Sprache des Traumes.* I once had a very instructive experience: a very intelligent lady had from the beginning long-drawn-out transference fantasies which appeared in the usual erotic guise. But she absolutely refused to admit their existence. Naturally she was betrayed by her dreams, in which, however, my person was always hidden under some other figure, often rather difficult to make out. A long series of such dreams finally compelled me to remark: "So, you see, it's always like that, the person you are really dreaming about is replaced and masked by someone else in the manifest dream." Till then she had obstinately denied this mechanism. But this time she could no longer evade it and had to admit my working rule—but only to play a trick on me. Next day she brought me a dream in which she and I appeared in a manifestly lascivious situation. I was naturally perplexed and thought of my rule. Her first association to the dream was the malicious question: "It's always true, isn't it, that the person you are really dreaming about is replaced by someone else in the manifest dream?"

646 Clearly, she had made use of her experience to find a protective formula by which she could express her fantasies openly in a quite innocent way.

647 This example shows at once how patients use insights they have gained from analysis. They use them for the purpose of symbolization. You get caught in your own net if you believe in fixed, unalterable symbols. That has happened to more than one psychoanalyst. It is therefore a fallacious and risky business

to try to exemplify any particular theory with dreams arising from an analysis. Proof can only come from the dreams of demonstrably uninfluenced persons. In such cases one would have to exclude at most telepathic thought-reading. But if you concede this possibility, you would have to subject many other things to a rigorous scrutiny, including judicial verdicts.

648 Although we must pay full attention to the element of suggestion, we should not go too far. The patient is not an empty sack into which we can stuff whatever we like; he brings his own particular contents with him which stubbornly resist suggestion and push themselves again and again to the fore. Analytic "suggestions" merely distort the expression, but not the content, as I have seen countless times. The expression varies without limit, but the content is fixed and can only be got at in the long run, and then with difficulty. Were it not so, suggestion therapy would be in every sense the most effective and rewarding and easiest therapy, a true panacea. Unfortunately it is not, as every honest hypnotist will readily admit.

649 To come back to your question as to whether it is possible for patients to trick the analyst by making deceptive use—perhaps involuntarily—of his mode of expression, this is indeed a very serious problem. The analyst must exercise all possible care and self-criticism not to let himself be led astray by his patient's dreams. One can say that patients almost invariably use in their dreams, to a greater or lesser extent, the mode of expression learnt in analysis. Interpretations of earlier symbols will themselves be used again as fresh symbols in later dreams. It often happens, for instance, that sexual situations which appeared in earlier dreams in symbolic form will appear "undisguised" in later ones—once more, be it noted, in symbolic form—as analysable expressions for ideas of a different nature hidden behind them. Thus the not infrequent dream of incestuous cohabitation is by no means an "undisguised" content, but a dream as freshly symbolic and capable of analysis as all others. You can only arrive at the paradoxical idea that such a dream is "undisguised" if you are pledged to the sexual theory of neurosis.

650 That the patient may mislead the analyst for a longer or shorter time by means of deliberate deception and misrepresentation is possible, as in all other branches of medicine. But

the patient injures himself most, since he has to pay for every deception or subterfuge with an aggravation of his symptoms, or with fresh ones. Deception is so obviously disadvantageous to himself that he can scarcely avoid relinquishing such a course for good.

651 The technique of analysis we can best postpone for oral discussion.

## *From Dr. Loÿ*

23 February 1913

652 From your letter of 18 February I would like first to single out the end, where you so aptly assign the element of suggestion its proper place in psychoanalysis: "The patient is not an empty sack into which we can stuff whatever we like; he brings his own particular contents with him, with which you have always to reckon afresh" [*sic*]. With this I fully agree, as my own experience confirms it. And you add: involuntary analytic suggestions will leave this content intact, but the expression, Proteus-like, can be distorted without limit. Hence it would be a kind of "mimicry," by which the patient seeks to escape the analyst who is driving him into a corner and for the moment seems to him an enemy. Until at last, through the joint work of patient and analyst—the former spontaneously yielding up his psychic content, the latter only interpreting and explaining—the analysis succeeds in bringing so much light into the darkness of the patient's psyche that he can see the true relationships and, without any preconceived plan of the analyst's, draw the right conclusions and apply them to his future life. This new life will follow the line of least resistance—or should we not rather say of least resistances—as a "compromise with all eventualities," in a just balancing of pain and pleasure. It is not for us to decide arbitrarily for the patient how matters stand and what will benefit him; his own nature decides. In other words, we should take over approximately the role of a midwife, who can only bring out into the light of day a child already alive, but who has to avoid a number of mistakes if the child is to remain alive and the mother is not to be injured.

653 All this is very clear to me because it is only an application to psychoanalytic procedure of a principle which should be

generally valid: Never do violence to Nature! Hence I also see that the psychoanalyst must follow his patient's apparently "erring ways" if the patient is ever to arrive at his own convictions and be freed once and for all from infantile reliance on authority. We ourselves as individuals have learnt and can only learn by making mistakes how to avoid them in the future, and mankind as a whole has created the conditions for its present and future stages of development quite as much by following the crooked path as by keeping to the straight one. Have not many neurotics—I do not know if you will agree, but I think so—become ill partly because their infantile faith in authority has gone to pieces? Now they stand before the wreckage of their faith, weeping over it, and terrified because they cannot find a substitute which would show them clearly where they have to turn. So they remain stuck between the infantilisms they are unwilling to renounce and the serious tasks of the present and future (moral conflict). I also see, particularly in such cases, how right you are in saying that it would be a mistake to try to replace their lost faith in authority by another faith in authority, which would be useful only as long as it lasted. This passes a verdict on the deliberate use of suggestive influence in psychoanalysis, and on regarding the "transference to the analyst" as the goal of analytic therapy. I no longer contest your dictum: "Every interference on the part of the analyst is a gross mistake in technique. So-called chance is the law and order of psychoanalysis." Further, I am in entire agreement when you say that altruism [*sic*] must necessarily be innate in man as a herd-animal. The contrary would be the thing to wonder at.

654 I am very much inclined to assume that not the egoistic but the altruistic instincts are primary. Love and trust of the child for the mother who feeds it, nurses, cherishes and pets it; love of man for wife, regarded as absorption in another's personality; love for offspring, care of them; love for kinsfolk, etc. Whereas the egoistic instincts owe their existence only to the desire for exclusive possession of the object of love, the desire to possess the mother exclusively, in opposition to the father and brother and sisters, the desire to have a woman for oneself alone, the desire for jewellery, clothes, etc. . . . But perhaps you will say I am being paradoxical and that the instincts, whether altruistic or egoistic, arise together in the heart of man, and that every

instinct is ambivalent by nature. But I ask: are our feelings and instincts really ambivalent? Are they perhaps bipolar? Can the qualities of emotions be compared at all? Is love really the opposite of hate?

655 Be that as it may, it is lucky that man carries his social imperatives within himself as an inborn necessity, otherwise our civilized humanity would be in a bad way, having to submit to laws imposed only from without: when the earlier religious faith in authority died out we would rapidly and infallibly fall into complete anarchy. We would then have to ask ourselves *whether it would not* be better to try to maintain by force an exclusively religious belief in authority, as the Middle Ages did. For the benefits of civilization, which strives to grant every individual as much outward freedom as is consistent with the freedom of others, would be well worth such a sacrifice as the sacrifice of free research. But the age of this use of force against nature is past, civilized mankind has abandoned these erroneous ways, not out of caprice, but obeying an inner need, and therefore we may look forward with joyful anticipation to the future. Mankind, advancing in knowledge and obeying its own law, will find its way across the ruins of faith in authority to the moral autonomy of the individual.

## *From Dr. Jung*

March 1913

656 At various places in your letters it has struck me that the problem of the "transference" seems to you particularly critical. Your feeling is entirely justified. The transference is indeed at present the central problem of analysis.

657 You know that Freud regards the transference as a projection of infantile fantasies upon the analyst. To that extent it is an infantile-erotic relationship. However, seen from outside, and superficially, the thing does not always look like an infantile-erotic relationship by any means. So long as it is a case of a so-called positive transference, you can as a rule recognize the infantile-erotic content of the transference without much difficulty. But if it is a so-called negative transference, you see nothing but violent resistances which sometimes disguise themselves in theoretical, seemingly critical or sceptical forms. In a certain

sense the determining factor in these relationships is the patient's relationship to authority, that is, in the last resort, to his father. In both forms of transference the analyst is treated as if he were the father—either with affection or with hostility. According to this view of the transference it acts as a resistance as soon as the question arises of resolving the infantile attitude. But this form of transference must be destroyed in so far as the aim of analysis is the patient's moral autonomy.

658 A lofty aim, you will say. Lofty indeed, and far off, but still not altogether so remote, since it actually corresponds to one of the predominating trends of our stage of civilization—the urge towards individualization, which might serve as a motto for our whole epoch. (Cf. Müller-Lyer, *The Family*.) Anyone who does not believe in this ultimate aim but still adheres to the old scientific causalism will naturally tend to take only the hostile element out of the transference and let the patient remain in a positive relationship to the father, in accordance with the ideals of a past epoch. As we know, the Catholic Church is one of the most powerful organizations based on this tendency. I do not venture to doubt that there are very many people who feel happier under the coercion of others than when forced to discipline themselves (see Shaw's *Man and Superman*). None the less, we would be doing our neurotic patients a grievous wrong if we tried to force them all into the category of the coerced. Among neurotics, there are not a few who do not require any reminders of their social duties and obligations, but are born and destined rather to be bearers of new cultural ideals. They are neurotic as long as they bow down before authority and refuse the freedom to which they are destined. As long as we look at life only retrospectively, as is the case in the psychoanalytic writings of the Viennese school, we shall never do justice to these persons and never bring them the longed-for deliverance. For in this way we train them only to be obedient children and thereby strengthen the very forces that made them ill—their conservative backwardness and submission to authority. Up to a point this is the right way to take with people suffering from an infantile insubordination who cannot *yet* adapt to authority. But the impulse which drives the others out of their conservative father-relationship is by no means an infantile wish for insubordination; it is a powerful urge to develop

their own personality, and the struggle for this is for them an imperative duty. Adler's psychology does much greater justice to this situation than Freud's.

659 For one type of person (called the infantile-rebel) a positive transference is, to begin with, an important achievement with a healing significance; for the other (the infantile-obedient) it is a dangerous backsliding, a convenient way of evading life's duties. For the first a negative transference denotes increased insubordination, hence a backsliding and an evasion of life's duties, for the second it is a step forward with a healing significance. (For the two types see Adler, "Trotz und Gehorsam," *Monatshefte für Pädagogik und Schulpolitik,* VIII, 1910.)

660 So the transference must, as you see, be evaluated quite differently according to the type of case.

661 The psychological process of transference—whether negative or positive—consists in a "libidinal investment" of the personality of the analyst, that is to say he stands for an emotional value. (As you know, by libido I mean very much what the ancients meant by the cosmogonic principle of Eros, or in modern language, "psychic energy.") The patient is bound to the analyst by ties of affection or resistance and cannot help following and imitating his psychic attitude. By this means he feels his way along (empathy). And with the best will in the world and for all his technical skill the analyst cannot prevent it, for empathy works surely and instinctively in spite of conscious judgment, be it never so strong. If the analyst himself is neurotic and insufficiently adapted to the demands of life or of his own personality, the patient will copy this defect and reflect it in his own attitudes: with what results you can imagine.

662 Accordingly I cannot regard the transference merely as a projection of infantile-erotic fantasies. No doubt that is what it is from *one* standpoint, but I also see in it, as I said in an earlier letter, a process of empathy and adaptation. From this standpoint, the infantile-erotic fantasies, in spite of their undeniable reality, appear rather as a means of comparison or as analogical images for something not yet understood than as independent wishes. This seems to me the real reason why they are unconscious. The patient, not knowing the right attitude, tries to grasp at the right relationship to the analyst by way of comparison and analogy with his infantile experiences. It is not

surprising that he gropes back to just the most intimate relationships of his childhood in the attempt to discover the appropriate formula for his relationship to the analyst, for this relationship is very intimate too but differs from the sexual relationship as much as does that of a child to its parents. This latter relationship—child to parent—which Christianity has everywhere set up as a symbolic formula for human relationships in general, serves to restore to the patient that direct feeling of human fellowship of which he has been deprived by the incursions of sexual and social valuations (valuations from the standpoint of power, etc.). The purely sexual and other more or less primitive and barbaric valuations militate against a direct, purely human relationship, and this creates a damming up of libido which may easily give rise to neurotic formations. Through analysis of the infantile content of the transference fantasies the patient is brought back to a remembrance of the childhood relationship, which, stripped of its infantile qualities, gives him a clear picture of a direct human relationship over and above merely sexual valuations, etc. I can only regard it as a misconception to judge the child-relationship retrospectively as a merely sexual one, even though a certain sexual content cannot be denied.

663 Recapitulating, I would like to say this of the positive transference:

The patient's libido fastens on the person of the analyst in the form of expectation, hope, interest, trust, friendship, and love. The transference first produces a projection of infantile fantasies, often with a predominantly erotic tinge. At this stage it is, as a rule, of a decidedly sexual character, even though the sexual component remains relatively unconscious. But this emotional process serves as a bridge for the higher aspect of empathy, whereby the patient becomes conscious of the inadequacy of his own attitude through recognition of the analyst's attitude, which is accepted as being adapted to life's demands and as normal. Through remembrance of the childhood relationship with the help of analysis the patient is shown the way which leads out of the subsidiary, purely sexual or power values acquired in puberty and reinforced by social prejudice. This road leads to a purely human relationship and to an intimacy based not on the existence of sexual or power factors but on the value of personality. That is the road to freedom which the analyst should show his patient.

664 I ought not to conceal from you at this point that the stubborn assertion of sexual values would not be maintained so tenaciously if they did not have a profound significance for that period of life in which propagation is of primary importance. The discovery of the value of human personality is reserved for a riper age. For young people the search for personality values is very often a pretext for evading their biological duty. Conversely, the exaggerated longing of an older person for the sexual values of youth is a short-sighted and often cowardly evasion of a duty which demands recognition of the value of personality and submission to the hierarchy of cultural values. The young neurotic shrinks back in terror from the expansion of life's duties, the old one from the dwindling of the treasures he has attained.

665 This view of the transference is, as you will have observed, closely connected with the acceptance of biological "duties." By this I mean the tendencies or determinants that produce culture in man with the same logic as in the bird they produce the artfully woven nest, and antlers in the stag. The purely causal, not to say materialistic views of the last few decades seek to explain all organic formation as the reaction of living matter, and though this is undoubtedly a heuristically valuable line of inquiry, as far as any real explanation goes it amounts only to a more or less ingenious postponement and apparent minimizing of the problem. I would remind you of Bergson's excellent criticism in this respect. External causes can account for at most half the reaction, the other half is due to the peculiar attributes of living matter itself, without which the specific reaction formation could never come about at all. We have to apply this principle also in psychology. The psyche does not merely *react,* it gives its own specific answer to the influences at work upon it, and at least half the resulting formation is entirely due to the psyche and the determinants inherent within it. Culture can never be understood as reaction to environment. That shallow explanation can safely be left to the past century. It is just these determinants that appear as psychological imperatives, and we have daily proof of their compelling power. What I call "biological duty" is identical with these determinants.

666 In conclusion, I must take up one point which seems to have caused you uneasiness. That is the *moral* question. Among our patients we observe so many so-called immoral impulses that the thought involuntarily forces itself on the psychotherapist how it would be if all these desires were gratified. You will have seen from my earlier letters that these desires should not be taken too seriously. Mostly they are boundlessly exaggerated demands which are thrust to the forefront by the patient's dammed-up libido, usually against his will. The canalizing of libido for the fulfilment of life's simple duties is in most cases sufficient to reduce the pressure of these desires to zero. But in certain cases it is a recognized fact that "immoral" tendencies are not got rid of by analysis, but appear more and more clearly until it becomes evident that they belong to the biological duties of the individual. This is particularly true of certain sexual demands aiming at an individual evaluation of sexuality. This is not a question for pathology, it is a social question of today which imperatively demands an ethical solution. For many it is a biological duty to work for a solution of this question, i.e., to find some sort of practical solution. (Nature, as we know, is not satisfied with theories.) Nowadays we have no real sexual morality, only a legalistic attitude to sexuality; just as the Middle Ages had no real morality of money-making but only prejudices and a legalistic point of view. We are not yet far enough advanced to distinguish between moral and immoral behaviour in the realm of free sexual activity. This is clearly expressed in the customary treatment, or rather ill-treatment, of unmarried mothers. All the repulsive hypocrisy, the high tide of prostitution and of venereal diseases, we owe to the barbarous, wholesale legal condemnation of certain kinds of sexual behaviour, and to our inability to develop a finer moral sense for the enormous psychological differences that exist in the domain of free sexual activity.

667 The existence of this exceedingly complicated and significant contemporary problem may serve to make clear to you why we so often find among our patients people who, because of their spiritual and social gifts, are quite specifically called to take an active part in the work of civilization—that is their biological destiny. We should never forget that what today seems to us a moral commandment will tomorrow be cast into the

melting-pot and transformed, so that in the near or distant future it may serve as a basis for new ethical formations. This much we ought to have learnt from the history of civilization, that the forms of morality belong to the category of transitory things. The finest psychological tact is needed with these sensitive natures if they are to turn the dangerous corner of infantile irresponsibility, indolence, or licentiousness, and to give the patient a clear and unclouded vision of the possibility of morally *autonomous* behaviour. Five per cent on money lent is fair interest, twenty per cent is despicable usury. We have to apply this view to the sexual situation as well.

668 So it comes about that there are many neurotics whose inner decency prevents them from being at one with present-day morality and who cannot adapt themselves so long as the moral code has gaps in it which it is the crying need of our age to fill. *We deceive ourselves greatly* if we think that many married women are neurotic merely because they are unsatisfied sexually or because they have not found the right man or because they have an infantile sexual fixation. The real reason in many cases is that they cannot recognize the cultural task that is waiting for them. We all have far too much the standpoint of the "nothing but" psychology, that is, we still think that the new future which is pressing in at the door can be squeezed into the framework of what is already known. And so these people see only the present and not the future. It was of profound psychological significance when Christianity first proclaimed that the orientation to the future was the redeeming principle for mankind. In the past nothing can be altered, and in the present little, but the future is ours and capable of raising life's intensity to the highest pitch. A little span of youth belongs to us, all the rest belongs to our children.

669 Thus your question about the significance of the loss of faith in authority answers itself. The neurotic is ill not because he has lost his old faith, but because he has not yet found a new form for his finest aspirations.

# PREFACES TO "COLLECTED PAPERS ON ANALYTICAL PSYCHOLOGY" [1]

## *First Edition*

670 This volume contains a selection of articles and pamphlets on analytical psychology written at intervals during the past fourteen years.[2] These years have seen the development of a new discipline and, as is usual in such a case, have involved many changes of viewpoint, conception, and formulation.

671 It is not my intention to present the fundamental concepts of analytical psychology in this book. The volume does, however, throw some light on a certain line of development which is especially characteristic of the Zurich school of psychoanalysis.

672 As is well known, the merit of discovering the new analytical method of general psychology belongs to Professor Freud of Vienna. His original views have had to undergo many important modifications, some of them owing to the work done at Zurich, in spite of the fact that he himself is far from agreeing with the standpoint of this school.

673 I cannot here explain the fundamental differences between

1 [Published in *Collected Papers on Analytical Psychology*, edited by Dr. Constance E. Long (London and New York, 1916; 2nd edn., 1917). The prefaces were probably written in German and translated by Dr. Long; they are published here with minor revisions.—EDITORS.]

2 [Contents of 1st edition and location in the Coll. Works: "On the Psychology and Pathology of So-called Occult Phenomena" (Vol. 1); "The Association Method": Lecture I, untitled, and Lecture II, "The Familial Constellations" (Vol. 2); Lecture III, "The Psychic Life of the Child" (Vol. 17, as "Psychic Conflicts in a Child"); "The Significance of the Father in the Destiny of the Individual," "A Contribution to the Psychology of Rumour," and "On the Significance of Number Dreams" (Vol. 4); "A Criticism of Bleuler's 'Theory of Schizophrenic Negativism'" (Vol. 3); "Psychoanalysis" and "On Psychoanalysis" (Vol. 4, as "Concerning Psychoanalysis" and "Psychoanalysis and Neurosis"); "On Some Crucial Points in Psychoanalysis" (Vol. 4); "On the Importance of the Unconscious in Psychopathology" (Vol. 3); "A Contribution to the Study of Psychological Types" (Vol. 6); "The Psychology of Dreams" (Vol. 8, as "General Aspects of Dream Psychology"); "The Content of the Psychoses" (Vol. 3); and "New Paths in Psychology" (Vol. 7, appendix; see n. 4, infra).—EDITORS.]

the two schools but would mention only the following: The Viennese School adopts an exclusively sexualistic standpoint while that of the Zurich School is symbolistic. The Viennese School interprets the psychological symbol semiotically, as a sign or token of certain primitive psychosexual processes. Its method is analytical and causal. The Zurich School recognizes the scientific possibility of such a conception but denies its exclusive validity, for it does not interpret the psychological symbol semiotically only but also symbolistically, that is, it attributes a positive value to the symbol.

674 The value of the symbol does not depend merely on historical causes; its chief importance lies in the fact that it has a meaning for the actual present and for the future, in their psychological aspects. For the Zurich School the symbol is not merely a sign of something repressed and concealed, but is at the same time an attempt to comprehend and to point the way to the further psychological development of the individual. Thus we add a prospective meaning to the retrospective value of the symbol.

675 The method of the Zurich School, therefore, is not only analytical and causal but synthetic and prospective, in recognition of the fact that the human mind is characterized by *fines* (aims) as well as by *causae*. This deserves particular emphasis, because there are two types of psychology, the one following the principle of hedonism, the other the power principle. The philosophical counterpart of the former type is scientific materialism and of the latter the philosophy of Nietzsche. The principle of the Freudian theory is hedonism, while the theory of Adler (one of Freud's earliest personal pupils) is founded on the power principle.

676 The Zurich School, recognizing the existence of these two types (also remarked by the late Professor William James), considers that the views of Freud and Adler are one-sided and valid only within the limits of their corresponding type. Both principles exist in every individual though not in equal proportions.

677 Thus, it is obvious that every psychological symbol has two aspects and should be interpreted in accordance with both principles. Freud and Adler interpret in the analytical and causal way, reducing to the infantile and primitive. Thus with Freud the conception of the "aim" is the fulfilment of the wish, while

with Adler it is the usurpation of power. In their practical analytical work both authors take the standpoint which brings to light only infantile and grossly egoistic aims.

678 The Zurich School is convinced that within the limits of a diseased mental attitude the psychology is such as Freud and Adler describe. It is, indeed, just on account of such an impossible and childish psychology that the individual is in a state of inner dissociation and hence neurotic. The Zurich School, therefore, in agreement with them so far, also reduces the psychological symbol (the fantasy-products of the patient) to his fundamental infantile hedonism or infantile desire for power. Freud and Adler content themselves with the result of mere reduction, which accords with their scientific biologism and naturalism.

679 But here a very important question arises. Can man obey the fundamental and primitive impulses of his nature without gravely injuring himself or his fellow beings? He cannot assert either his sexual desire or his desire for power unlimitedly in the face of limits which are very restrictive. The Zurich School has in view the end-result of analysis, and it regards the fundamental thoughts and impulses of the unconscious as symbols, indicative of a definite line of future development. We must admit, however, that there is *no scientific justification* for such a procedure, because our present-day science is based wholly on causality. But causality is only one principle, and psychology cannot be exhausted by causal methods only, because the mind lives by aims as well. Besides this controversial philosophical argument we have another of much greater value in favour of our hypothesis, namely that of *vital necessity*. It is impossible to live according to the promptings of infantile hedonism or according to a childish desire for power. If these are to be given a place they must be taken symbolically. Out of the symbolic application of infantile trends there evolves an attitude which may be termed philosophic or religious, and these terms characterize sufficiently well the lines of the individual's further development. The individual is not just a fixed and unchangeable complex of psychological facts; he is also an extremely variable entity. By an exclusive reduction to causes the primitive trends of a personality are reinforced; this is helpful only when these primitive tendencies are balanced by a recognition of their symbolic value. Analysis and reduction lead to causal truth; this by

itself does not help us to live but only induces resignation and hopelessness. On the other hand, the recognition of the intrinsic value of a symbol leads to constructive truth and helps us to live; it inspires hopefulness and furthers the possibility of future development.

680 The functional importance of the symbol is clearly shown in the history of civilization. For thousands of years the religious symbol proved a most efficacious device in the moral education of mankind. Only a prejudiced mind could deny such an obvious fact. Concrete values cannot take the place of the symbol; only new and more effective symbols can be substituted for those that are antiquated and outworn and have lost their efficacy through the progress of intellectual analysis and understanding. The further development of the individual can be brought about only by means of symbols which represent something far in advance of himself and whose intellectual meanings cannot yet be grasped entirely. The individual unconscious produces such symbols, and they are of the greatest possible value in the moral development of the personality.

681 Man almost invariably has philosophic and religious views concerning the meaning of the world and of his own life. There are some who are proud to have none. But these are exceptions outside the common path of mankind; they lack an important function which has proved itself to be indispensable to the human psyche.

682 In such cases we find in the unconscious, instead of modern symbolism, an antiquated, archaic view of the world and of life. If a necessary psychological function is not represented in the sphere of consciousness it exists in the unconscious in the form of an archaic or embryonic prototype.

683 This brief résumé may show the reader what he may expect *not* to find in this collection of papers. The essays are stations on the way toward the more general views developed above.

*Küsnacht/Zurich, January 1916*

## *Second Edition*

684 In agreement with my honoured collaborator, Dr. C. E. Long, I have made certain additions to the second edition of

this book. It should especially be noted that a new chapter on "The Conception of the Unconscious"[3] has been added. This is a lecture I gave early in 1916 to the Zurich Society for Analytical Psychology. It provides a general survey of a most important problem in practical analysis, namely the relation of the ego to the psychological non-ego. Chapter XIV, "The Psychology of the Unconscious Processes," [4] has been fundamentally revised, and I have taken the opportunity to incorporate an article [5] that describes the results of more recent researches.

685 In accordance with my usual method of working, my description is as generalized as possible. My habit in daily practice is to confine myself for some time to studying the human material. I then abstract as general a formula as possible from the data collected, obtaining from it a point of view and applying it in my practical work until it has been either confirmed, modified, or else abandoned. If it is confirmed, I publish it as a general viewpoint without giving the empirical material. I introduce the material amassed in the course of my practice only in the form of example or illustration. I therefore beg the reader not to consider the views I present as mere fabrications of my brain. They are, as a matter of fact, the results of extensive experience and ripe reflection.

686 These additions will enable the reader of the second edition to familiarize himself with the recent views of the Zurich School.

687 As regards the criticism encountered by the first edition of this work, I was pleased to find my writings were received with

3 [This was a translation of the original version of "The Relations between the Ego and the Unconscious." Later in 1916 the German original was translated into French under the title "La Structure de l'inconscient." See *Two Essays on Analytical Psychology*, 2nd edn., pp. 123ff. and p. 269, n. 1.—EDITORS.]

4 [A revised and expanded version of "New Paths in Psychology" (orig. in *Raschers Jahrbuch für Schweizer Art und Kunst*, Zurich, 1912). In 1926 it was again expanded and published under the title *Das Unbewusste im normalen und kranken Seelenleben*. A revised and expanded version of this appeared in 1942 as *Über die Psychologie des Unbewussten*. See *Two Essays on Analytical Psychology*, 2nd edn., pp. 3ff. and p. 245, n. 1.—EDITORS.]

5 [Part II, untitled, of "The Content of the Psychoses," Ch. XIII in the *Collected Papers*. This was originally written in English and published as "On Psychological Understanding," *Journal of Abnormal Psychology* (Boston), IX (1915). Later in 1914, translated into German and published as a supplement to *Der Inhalt der Psychose*. See *The Psychogenesis of Mental Disease*, pp. 179ff.—EDITORS.]

much more open-mindedness among English critics than was the case in Germany, where they are met with the silence born of contempt. I am particularly grateful to Dr. Agnes Savill for an exceptionally understanding criticism in the *Medical Press* My thanks are also due to Dr. T. W. Mitchell for an exhaustive review in the *Proceedings of the Society for Psychical Research.*[6] This critic takes exception to my heresy respecting causality. He considers that I am entering upon a perilous, because unscientific, course when I question the sole validity of the causal viewpoint in psychology. I sympathize with him, but in my opinion the nature of the human mind compels us to take the finalistic view. It cannot be disputed that, psychologically speaking, we are living and working day by day according to the principle of directed aim or purpose as well as that of causality. A psychological theory must necessarily adapt itself to this fact. What is plainly directed towards a goal cannot be given an exclusively causalistic explanation, otherwise we should be led to the conclusion expressed in Moleschott's famous dictum: "Man ist was er isst" (Man *is* what he eats). We must always bear in mind that *causality is a point of view.* It affirms the inevitable and immutable relation of a series of events: *a-b-c-z.* Since this relation is fixed, and according to the causal point of view must necessarily be so, looked at logically the order may also be reversed. *Finality is also a point of view,* and it is empirically justified by the existence of series of events in which the causal connection is indeed evident *but the meaning of which only becomes intelligible in terms of end-products (final effects).* Ordinary life furnishes the best instances of this. The causal explanation must be mechanistic if we are not to postulate a metaphysical entity as first cause. For instance, if we adopt Freud's sexual theory and assign primary importance psychologically to the function of the genital glands, the brain is seen as an appendage of the genital glands. If we approach the Viennese concept of sexuality, with all its vague omnipotence, in a strictly scientific manner and reduce it to its physiological basis, we shall arrive at the first cause, according to which psychic life is for the most, or the most important part, tension and relaxation of the genital glands. If we assume for the moment that this mechanistic

6 [Savill, "Psychoanalysis" (1916); Mitchell (1916).—EDITORS.]

explanation is "true," it would be the sort of truth which is exceptionally tiresome and rigidly limited in scope. A similar statement would be that the genital glands cannot function without adequate *nourishment,* the inference being that sexuality is a subsidiary function of nutrition. The truth of this forms an important chapter in the biology of the lower forms of life.

688 But if we wish to work in a really psychological way we shall want to know the *meaning* of psychological phenomena. After learning what kinds of steel the various parts of a locomotive are made of, and what iron-works and mines they come from, we do not really know anything about the locomotive's *function,* that is to say its *meaning*. But "function" as conceived by modern science is by no means exclusively a causal concept; it is especially a final or "teleological" one. For it is impossible to consider the psyche from the causal standpoint only; we are obliged to consider it also from the final point of view. As Dr. Mitchell remarks, it is impossible to think of causal determination as having at the same time a finalistic reference. That would be an obvious contradiction. But the theory of cognition does not need to remain on a pre-Kantian level. It is well known that Kant showed very clearly that the mechanistic and the teleological viewpoints are not *constituent* (objective) principles—as it were, qualities of the object—but that they are purely *regulative* (subjective) principles of thought, and, as such, not mutually inconsistent. I can, for example, easily conceive the following thesis and antithesis:

*Thesis:* Everything came into existence according to mechanistic laws.

*Antithesis:* Some things did not come into existence according to mechanistic laws only.

Kant says to this: Reason cannot prove either of these principles because *a priori* the purely empirical laws of nature cannot give us a determinative principle regarding the potentiality of events.

689 As a matter of fact, modern physics has necessarily been converted from the idea of pure mechanism to the finalistic concept of the conservation of energy, because the mechanistic explanation recognizes only reversible processes whereas the actual truth is that the processes of nature are irreversible. This fact led to the concept of an energy that tends towards relief of tension and hence towards a definitive final state.

690 Obviously, I consider both these points of view necessary, the causal as well as the final, but would at the same time stress that since Kant's time we have come to realize that the two viewpoints are not antagonistic if they are regarded as regulative principles of thought and not as constituent principles of the process of nature itself.

691 In speaking of the reviews of this book I must mention some that seem to me wide of the mark. I was once again struck by the fact that certain critics cannot distinguish between the theoretical explanation given by the author and the fantastic ideas produced by the patient. One of my critics is guilty of this confusion when discussing "On the Significance of Number Dreams." The associations to the quotation from the Bible in this paper are, as every attentive reader will perceive, not arbitrary explanations of my own but a cryptomnesic conglomeration emanating not from my brain at all but from that of the patient. Surely it is not difficult to see that this conglomeration of numbers corresponds exactly to the unconscious psychological function from which the whole mysticism of numbers originated, Pythagorean, cabalistic, and so forth, back to very early times.

692 I am grateful to my serious reviewers, and should like here to express my thanks also to Mrs. Harold F. McCormick for her generous help in the production of this book.

*June 1917*

# INTRODUCTION TO KRANEFELDT'S "SECRET WAYS OF THE MIND"[1]

745 At the present time, one can well say, it is still quite impossible to draw up a comprehensive and hence a proper picture of all that commonly goes by the much abused name "psychoanalysis." What the layman usually understands by "psychoanalysis"—a medical dissection of the soul for the purpose of disclosing hidden causes and connections—touches only a small part of the phenomena in question. Even if we regard psychoanalysis from a wider angle—in agreement with Freud's conception of it—as essentially a medical instrument for the cure of neurosis, this broader point of view still does not exhaust the nature of the subject. Above all, psychoanalysis in the strictly Freudian sense is not only a therapeutic method but a psychological theory, which does not confine itself in the least to the neuroses and to psychopathology in general but attempts also to bring within its province the normal phenomenon of the dream and, besides this, wide areas of the humane sciences, of literature and the creative arts, as well as biography, mythology, folklore, comparative religion, and philosophy.

746 It is a somewhat curious fact in the history of science—but one that is in keeping with the peculiar nature of the psychoanalytic movement—that Freud, the creator of psychoanalysis (in the narrower sense), insists on identifying the method with his sexual theory, thus placing upon it the stamp of dogmatism. This declaration of "scientific" infallibility caused me, at the time, to break with Freud, for to me dogma and science are incommensurable quantities which damage one another by mutual contamination. Dogma as a factor in religion is of ines-

[1] [Originally published in W. M. Kranefeldt's *Die Psychoanalyse* (Berlin and Leipzig, 1930). Translated by Ralph M. Eaton in the English version of the volume, *Secret Ways of the Mind* (New York, 1932; London, 1934). The present translation is of the original, but reference was made to the Eaton version. —EDITORS.]

timable value precisely because of its absolute standpoint. But when science dispenses with criticism and scepticism it degenerates into a sickly hot-house plant. One of the elements necessary to science is extreme uncertainty. Whenever science inclines towards dogma and shows a tendency to be impatient and fanatical, it is concealing a doubt which in all probability is justified and explaining away an uncertainty which is only too well founded.

747 I emphasize this unfortunate state of affairs not because I want to make a critical attack on Freud's theories, but rather to point out to the unbiased reader the significant fact that Freudian psychoanalysis, apart from being a scientific endeavour and a scientific achievement, is a psychic symptom which has proved to be more powerful than the analytical art of the master himself. As Maylan's book on "Freud's tragic complex" [2] has shown, it would not be at all difficult to derive Freud's tendency to dogmatize from the premises of his own personal psychology —indeed, he taught this trick to his disciples and practised it more or less successfully himself—but I do not wish to turn his own weapons against him. In the end no one can completely outgrow his personal limitations; everyone is more or less imprisoned by them—especially when he practises psychology.

748 I find these technical defects uninteresting and believe it is dangerous to lay too much stress on them, as it diverts attention from the one important fact: that even the loftiest mind is most limited and dependent just at the point where it seems to be freest. In my estimation the creative spirit in man is not his personality at all but rather a sign or symptom of a contemporary movement of thought. His personality is important only as the mouthpiece of a conviction arising out of an unconscious, collective background—a conviction that robs him of his freedom, forces him to sacrifice himself and to make mistakes which he would criticize mercilessly in others. Freud is borne along by a particular current of thought which can be traced back to the Reformation. Gradually it freed itself from innumerable veils and disguises, and it is now turning into the kind of psychology which Nietzsche foresaw with prophetic insight—the discovery of the psyche as a new fact. Some day we shall be able to

2 [*Freuds tragischer Komplex: Eine Analyse der Psychoanalyse* (1929).—EDITORS.]

see by what tortuous paths modern psychology has made its way from the dingy laboratories of the alchemists, via mesmerism and magnetism (Kerner, Ennemoser, Eschimayer, Baader, Passavant, and others), to the philosophical anticipations of Schopenhauer, Carus, and von Hartmann; and how, from the native soil of everyday experience in Liébeault and, still earlier, in Quimby (the spiritual father of Christian Science),[3] it finally reached Freud through the teachings of the French hypnotists. This current of ideas flowed together from many obscure sources, gaining rapidly in strength in the nineteenth century and winning many adherents, amongst whom Freud is not an isolated figure.

749 What is designated today by the catchword "psychoanalysis" is not in reality a uniform thing, but comprises in itself many different aspects of the great psychological problem of our age. Whether or not the public at large is conscious of this problem does not alter the fact of its existence. In our time the psyche has become something of a problem for everyone. Psychology has acquired a power of attraction which is really astounding. It explains the surprising, world-wide spread of Freudian psychoanalysis, which has had a success comparable only to that of Christian Science, theosophy, and anthroposophy—comparable not only in its success but also in its essence, for Freud's dogmatism comes very close to the attitude of religious conviction that characterizes these movements. Moreover, all four movements are decidedly psychological. When we add to this the almost unbelievable rise of occultism in every form in all civilized parts of the Western world, we begin to get a picture of this current of thought, everywhere a little taboo yet nonetheless compelling. Similarly, modern medicine shows significant leanings towards the spirit of Paracelsus, and is becoming increasingly aware of the importance of the psyche in somatic diseases. Even the traditionalism of criminal law is beginning to yield to the claims of psychology, as we can see from the suspension of sentences and the more and more frequent practice of calling in psychological experts.

750 So much for the positive aspects of this psychological move-

3 [Phineas Parkhurst Quimby (1802–66), American hypnotist and mental healer, consulted by Mary Baker Eddy, whose ideas he is thought to have influenced. —EDITORS.]

ment. But these aspects are balanced on the other side by equally characteristic negative ones. Already at the time of the Reformation the conscious mind had begun to break away from the metaphysical certainties of the Gothic age, and this separation became more acute and widespread with every passing century. At the beginning of the eighteenth century the world saw the truths of Christianity publicly dethroned for the first time, and at the beginning of the twentieth the government of one of the largest countries on earth is making every effort to stamp out the Christian faith as if it were a disease. Meanwhile, the intellect of the white man as a whole has outgrown the authority of Catholic dogma, and Protestantism has succeeded in splitting itself into more than four hundred denominations through the most trivial quibbles. These are obvious negative aspects, and they explain why people increasingly flock to any movement from which they expect a helpful truth to come.

751 Religions are the great healing-systems for the ills of the soul. Neuroses and similar illnesses arise, one and all, from psychic complications. But once a dogma is disputed and questioned, it has lost its healing power. A person who no longer believes that a God who knows suffering will have mercy on him, will help and comfort him and give his life a meaning, is weak and a prey to his own weakness and becomes neurotic. The innumerable pathological elements in the population constitute one of the most powerful factors that lend support to the psychological tendencies of our time.

752 Another and by no means unimportant contingent is formed by all those who, after a period of belief in authority, have awakened with a kind of resentment and find a satisfaction mixed with self-torture in advocating a so-called new truth which is destructive of their old, still-smouldering convictions. Such people can never keep their mouths shut and, because of the weakness of their conviction and their fear of isolation, must always flock together in proselytizing bands, thus at least making up in quantity for their doubtful quality.

753 Finally, there are those who are earnestly searching for something, who are thoroughly convinced that the soul is the seat of all psychic sufferings and at the same time the dwelling-place of all the healing truths that have ever been announced as glad tidings to suffering humanity. From the soul come the most

senseless conflicts, yet we also look to it for a solution or at least a valid answer to the tormenting question: why?

754 One does not have to be neurotic to feel the need of healing, and this need exists even in people who deny with the deepest conviction that any such healing is possible. In a weak moment they cannot help glancing inquisitively into a book on psychology, even if only to find a recipe for adroitly bringing a refractory marriage partner to reason.

755 These entirely different interests on the part of the public are reflected in the variations on the theme of "psychoanalysis." The Adlerian school, which grew up side by side with Freud, lays particular stress on the social aspect of the psychic problem and, accordingly, has differentiated itself more and more into a system of social education. It denies, not only in theory but in practice, all the essentially Freudian elements of psychoanalysis, so much so that with the exception of a few theoretical principles the original points of contact with the Freudian school are almost unrecognizable. For this reason Adler's "individual psychology" can no longer be included in the concept of "psychoanalysis." It is an independent system of psychology, the expression of a different temperament and a wholly different view of the world.

756 No one who is interested in "psychoanalysis" and who wants to get anything like an adequate survey of the whole field of modern psychiatry should fail to study the writings of Adler. He will find them extremely stimulating, and in addition he will make the valuable discovery that exactly the same case of neurosis can be explained in an equally convincing way from the standpoint of Freud or of Adler, despite the fact that the two methods of explanation seem diametrically opposed to one another. But things that fall hopelessly apart in theory lie close together without contradiction in the paradoxical soul of man: every human being has a power instinct as well as a sexual instinct. Consequently, he displays both of these psychologies, and every psychic impulse in him has subtle overtones coming from the one side as much as the other.

757 Since it has not been established how many primary instincts exist in man or in animals, the possibility at once arises that an ingenious mind might discover a few more psychologies, apparently contradicting all the rest and yet productive of highly

satisfactory explanations. But these discoveries are not just a simple matter of sitting down and evolving a new psychological system out of, shall we say, the artistic impulse. Neither Freud's nor Adler's psychology came into existence in this way. Rather, as if they were fated by an inner necessity, both investigators confessed their ruling principle, putting on record their own personal psychology and hence also their way of observing other people. This is a question of deep experience and not an intellectual conjuring-trick. One could wish that there were more confessions of this sort; they would give us a more complete picture of the psyche's potentialities.

758 My own views and the school I have founded are equally psychological, and are therefore subject to the same limitations and criticisms that I have allowed myself to urge against these other psychologists. So far as I myself can pass judgment on my own point of view, it differs from the psychologies discussed above in this respect, that it is not monistic but, if anything, dualistic, being based on the principle of opposites, and possibly pluralistic, since it recognizes a multiplicity of relatively autonomous psychic complexes.

759 It will be seen that I have deduced a theory from the fact that contradictory and yet satisfactory explanations are possible. Unlike Freud and Adler, whose principles of explanation are essentially reductive and always return to the infantile conditions that limit human nature, I lay more stress on a constructive or synthetic explanation, in acknowledgment of the fact that tomorrow is of more practical importance than yesterday, and that the Whence is less essential than the Whither. For all my respect for history, it seems to me that no insight into the past and no re-experiencing of pathogenic reminiscences—however powerful it may be—is as effective in freeing man from the grip of the past as the construction of something new. I am of course very well aware that, without insight into the past and without an integration of significant memories that have been lost, nothing new and viable can be created. But I consider it a waste of time and a misleading prejudice to rummage in the past for the alleged specific causes of illness; for neuroses, no matter what the original circumstances from which they arose, are conditioned and maintained by a wrong attitude which is present all the time and which, once it is recognized, must be

corrected *now* and not in the early period of infancy. Nor is it enough merely to bring the causes into consciousness, for the cure of neurosis is, in the last analysis, a moral problem and not the magic effect of rehearsing old memories.

760 My views differ further from those of Freud and Adler in that I give an essentially different value to the unconscious. Freud, who attributes an infinitely more important role to the unconscious than Adler (this school allows it to disappear completely into the background), has a more religious temperament than Adler and for this reason he naturally concedes an autonomous, if negative, function to the psychic non-ego. In this respect I go several steps further than Freud. For me the unconscious is not just a receptacle for all unclean spirits and other odious legacies from the dead past—such as, for instance, that deposit of centuries of public opinion which constitutes Freud's "superego." It is in very truth the eternally living, creative, germinal layer in each of us, and though it may make use of age-old symbolical images it nevertheless intends them to be understood in a new way. Naturally a new meaning does not come ready-made out of the unconscious, like Pallas Athene springing fully-armed from the head of Zeus; a living effect is achieved only when the products of the unconscious are brought into serious relationship with the conscious mind.

761 In order to interpret the products of the unconscious, I also found it necessary to give a quite different reading to dreams and fantasies. I did not reduce them to personal factors, as Freud does, but—and this seemed indicated by their very nature—I compared them with the symbols from mythology and the history of religion, in order to discover the meaning they were trying to express. This method did in fact yield extremely interesting results, not least because it permitted an entirely new reading of dreams and fantasies, thus making it possible to unite the otherwise incompatible and archaic tendencies of the unconscious with the conscious personality. This union had long seemed to me the end to strive for, because neurotics (and many normal people, too) suffer at bottom from a dissociation between conscious and unconscious. As the unconscious contains not only the sources of instinct and the whole prehistoric nature of man right down to the animal level, but also, along with these, the creative seeds of the future and the

roots of all constructive fantasies, a separation from the unconscious through neurotic dissociation means nothing less than a separation from the source of all life. It therefore seemed to me that the prime task of the therapist was to re-establish this lost connection and the life-giving co-operation between conscious and unconscious. Freud depreciates the unconscious and seeks safety in the discriminating power of consciousness. This approach is generally mistaken and leads to desiccation and rigidity wherever a firmly established consciousness already exists; for, by holding off the antagonistic and apparently hostile elements in the unconscious, it denies itself the vitality it needs for its own renewal.

762 Freud's approach is not always mistaken, however, for consciousness is not always firmly established. This presupposes a good deal of experience of life and a certain amount of maturity. Young people, who are very far from knowing who they really are, would run a great risk if they obscured their knowledge of themselves still further by letting the "dark night of the soul" pour into their immature, labile consciousness. Here a certain depreciation of the unconscious is justified. Experience has convinced me that there are not only different temperaments ("types"), but different stages of psychological development, so that one can well say that there is an essential difference between the psychology of the first and the second half of life. Here again I differ from the others in maintaining that the same psychological criteria are not applicable to the different stages of life.

763 If, to all these considerations, one adds the further fact that I distinguish between extraverts and introverts, and again distinguish each of them by the criterion of its most differentiated function (of which I can clearly make out four), it will be evident that hitherto my main concern as an investigator in the field of psychology has been to break in rudely upon a situation which, seen from the other two standpoints, is simple to the point of monotony, and to call attention to the inconceivable complexity of the psyche as it really is.

764 Most people have wanted to ignore these complexities, and have frankly deplored their existence. But would any physiologist assert that the body is simple? Or that a living molecule of albumen is simple? If the human psyche is anything, it must be of unimaginable complexity and diversity, so that it cannot

possibly be approached through a mere psychology of instinct. I can only gaze with wonder and awe at the depths and heights of our psychic nature. Its non-spatial universe conceals an untold abundance of images which have accumulated over millions of years of living development and become fixed in the organism. My consciousness is like an eye that penetrates to the most distant spaces, yet it is the psychic non-ego that fills them with non-spatial images. And these images are not pale shadows, but tremendously powerful psychic factors. The most we may be able to do is misunderstand them, but we can never rob them of their power by denying them. Beside this picture I would like to place the spectacle of the starry heavens at night, for the only equivalent of the universe within is the universe without; and just as I reach this world through the medium of the body, so I reach that world through the medium of the psyche.

765 Thus I cannot regret the complications introduced into psychology by my own contributions, for scientists have always deceived themselves very thoroughly when they thought they had discovered how simple things are.

766 In this introduction I hope I have conveyed to the reader that the psychological endeavours summed up in the layman's idea of "psychoanalysis" ramify very much further historically, socially, and philosophically than the term indicates. It may also become clear that the field of research presented in this book is far from being a distinct, easily delimited territory. On the contrary it is a growing science, which is only just beginning to leave its medical cradle and become a psychology of human nature.

767 The exposition that now follows is not intended to describe the whole range of present-day psychological problems. It confines itself to surveying the beginnings of modern psychology and the elementary problems which fall chiefly within the province of the physician. I have included in my introduction a number of wider considerations so as to give the reader a more general orientation.

# FREUD AND JUNG: CONTRASTS[1]

768 The difference between Freud's views and my own ought really to be dealt with by someone who stands outside the orbit of those ideas which go under our respective names. Can I be credited with sufficient impartiality to rise above my own ideas? Can any man do this? I doubt it. If I were told that someone had rivalled Baron Munchausen by accomplishing such a feat, I should feel sure that his ideas were borrowed ones.

769 It is true that widely accepted ideas are never the personal property of their so-called author; on the contrary, he is the bondservant of his ideas. Impressive ideas which are hailed as truths have something peculiar about them. Although they come into being at a definite time, they are and have always been timeless; they arise from that realm of creative psychic life out of which the ephemeral mind of the single human being grows like a plant that blossoms, bears fruit and seed, and then withers and dies. Ideas spring from something greater than the personal human being. Man does not make his ideas; we could say that man's ideas make him.

770 Ideas are, inevitably, a fatal confession, for they bring to light not only the best in us, but our worst insufficiencies and personal shortcomings as well. This is especially the case with ideas about psychology. Where should they come from except from our most subjective side? Can our experience of the objective world ever save us from our subjective bias? Is not every experience, even in the best of circumstances, at least fifty-per-cent subjective interpretation? On the other hand, the subject is also an objective fact, a piece of the world; and what

1 [Originally published as "Der Gegensatz Freud und Jung," *Kölnische Zeitung* (Cologne), May 7, 1929, p. 4. Reprinted in *Seelenprobleme der Gegenwart* (Zurich, 1931), and translated by W. S. Dell and Cary F. Baynes, under the present title, in *Modern Man in Search of a Soul* (London and New York, 1933). The original German text is retranslated here, though reference has been made to the 1933 translation.—EDITORS.]

comes from him comes, ultimately, from the stuff of the world itself, just as the rarest and strangest organism is none the less supported and nourished by the earth which is common to all. It is precisely the most subjective ideas which, being closest to nature and to our own essence, deserve to be called the truest. But: "What is truth?"

771 For the purposes of psychology, I think it best to abandon the notion that we are today in anything like a position to make statements about the nature of the psyche that are "true" or "correct." The best that we can achieve is true expression. By true expression I mean an open avowal and detailed presentation of everything that is subjectively observed. One person will stress the *forms* into which he can work this material, and will therefore believe that he is the creator of what he finds within himself. Another will lay most weight on *what* is observed; he will therefore speak of it as a phenomenon, while remaining conscious of his own receptive attitude. The truth probably lies between the two: true expression consists in giving form to what is observed.

772 The modern psychologist, however ambitious, can hardly claim to have achieved more than this. Our psychology is the more or less successfully formulated confession of a few individuals, and so far as each of them conforms more or less to a type, his confession can be accepted as a fairly valid description of a large number of people. And since those who conform to other types none the less belong to the human species, we may conclude that this description applies, though less fully, to them too. What Freud has to say about sexuality, infantile pleasure, and their conflict with the "reality principle," as well as what he says about incest and the like, can be taken as the truest expression of his personal psychology. It is the successful formulation of what he himself subjectively observed. I am no opponent of Freud's; I am merely presented in that light by his own short-sightedness and that of his pupils. No experienced psychiatrist can deny having met with dozens of cases whose psychology answers in all essentials to that of Freud. By his own subjective confession, Freud has assisted at the birth of a great truth about man. He has devoted his life and strength to the construction of a psychology which is a formulation of his own being.

773 Our way of looking at things is conditioned by what we are. And since other people have a different psychology, they see things differently and express themselves differently. Adler, one of Freud's earliest pupils, is a case in point. Working with the same empirical material as Freud, he approached it from a totally different standpoint. His way of looking at things is at least as convincing as Freud's, because he too represents a psychology of a well-known type. I know that the followers of both schools flatly assert that I am in the wrong, but I may hope that history and all fair-minded persons will bear me out. Both schools, to my way of thinking, deserve reproach for overemphasizing the pathological aspect of life and for interpreting man too exclusively in the light of his defects. A convincing example of this in Freud's case is his inability to understand religious experience, as is clearly shown in his book *The Future of an Illusion.*

774 For my part, I prefer to look at man in the light of what in him is healthy and sound, and to free the sick man from just that kind of psychology which colours every page Freud has written. I cannot see how Freud can ever get beyond his own psychology and relieve the patient of a suffering from which the doctor himself still suffers. It is the psychology of neurotic states of mind, definitely one-sided, and its validity is really confined to those states. Within these limits it is true and valid even when it is in error, for error also belongs to the picture and carries the truth of a confession. But it is not a psychology of the healthy mind, and—this is a symptom of its morbidity—it is based on an uncriticized, even an unconscious, view of the world which is apt to narrow the horizon of experience and limit one's vision. It was a great mistake on Freud's part to turn his back on philosophy. Not once does he criticize his assumptions or even his personal psychic premises. Yet to do so was necessary, as may be inferred from what I have said above; for had he critically examined his own foundations he would never have been able to put his peculiar psychology so naïvely on view as he did in *The Interpretation of Dreams.* At all events, he would have had a taste of the difficulties I have met with. I have never refused the bitter-sweet drink of philosophical criticism, but have taken it with caution, a little at a time. All too little, my opponents will say; almost too much, my own feeling

tells me. All too easily does self-criticism poison one's naïveté, that priceless possession, or rather gift, which no creative person can do without. At any rate, philosophical criticism has helped me to see that every psychology—my own included—has the character of a subjective confession. And yet I must prevent my critical powers from destroying my creativeness. I know well enough that every word I utter carries with it something of myself—of my special and unique self with its particular history and its own particular world. Even when I deal with empirical data I am necessarily speaking about myself. But it is only by accepting this as inevitable that I can serve the cause of man's knowledge of man—the cause which Freud also wished to serve and which, in spite of everything, he has served. Knowledge rests not upon truth alone, but upon error also.

775 It is perhaps here, where the question arises of recognizing that every psychology which is the work of one man is subjectively coloured, that the line between Freud and myself is most sharply drawn.

776 A further difference seems to me to consist in this, that I try to free myself from all unconscious and therefore uncriticized assumptions about the world in general. I say "I try," for who can be sure that he has freed himself from all of his unconscious assumptions? I try to save myself from at least the crassest prejudices, and am therefore disposed to recognize all manner of gods provided only that they are active in the human psyche. I do not doubt that the natural instincts or drives are forces of propulsion in psychic life, whether we call them sexuality or the will to power; but neither do I doubt that these instincts come into collision with the spirit, for they are continually colliding with something, and why should not this something be called "spirit"? I am far from knowing what spirit is in itself, and equally far from knowing what instincts are. The one is as mysterious to me as the other; nor can I explain the one as a misunderstanding of the other. There are no misunderstandings in nature, any more than the fact that the earth has only one moon is a misunderstanding; misunderstandings are found only in the realm of what we call "understanding." Certainly instinct and spirit are beyond my understanding. They are terms which we posit for powerful forces whose nature we do not know.

777 My attitude to all religions is therefore a positive one. In their symbolism I recognize those figures which I have met with in the dreams and fantasies of my patients. In their moral teachings I see efforts that are the same as or similar to those made by my patients when, guided by their own insight or inspiration, they seek the right way to deal with the forces of psychic life. Ceremonial ritual, initiation rites, and ascetic practices, in all their forms and variations, interest me profoundly as so many techniques for bringing about a proper relation to these forces. My attitude to biology is equally positive, and to the empiricism of natural science in general, in which I see a herculean attempt to understand the psyche by approaching it from the outside world, just as religious gnosis is a prodigious attempt of the human mind to derive knowledge of the cosmos from within. In my picture of the world there is a vast outer realm and an equally vast inner realm; between these two stands man, facing now one and now the other, and, according to temperament and disposition, taking the one for the absolute truth by denying or sacrificing the other.

778 This picture is hypothetical, of course, but it offers a hypothesis which is so valuable that I will not give it up. I consider it heuristically and empirically justified and, moreover, it is confirmed by the *consensus gentium*. This hypothesis certainly came to me from an inner source, though I might imagine that empirical findings had led to its discovery. Out of it has grown my theory of types, and also my reconciliation with views as different from my own as those of Freud.

779 I see in all that happens the play of opposites, and derive from this conception my idea of psychic energy. I hold that psychic energy involves the play of opposites in much the same way as physical energy involves a difference of potential, that is to say the existence of opposites such as warm and cold, high and low, etc. Freud began by taking sexuality as the only psychic driving force, and only after my break with him did he take other factors into account. For my part, I have summed up the various psychic drives or forces—all constructed more or less *ad hoc*—under the concept of energy, in order to eliminate the almost unavoidable arbitrariness of a psychology that deals purely with power-drives. I therefore speak not of separate

drives or forces but of "value intensities." [2] By this I do not mean to deny the importance of sexuality in psychic life, though Freud stubbornly maintains that I do deny it. What I seek is to set bounds to the rampant terminology of sex which vitiates all discussion of the human psyche, and to put sexuality itself in its proper place.

780 Common-sense will always return to the fact that sexuality is only one of the biological instincts, only one of the psychophysiological functions, though one that is without doubt very far-reaching and important. But—what happens when we can no longer satisfy our hunger? There is, quite obviously, a marked disturbance today in the psychic sphere of sex, just as, when a tooth really hurts, the whole psyche seems to consist of nothing but toothache. The kind of sexuality described by Freud is that unmistakable sexual obsession which shows itself whenever a patient has reached the point where he needs to be forced or tempted out of a wrong attitude or situation. It is an overemphasized sexuality piled up behind a dam, and it shrinks at once to normal proportions as soon as the way to development is opened. Generally it is being caught in the old resentments against parents and relations and in the boring emotional tangles of the "family romance" that brings about the damming up of life's energies, and this stoppage unfailingly manifests itself in the form of sexuality called "infantile." It is not sexuality proper, but an unnatural discharge of tensions that really belong to quite another province of life. That being so, what is the use of paddling about in this flooded country? Surely, straight thinking will grant that it is more important to open up drainage canals, that is, to find a new attitude or way of life which will offer a suitable gradient for the pent-up energy. Otherwise a vicious circle is set up, and this is in fact what Freudian psychology appears to do. It points no way that leads beyond the inexorable cycle of biological events. In despair we would have to cry out with St. Paul: "Wretched man that I am, who will deliver me from the body of this death?" And the spiritual man in us comes forward, shaking his head, and says in Faust's words: "Thou art conscious only of the single urge," namely of the fleshly bond leading back to father and mother or

2 Cf. "On Psychic Energy," pars. 14ff.

forward to the children that have sprung from our flesh—"incest" with the past and "incest" with the future, the original sin of perpetuation of the "family romance." There is nothing that can free us from this bond except that opposite urge of life, the spirit. It is not the children of the flesh, but the "children of God," who know freedom. In Ernst Barlach's tragedy *The Dead Day,* the mother-daemon says at the end: "The strange thing is that man will not learn that God is his father." That is what Freud would never learn, and what all those who share his outlook forbid themselves to learn. At least, they never find the key to this knowledge. Theology does not help those who are looking for the key, because theology demands faith, and faith cannot be made: it is in the truest sense a gift of grace. We moderns are faced with the necessity of rediscovering the life of the spirit; we must experience it anew for ourselves. It is the only way in which to break the spell that binds us to the cycle of biological events.

781 My position on this question is the third point of difference between Freud's views and my own. Because of it I am accused of mysticism. I do not, however, hold myself responsible for the fact that man has, always and everywhere, spontaneously developed a religious function, and that the human psyche from time immemorial has been shot through with religious feelings and ideas. Whoever cannot see this aspect of the human psyche is blind, and whoever chooses to explain it away, or to "enlighten" it away, has no sense of reality. Or should we see in the father-complex which shows itself in all members of the Freudian school, and in its founder as well, evidence of a notable release from the fatalities of the family situation? This father-complex, defended with such stubbornness and oversensitivity, is a religious function misunderstood, a piece of mysticism expressed in terms of biological and family relationships. As for Freud's concept of the "superego," it is a furtive attempt to smuggle the time-honoured image of Jehovah in the dress of psychological theory. For my part, I prefer to call things by the names under which they have always been known.

782 The wheel of history must not be turned back, and man's advance toward a spiritual life, which began with the primitive rites of initiation, must not be denied. It is permissible for science to divide up its field of inquiry and to operate with

limited hypotheses, for science must work in that way; but the human psyche may not be so parcelled out. It is a whole which embraces consciousness, and it is the mother of consciousness. Scientific thought, being only one of the psyche's functions, can never exhaust all its potentialities. The psychotherapist must not allow his vision to be coloured by pathology, he must never allow himself to forget that the ailing mind is a human mind and that, for all its ailments, it unconsciously shares the whole psychic life of man. He must even be able to admit that the ego is sick for the very reason that it is cut off from the whole, and has lost its connection not only with mankind but with the spirit. The ego is indeed the "place of fears," as Freud says in *The Ego and the Id,* but only so long as it has not returned to its "father" and "mother." Freud founders on the question of Nicodemus: "How can a man be born when he is old? Can he enter the second time into his mother's womb, and be born?" (John 3:4). History repeats itself, for—to compare small things with great—the question reappears today in the domestic quarrel of modern psychology.

783 For thousands of years, rites of initiation have been teaching rebirth from the spirit; yet, strangely enough, man forgets again and again the meaning of divine procreation. Though this may be poor testimony to the strength of the spirit, the penalty for misunderstanding is neurotic decay, embitterment, atrophy, and sterility. It is easy enough to drive the spirit out of the door, but when we have done so the meal has lost its savour—the salt of the earth. Fortunately, we have proof that the spirit always renews its strength in the fact that the essential teaching of the initiations is handed on from generation to generation. Ever and again there are human beings who understand what it means that God is their father. The equal balance of the flesh and the spirit is not lost to the world.

784 The contrast between Freud and myself goes back to essential differences in our basic assumptions. Assumptions are unavoidable, and this being so it is wrong to pretend that we have no assumptions. That is why I have dealt with fundamental questions; with these as a starting-point, the manifold and detailed differences between Freud's views and my own can best be understood.

# APPENDIX

# ANSWERS TO QUESTIONS ON FREUD[1]

On 24 July 1953, the representative of the *New York Times* in Geneva, Michael L. Hoffman, sent Jung the following questionnaire in connection with a projected article on Freud:

1. What part of Freud's work do you accept?
2. What was the role of Freud's work and views in the development of your own analytical psychology?
3. In your opinion does Freudian sexuality play any part in the aetiology of neuroses?
4. Would you care to make any estimate of Freud's contribution to our knowledge of the psyche?
5. Would you care to comment on the value of Freud's procedure as a therapeutic procedure?

As it is impossible to deal with a critique of Freud's work in a short article I have to restrict myself to concise answers.

1. I accept the facts Freud has discovered, but accept his theory only partially.

2. The facts of repression, substitution, symbolization, and systematic amnesia described by Freud coincided with the results of my association experiments (1902–4). Later on (1906) I discovered similar phenomena in schizophrenia. I accepted in those years all of Freud's views, but I could not make up my mind to accept the sexual theory of neurosis and still less of psychosis, no matter how much I tried. I came to the conclusion (1910) that Freud's one-sided emphasis on sex must be a subjective prejudice.

3. It is obvious that the sexual instinct plays a considerable role everywhere in life, and thus also in neurosis, and it is equally obvious that the power-drive, the many forms of fear, and

[1] [Jung wrote this reply to the *New York Times* questions on 7 Aug. 1953. So far as is known, Jung's answers were not published nor used in any form. This statement is published in Coll. Works, Vol. 18.]

the individual necessities are of equal importance. I object only to the uniqueness of sexuality as suggested by Freud.

4. Freud's contribution to our knowledge of the psyche is without doubt of the greatest importance. It yields an insight into the dark recesses of the human mind and character which can only be compared to Nietzsche's *Genealogy of Morals.* In this respect Freud was one of the great cultural critics of the nineteenth century. His specific resentment explains the one-sidedness of his explanatory principle.

One could not say that Freud is the discoverer of the unconscious—C. G. Carus and Eduard von Hartmann were before him and Pierre Janet was his contemporary—but he certainly showed a way to the unconscious and a definite possibility of investigating its contents. In this respect his book on dream interpretation proved to be most helpful, although from a scientific standpoint it is most objectionable.

5. The question of psychological therapy is exceedingly complex. We know for certain that just any method or any procedure or any theory, seriously believed, conscientiously applied, and supported by a humanly congenial understanding, can have a most remarkable therapeutic effect. Therapeutic efficacy is by no means the prerogative of any particular system; what counts is the character and the attitude of the therapist. For this reason I tell my pupils: you must know the best you can about the psychology of neurotic individuals as well as of yourself. If it is the best, you are likely to believe it, and then you can be serious enough to apply what you know with devotion and responsibility. If it is the best *you* know, then you will always entertain a reasonable doubt whether somebody else might not know better than yourself, and out of sheer compassion with your patient you will make sure that you don't lead him astray. Therefore you will never forget to inquire how far he agrees or disagrees with you. When he disagrees you are stuck, and if this fact is overlooked both doctor and patient are fooled.

Theory is important in the first place for science. In practice you can apply as many theories as there are individuals. If you are honest you will preach your individual gospel, even if you don't know it. If you are right, it will be good enough. If you are wrong, even the best theory will be equally wrong. Nothing is worse than the right means in the hands of the wrong man. Never forget that the analysis of a patient analyses yourself, as you are just as much in it as he is.

I am afraid psychotherapy is a very responsible business and anything but an impersonal application of a convenient medical method. There was a time when the surgeon did not even think of washing his hands before an operation, and the time is still with us when doctors believe they are not personally concerned when they apply psychotherapeutic methods.

For this reason I object to any kind of prejudice in the therapeutical approach. In Freud's case I disagree with his materialism, his credulity (trauma theory), his fanciful assumptions (totem and taboo theory) and his asocial, merely biological point of view (theory of neurosis).

This is a mere outline of critical viewpoints. I myself regard such statements as futile, since it is much more important to put forward facts that demand an altogether different conception of the psyche, i.e., new facts unknown to Freud and his school.

It has never been my purpose to criticize Freud, to whom I owe so much. I have been far more interested in the continuation of the road he tried to build, namely the further investigation of the unconscious so sadly neglected by his own school.

# BIBLIOGRAPHY

## LIST OF PERIODICALS CITED, WITH ABBREVIATIONS

*Amer. J. Psychol.* = *American Journal of Psychology.* Baltimore.

*Arch. Psychol. Suisse rom.* = *Archives de psychologie de la Suisse romande.* Geneva.

*J. abnorm. Psychol.* = *Journal of Abnormal Psychology.* Boston.

*Jb. psychoanal. psychopath. Forsch.* = *Jahrbuch für psychoanalytische und psychopathologische Forschungen.* Vienna and Leipzig.

*Proc. Soc. psych. Res., Lond.* = *Proceedings of the Society for Psychical Research.* London.

*Psychiat.-neurol. Wschr.* = *Psychiatrisch-neurologische Wochenschrift.* Halle.

*Z. ReligPsychol.* = *Zeitschrift für Religionspsychologie.* Halle.

# BIBLIOGRAPHY

ABRAHAM, KARL. *Dreams and Myths.* Translated by William Alanson White. (Nervous and Mental Disease Monograph Series, 15.) New York, 1913.

———. "The Psycho-Sexual Differences between Hysteria and Dementia Praecox." In: *Selected Papers.* Translated by Douglas Bryan and Alix Strachey. (International Psycho-Analytical Library, 13.) London, 1927.

BOAS, FRANZ. *Indianische Sagen von der Nord-pacifischen Küste Amerikas.* Berlin, 1895.

BREUER, JOSEF, and FREUD, SIGMUND. *Studies on Hysteria.* Translated by James and Alix Strachey. (Complete Psychological Works of Sigmund Freud, Standard Edition, 2.) London, 1955. (Original: *Studien über Hysterie,* 1895.)

FRANK, LUDWIG. *Affektstörungen. Studien über ihre Ätiologie und Therapie.* (Monographien aus dem Gesamtgebiete der Neurologie und Psychiatrie, 4.) Berlin, 1913.

FREUD, SIGMUND. "Character and Anal Erotism." Translated by R. C. McWatters. In: Standard Edn.,* 9. 1959. (Original: "Charakter und Analerotik," *Psychiat.-neurol. Wschr.,* IX (1907).)

———. *Collected Papers.* (International Psycho-Analytical Library, 7–10, 37.) London, 1924–50. 5 vols.

———. *The Ego and the Id.* Translated by Joan Riviere. In: Standard Edn.,* 19. 1961. (Original: *Das Ich und das Es.* 1923.)

———. "Five Lectures on Psycho-Analysis." (Delivered on the Occasion of the Celebration of the Twentieth Anniversary of the Foundation of Clark University, Worcester, Mass., September 1909.) Translated by James Strachey. In: Standard Edn.,* 11. 1957. (Original: *Ueber Psychoanalyse.* 1910.)

———. "Fragment of an Analysis of a Case of Hysteria." Translated

* The Standard Edition of the Complete Psychological Works of Sigmund Freud, translated under the general editorship of James Strachey. London.

by Alix and James Strachey. In: Standard Edn.,* 7. 1953. (Original: "Bruchstücke einer Hysterie-Analyse." 1905.)

———. "Freud's Psycho-Analytic Procedure." Translated by J. Bernays. In: Standard Edn.,* 7. 1953. (Original: "Die Freud'sche Psychoanalytische Methode." 1904.)

———. *The Future of an Illusion.* Translated by W. D. Robson-Scott. In: Standard Edn.,* 21. 1961. (Original: *Die Zukunft einer Illusion.* 1927.)

———. *The Interpretation of Dreams.* Translated by James Strachey. Standard Edn.,* 4, 5. 1953. (Original: *Die Traumdeutung.* 1900.)

———. *Jokes and Their Relation to the Unconscious.* Standard Edn.,* 8. 1960. (Original: *Der Witz und seine Beziehung zum Unbewussten.* 1905.)

———. "The Neuro-Psychoses of Defence." Translated by John Rickman. In: Standard Edn.,* 3. 1962. (Original: *Die Abwehrneuropsychosen.* 1894.)

———. "Obsessive Acts and Religious Practices." Translated by R. C. McWatters. In: Standard Edn.,* 9. 1959. (Original: "Zwangshandlungen und Religionsübung," *Z. ReligPsychol.*, I (1907).)

———. "On Beginning the Treatment (Further Recommendations on the Technique of Psycho-Analysis I)." In: Standard Edn.,* 12. 1958.

———. "On Psychotherapy." Translated by J. Bernays. In: Standard Edn.,* 7. 1953. (Original: "Über Psychotherapie." 1904.)

———. "The Origin and Development of Psychoanalysis." See "Five Lectures on Psycho-Analysis."

———. "Psycho-Analytic Notes on an Autobiographical Account of a Case of Paranoia (Dementia Paranoides)." Translated by Alix and James Strachey. In: Standard Edn.,* 12. 1958. (Original: "Psychoanalytische Bemerkungen über einen autobiographisch beschriebenen Fall von Paranoia (Dementia Paranoides)." 1911.)

———. *The Psychopathology of Everyday Life.* Translated by Alan Tyson. Standard Edn.,* 6. 1960. (Original: *Zur Psychopathologie des Alltagslebens.* 1901.)

———. "Recommendations to Physicians Practising Psycho-Analysis." Translated by Joan Riviere. In: Standard Edn.,* 12. 1958.

(Original: "Ratschläge für den Arzt bei der psychoanalytischen Behandlung." 1912.)

———. *Sammlung kleiner Schriften zur Neurosenlehre*, Vienna, 1906–22. 5 vols. (Mostly translated in *Collected Papers*, q.v.)

———. "Three Essays on the Theory of Sexuality." Translated by James Strachey. Standard Edn.,* 7. 1953. (Original: *Drei Abhandlungen zur Sexualtheorie*. 1905.)

FÜRST, EMMA. "Statistical Investigations on Word-Associations and on Familial Agreement in Reaction Type among Uneducated Persons." In: C. G. JUNG (ed.). *Studies in Word-Association*. Translated by M. D. Eder. London, 1918; New York, 1919.

GOETHE, JOHANN WOLFGANG VON. *Faust: Part One*. Translated by Philip Wayne. (Penguin Classics.) Harmondsworth, 1956.

JAMES, WILLIAM. *Pragmatism*. London and Cambridge (Mass.), 1907.

JONES, ERNEST. "Freud's Theory of Dreams," *Amer. J. Psychol.*, XXI (1910), 283–308.

———. *On the Nightmare*. (International Psycho-Analytical Library, 20.) London, 1931.

———. "Remarks on Dr Morton Prince's article 'The Mechanism and Interpretation of Dreams.'" *J. abnorm. Psychol.*, V (1910–11), 328–36.

———. *Sigmund Freud: Life and Work*. London, 1953–57. 3 vols. (Also pub. New York separately. Refs. are to the London edn.)

JUNG, CARL GUSTAV. *Collected Papers on Analytical Psychology*. Edited by Constance Long, translated by various persons. London and New York, 1916; 2nd edn., 1917.

———. *Freud and Psychoanalysis*. (Collected Works, 4.) 1961.

———. "New Paths in Psychology." In: *Two Essays on Analytical Psychology*, q.v.

———. "On Psychic Energy." In: *The Structure and Dynamics of the Psyche*. (Collected Works, 8.) 1960; 2nd edn., 1969.

———. "On Psychological Understanding." In: *The Psychogenesis of Mental Disease*, q.v.

———. "Psychic Conflicts in a Child." In: *The Development of Personality*. (Collected Works, 17.) 1954.

———. *The Psychogenesis of Mental Disease*. (Collected Works, 3.) 1960.

———. "The Psychology of the Transference." In: *The Practice of Psychotherapy*. (Collected Works, 16.) 1954; 2nd edn., 1966.

JUNG, CARL GUSTAV. *Symbols of Transformation.* (Collected Works, 5.) 1956; 2nd edn., 1967.

———. *Two Essays on Analytical Psychology.* (Collected Works, 7.) 1953; 2nd edn., 1966.

MAEDER, ALPHONSE. "Contributions à la psychologie de la vie quotidienne," *Arch. Psychol. Suisse rom.*, VI (1906–7), 148 ff., and VII (1907–8), 283 ff.

———. "Essai d'interprétation de quelques rêves," *Arch. Psychol. Suisse rom.*, VI (1906–7), 354 ff.

———. "Die Symbolik in den Legenden, Märchen, Gebräuchen und Träumen," *Psychiat.-neurol. Wschr.*, X (1908).

MAYLAN, CHARLES E. *Freuds tragischer Komplex: Eine Analyse der Psychoanalyse.* Munich, 1929.

MITCHELL, T. WEIR. Review of "Collected Papers on Analytical Psychology," *Proc. Soc. psych. Res., Lond.*, XXIX (1916), 191–95.

PAGE, H. W. "Shock from Fright." In: HACK TUKE. *Dictionary of Psychological Medicine.* London, 1892.

———. *Injuries of the Spine and Spinal Cord without Apparent Mechanical Lesions, and Nervous Shocks—Their Surgical and Medico-Legal Aspects.* London and Philadelphia, 1883.

RANK, OTTO. *The Myth of the Birth of the Hero.* Translated by William Alanson White. (Nervous and Mental Disease Monograph Series, 18.) New York, 1914.

———. "Ein Traum, der sich selbst deutet," *Jb. psychoanal. psychopath. Forsch.*, II (1910), 465–540.

RIKLIN, FRANZ. *Wishfulfilment and Symbolism in Fairy Tales.* Translated by William Alanson White. (Nervous and Mental Disease Monograph Series, 21.) New York, 1915.

SALLUST (C. Sallustius Crispus). [*Works.*] With an English translation by J. C. Rolfe. (Loeb Classical Library.) London and New York, 1921.

SAVILL, AGNES. "Psychoanalysis," *Med. Pr.*, CLII (1916), 446–48.

SILBERER, HERBERT. "Phantasie und Mythos," *Jb. psychoanal. psychopath. Forsch.*, II (1910), 541–622.

———. *Problems of Mysticism and Its Symbolism.* Translated by Smith Ely Jelliffe. New York, 1917.

SPIELREIN, SABINA. "Über den psychologischen Inhalt eines Falls von Schizophrenie," *Jb. psychoanal. psychopath. Forsch.*, III (1912), 329–400.

# INDEX

# INDEX

G



H

K



L

T

# THE COLLECTED WORKS OF

# *C. G. JUNG*

THE PUBLICATION of the first complete edition, in English, of the works of C. G. Jung was undertaken by Routledge and Kegan Paul, Ltd., in England and by Bollingen Foundation in the United States. The American edition is number XX in Bollingen Series, which since 1967 has been published by Princeton University Press. The edition contains revised versions of works previously published, such as *Psychology of the Unconscious*, which is now entitled *Symbols of Transformation*; works originally written in English, such as *Psychology and Religion*; works not previously translated, such as *Aion*; and, in general, new translations of virtually all of Professor Jung's writings. Prior to his death, in 1961, the author supervised the textual revision, which in some cases is extensive. Sir Herbert Read (d. 1968), Dr. Michael Fordham, and Dr. Gerhard Adler compose the Editorial Committee; the translator is R. F. C. Hull (except for Volume 2) and William McGuire is executive editor.

The price of the volumes varies according to size; they are sold separately, and may also be obtained on standing order. Several of the volumes are extensively illustrated. Each volume contains an index and in most a bibliography; the final volume will contain a complete bibliography of Professor Jung's writings and a general index to the entire edition.

In the following list, dates of original publication are given in parentheses (of original composition, in brackets). Multiple dates indicate revisions.

*1. PSYCHIATRIC STUDIES

On the Psychology and Pathology of So-Called Occult Phenomena (1902)

On Hysterical Misreading (1904)

Cryptomnesia (1905)

On Manic Mood Disorder (1903)

A Case of Hysterical Stupor in a Prisoner in Detention (1902)

On Simulated Insanity (1903)

A Medical Opinion on a Case of Simulated Insanity (1904)

A Third and Final Opinion on Two Contradictory Psychiatric Diagnoses (1906)

On the Psychological Diagnosis of Facts (1905)

†2. EXPERIMENTAL RESEARCHES

*Translated by Leopold Stein in collaboration with Diana Riviere*

STUDIES IN WORD ASSOCIATION (1904–7, 1910)

The Associations of Normal Subjects (by Jung and F. Riklin)

An Analysis of the Associations of an Epileptic

The Reaction-Time Ratio in the Association Experiment

Experimental Observations on the Faculty of Memory

Psychoanalysis and Association Experiments

The Psychological Diagnosis of Evidence

Association, Dream, and Hysterical Symptom

The Psychopathological Significance of the Association Experiment

Disturbances in Reproduction in the Association Experiment

The Association Method

The Family Constellation

PSYCHOPHYSICAL RESEARCHES (1907–8)

On the Psychophysical Relations of the Association Experiment

Psychophysical Investigations with the Galvanometer and Pneumograph in Normal and Insane Individuals (by F. Peterson and Jung)

Further Investigations on the Galvanic Phenomenon and Respiration in Normal and Insane Individuals (by C. Ricksher and Jung)

Appendix: Statistical Details of Enlistment (1906); New Aspects of Criminal Psychology (1908); The Psychological Methods of Investigation Used in the Psychiatric Clinic of the University of Zurich (1910); On the Doctrine of Complexes ([1911] 1913); On the Psychological Diagnosis of Evidence (1937)

* Published 1957; 2nd edn., 1970. † Published 1973.

*3. THE PSYCHOGENESIS OF MENTAL DISEASE

The Psychology of Dementia Praecox (1907)
The Content of the Psychoses (1908/1914)
On Psychological Understanding (1914)
A Criticism of Bleuler's Theory of Schizophrenic Negativism (1911)
On the Importance of the Unconscious in Psychopathology (1914)
On the Problem of Psychogenesis in Mental Disease (1919)
Mental Disease and the Psyche (1928)
On the Psychogenesis of Schizophrenia (1939)
Recent Thoughts on Schizophrenia (1957)
Schizophrenia (1958)

†4. FREUD AND PSYCHOANALYSIS

Freud's Theory of Hysteria: A Reply to Aschaffenburg (1906)
The Freudian Theory of Hysteria (1908)
The Analysis of Dreams (1909)
A Contribution to the Psychology of Rumour (1910–11)
On the Significance of Number Dreams (1910–11)
Morton Prince, "The Mechanism and Interpretation of Dreams": A Critical Review (1911)
On the Criticism of Psychoanalysis (1910)
Concerning Psychoanalysis (1912)
The Theory of Psychoanalysis (1913)
General Aspects of Psychoanalysis (1913)
Psychoanalysis and Neurosis (1916)
Some Crucial Points in Psychoanalysis: A Correspondence between Dr. Jung and Dr. Loÿ (1914)
Prefaces to "Collected Papers on Analytical Psychology" (1916, 1917)
The Significance of the Father in the Destiny of the Individual (1909/1949)
Introduction to Kranefeldt's "Secret Ways of the Mind" (1930)
Freud and Jung: Contrasts (1929)

‡5. SYMBOLS OF TRANSFORMATION (1911–12/1952)

PART I

*Introduction*
Two Kinds of Thinking
The Miller Fantasies: Anamnesis
The Hymn of Creation
The Song of the Moth

(*continued*)

* Published 1960. † Published 1961.
‡ Published 1956; 2nd edn., 1967. (65 plates, 43 text figures.)

5. (*continued*)

PART II

Introduction

The Concept of Libido

The Transformation of Libido

The Origin of the Hero

Symbols of the Mother and of Rebirth

The Battle for Deliverance from the Mother

The Dual Mother

The Sacrifice

Epilogue

Appendix: The Miller Fantasies

*6. PSYCHOLOGICAL TYPES (1921)

Introduction

The Problem of Types in the History of Classical and Medieval Thought

Schiller's Ideas on the Type Problem

The Apollinian and the Dionysian

The Type Problem in Human Character

The Type Problem in Poetry

The Type Problem in Psychopathology

The Type Problem in Aesthetics

The Type Problem in Modern Philosophy

The Type Problem in Biography

General Description of the Types

Definitions

Epilogue

Four Papers on Psychological Typology (1913, 1925, 1931, 1936)

†7. TWO ESSAYS ON ANALYTICAL PSYCHOLOGY

On the Psychology of the Unconscious (1917/1926/1943)

The Relations between the Ego and the Unconscious (1928)

Appendix: New Paths in Psychology (1912); The Structure of the Unconscious (1916) (new versions, with variants, 1966)

‡8. THE STRUCTURE AND DYNAMICS OF THE PSYCHE

On Psychic Energy (1928)

The Transcendent Function ([1916]/1957)

A Review of the Complex Theory (1934)

The Significance of Constitution and Heredity in Psychology (1929)

* Published 1971.

† Published 1953; 2nd edn., 1966.

‡ Published 1960; 2nd edn., 1969.

Psychological Factors Determining Human Behavior (1937)
Instinct and the Unconscious (1919)
The Structure of the Psyche (1927/1931)
On the Nature of the Psyche (1947/1954)
General Aspects of Dream Psychology (1916/1948)
On the Nature of Dreams (1945/1948)
The Psychological Foundations of Belief in Spirits (1920/1948)
Spirit and Life (1926)
Basic Postulates of Analytical Psychology (1931)
Analytical Psychology and *Weltanschauung* (1928/1931)
The Real and the Surreal (1933)
The Stages of Life (1930–1931)
The Soul and Death (1934)
Synchronicity: An Acausal Connecting Principle (1952)
Appendix: On Synchronicity (1951)

*9. PART I. THE ARCHETYPES AND THE COLLECTIVE UNCONSCIOUS

Archetypes of the Collective Unconscious (1934/1954)
The Concept of the Collective Unconscious (1936)
Concerning the Archetypes, with Special Reference to the Anima Concept (1936/1954)
Psychological Aspects of the Mother Archetype (1938/1954)
Concerning Rebirth (1940/1950)
The Psychology of the Child Archetype (1940)
The Psychological Aspects of the Kore (1941)
The Phenomenology of the Spirit in Fairytales (1945/1948)
On the Psychology of the Trickster-Figure (1954)
Conscious, Unconscious, and Individuation (1939)
A Study in the Process of Individuation (1934/1950)
Concerning Mandala Symbolism (1950)
Appendix: Mandalas (1955)

*9. PART II. AION (1951)

RESEARCHES INTO THE PHENOMENOLOGY OF THE SELF

The Ego
The Shadow
The Syzygy: Anima and Animus
The Self
Christ, a Symbol of the Self
The Sign of the Fishes

(*continued*)

* Published 1959; 2nd edn., 1968. (Part I: 79 plates, with 29 in colour.)

9. *(continued)*

The Prophecies of Nostradamus
The Historical Significance of the Fish
The Ambivalence of the Fish Symbol
The Fish in Alchemy
The Alchemical Interpretation of the Fish
Background to the Psychology of Christian Alchemical Symbolism
Gnostic Symbols of the Self
The Structure and Dynamics of the Self
Conclusion

*10. CIVILIZATION IN TRANSITION

The Role of the Unconscious (1918)
Mind and Earth (1927/1931)
Archaic Man (1931)
The Spiritual Problem of Modern Man (1928/1931)
The Love Problem of a Student (1928)
Woman in Europe (1927)
The Meaning of Psychology for Modern Man (1933/1934)
The State of Psychotherapy Today (1934)
Preface and Epilogue to "Essays on Contemporary Events" (1946)
Wotan (1936)
After the Catastrophe (1945)
The Fight with the Shadow (1946)
The Undiscovered Self (Present and Future) (1957)
Flying Saucers: A Modern Myth (1958)
A Psychological View of Conscience (1958)
Good and Evil in Analytical Psychology (1959)
Introduction to Wolff's "Studies in Jungian Psychology" (1959)
The Swiss Line in the European Spectrum (1928)
Reviews of Keyserling's "America Set Free" (1930) and "La Révolution Mondiale" (1934)
The Complications of American Psychology (1930)
The Dreamlike World of India (1939)
What India Can Teach Us (1939)
Appendix: Documents (1933–1938)

†11. PSYCHOLOGY AND RELIGION: WEST AND EAST

WESTERN RELIGION

Psychology and Religion (The Terry Lectures) (1938/1940)

* Published 1964; 2nd edn., 1970. (8 plates.)
† Published 1958; 2nd edn., 1969.

A Psychological Approach to the Dogma of the Trinity (1942/1948)
Transformation Symbolism in the Mass (1942/1954)
Forewords to White's "God and the Unconscious" and Werblowsky's "Lucifer and Prometheus" (1952)
Brother Klaus (1933)
Psychotherapists or the Clergy (1932)
Psychoanalysis and the Cure of Souls (1928)
Answer to Job (1952)

EASTERN RELIGION

Psychological Commentaries on "The Tibetan Book of the Great Liberation" (1939/1954) and "The Tibetan Book of the Dead" (1935/1953)
Yoga and the West (1936)
Foreword to Suzuki's "Introduction to Zen Buddhism" (1939)
The Psychology of Eastern Meditation (1943)
The Holy Men of India: Introduction to Zimmer's "Der Weg zum Selbst" (1944)
Foreword to the "I Ching" (1950)

*12. PSYCHOLOGY AND ALCHEMY (1944)
Prefatory note to the English Edition ([1951?] added 1967)
Introduction to the Religious and Psychological Problems of Alchemy
Individual Dream Symbolism in Relation to Alchemy (1936)
Religious Ideas in Alchemy (1937)
Epilogue

†13. ALCHEMICAL STUDIES
Commentary on "The Secret of the Golden Flower" (1929)
The Visions of Zosimos (1938/1954)
Paracelsus as a Spiritual Phenomenon (1942)
The Spirit Mercurius (1943/1948)
The Philosophical Tree (1945/1954)

‡14. MYSTERIUM CONIUNCTIONIS (1955-56)

AN INQUIRY INTO THE SEPARATION AND SYNTHESIS OF PSYCHIC OPPOSITES IN ALCHEMY

The Components of the Coniunctio
The Paradoxa
The Personification of the Opposites
Rex and Regina *(continued)*

* Published 1953; 2nd edn., completely revised, 1968. (270 illustrations.)
† Published 1968. (50 plates, 4 text figures.)
‡ Published 1963; 2nd edn., 1970. (10 plates.)

14. *(continued)*
Adam and Eve
The Conjunction

*15. THE SPIRIT IN MAN, ART, AND LITERATURE
Paracelsus (1929)
Paracelsus the Physician (1941)
Sigmund Freud in His Historical Setting (1932)
In Memory of Sigmund Freud (1939)
Richard Wilhelm: In Memoriam (1930)
On the Relation of Analytical Psychology to Poetry (1922)
Psychology and Literature (1930/1950)
"Ulysses": A Monologue (1932)
Picasso (1932)

†16. THE PRACTICE OF PSYCHOTHERAPY
GENERAL PROBLEMS OF PSYCHOTHERAPY
Principles of Practical Psychotherapy (1935)
What Is Psychotherapy? (1935)
Some Aspects of Modern Psychotherapy (1930)
The Aims of Psychotherapy (1931)
Problems of Modern Psychotherapy (1929)
Psychotherapy and a Philosophy of Life (1943)
Medicine and Psychotherapy (1945)
Psychotherapy Today (1945)
Fundamental Questions of Psychotherapy (1951)
SPECIFIC PROBLEMS OF PSYCHOTHERAPY
The Therapeutic Value of Abreaction (1921/1928)
The Practical Use of Dream-Analysis (1934)
The Psychology of the Transference (1946)
Appendix: The Realities of Practical Psychotherapy ([1937] added, 1966)

‡17. THE DEVELOPMENT OF PERSONALITY
Psychic Conflicts in a Child (1910/1946)
Introduction to Wickes's "Analyses der Kinderseele" (1927/1931)
Child Development and Education (1928)
Analytical Psychology and Education: Three Lectures (1926/1946)
The Gifted Child (1943)
The Significance of the Unconscious in Individual Education (1928)

* Published 1966.
† Published 1954; 2nd edn., revised and augmented, 1966. (13 illustrations.)
‡ Published 1954.

The Development of Personality (1934)
Marriage as a Psychological Relationship (1925)

18. THE SYMBOLIC LIFE
Miscellaneous Writings

19. BIBLIOGRAPHY OF C. G. JUNG'S WRITINGS

20. GENERAL INDEX TO THE COLLECTED WORKS

*See also*:

C. G. JUNG: LETTERS
Selected and edited by Gerhard Adler, in collaboration with Aniela Jaffé.
Translations from the German by R.F.C. Hull.
VOL. 1: 1906–1950
VOL. 2: 1951–1961

THE FREUD/JUNG LETTERS
The Correspondence between Sigmund Freud and C. G. Jung
Translated by Ralph Manheim and R.F.C. Hull
Edited by William McGuire

## Also available in Princeton/Bollingen Paperbacks

ON THE NATURE OF THE PSYCHE by C. G. Jung, trans. by R.F.C. Hull, Extracted from *The Structure and Dynamics of the Psyche*, Vol. 8, Collected Works (P/B #157)

The PSYCHOLOGY OF THE TRANSFERENCE by C. G. Jung, trans. by R.F.C. Hull, Extracted from *The Practice of Psychotherapy*, Vol. 16, Collected Works (P/B #158)

PSYCHOLOGY AND EDUCATION by C. G. Jung, trans. by R.F.C. Hull, Extracted from *The Development of Personality*, Vol. 17, Collected Works (P/B #159)

ESSAYS ON A SCIENCE OF MYTHOLOGY by C. G. Jung and C. Kerényi, trans. by R.F.C. Hull (P/B #180)

THE ORIGINS AND HISTORY OF CONSCIOUSNESS by Erich Neumann, trans. by R.F.C. Hull (P/B Paperback #204)

FOUR ARCHETYPES: MOTHER/REBIRTH/SPIRIT/TRICKSTER by C. G. Jung, trans. by R.F.C. Hull, Extracted from *The Archetypes and the Collective Unconscious*, Vol. 9, part I, Collected Works (P/B #215)

AMOR AND PSYCHE: THE PSYCHIC DEVELOPMENT OF THE FEMININE by Erich Neumann, trans. by Ralph Manheim (P/B #239)

ART AND THE CREATIVE UNCONSCIOUS by Erich Neumann, trans. by R.F.C. Hull (P/B #240)

COMPLEX/ARCHETYPE/SYMBOL IN THE PSYCHOLOGY OF C. G. JUNG by Jolande Jacobi, trans. by Ralph Manheim (P/B #241)

THE SPIRIT IN MAN, ART, AND LITERATURE by C. G. Jung, trans. by R.F.C. Hull, Vol. 15, Collected Works (P/B #252)

THE GREAT MOTHER by Erich Neumann, trans. by Ralph Manheim (P/B #265)

MANDALA SYMBOLISM by C. G. Jung, trans. by R.F.C. Hull, Extracted from *The Archetypes and the Collective Unconscious*, Vol. 9, part I, Collected Works (P/B #266)

TWO ESSAYS ON ANALYTICAL PSYCHOLOGY by C. G. Jung, trans. by R.F.C. Hull, Vol. 7, Collected Works (P/B #268)

ANSWER TO JOB by C. G. Jung, trans. by R.F.C. Hull, Extracted from *Psychology and Religion: West and East*, Vol. 11, Collected Works (P/B #283)

PSYCHOLOGICAL REFLECTIONS: A NEW ANTHOLOGY OF HIS WRITINGS, 1905–1961 by C. G. Jung, ed. by Jolande Jacobi and R.F.C. Hull (P/B #284)

PSYCHIC ENERGY: ITS SOURCE AND ITS TRANSFORMATION by M. Esther Harding (P/B #296)

SYNCHRONICITY: AN ACAUSAL CONNECTING PRINCIPLE by C. G. Jung, trans. by R.F.C. Hull, Extracted from *The Structure and Dynamics of the Psyche*, Vol. 8, Collected Works (P/B #297)

DREAMS by C. G. Jung, trans. by R.F.C. Hull, Extracted from *Freud and Psychoanalysis*, Vol. 4; *The Structure and Dynamics of the Psyche*, Vol. 8; *Psychology and Alchemy*, Vol. 12; and *The Practice of Psychotherapy*, Vol. 16; all in the Collected Works (P/B #298)

THE 'I' AND THE 'NOT-I': A STUDY IN THE DEVELOPMENT OF CONSCIOUSNESS by M. Esther Harding (P/B #307)

THE PSYCHOANALYTIC YEARS by C. G. Jung, trans. by R.F.C. Hull, Extracted from *Experimental Researches*, Vol. 2; *Freud and Psychoanalysis*, Vol. 4; and *The Development of Personality*, Vol. 17; all in the Collected Works (P/B #314)

THE PSYCHOLOGY OF DEMENTIA PRAECOX by C. G. Jung, trans. by R.F.C. Hull, Extracted from *The Psychogenesis of Mental Disease*, Vol. 3, Collected Works (P/B #315)

CRITIQUE OF PSYCHOANALYSIS by C. G. Jung, trans. by R.F.C. Hull, Extracted from *Freud and Psychoanalysis*, Vol. 4; and *The Symbolic Life*, Vol. 18; both in the Collected Works (P/B #329)

GPSR Authorized Representative: Easy Access System Europe - Mustamäe tee 50, 10621 Tallinn, Estonia, gpsr.requests@easproject.com

www.ingramcontent.com/pod-product-compliance
Lightning Source LLC
LaVergne TN
LVHW011119300926
849160LV00008B/442

* 9 7 8 0 6 9 1 6 1 7 1 6 9 *